Writings in Jazz

Sixth Edition

Nathan T. Davis

University of Pittsburgh

KENDALL/HUNT PUBLISHING COMPANY
4050 Westmark Drive   Dubuque, Iowa 52002

The University of Pittsburgh International Academy of Jazz Hall of Fame, established in 1976, was the first jazz hall of fame established by a major university in the world.

Cover photo courtesy of Eric White.

All musical examples in the text are by Nathan T. Davis

Copyright © 2002 by Kendall/Hunt Publishing Company

Library of Congress Control Number: 2001098086

ISBN 0-7872-9101-3

Printed in the United States of America
10   9   8   7   6   5   4   3   2   1

Contents

Foreword

Music has been one means of measuring the development of a society or culture. Since the sixties, the study of culture and its components and structure has been one of the top priorities in the pursuit of educational excellence.

Over the last decade many books and pamphlets have been published on African-American music and the major role it has played in forming American culture. Of all these publications, only a few have the breadth or depth to be considered a truly historical treatise. This book fills a gap in the dearth of comprehensive material on such a vital subject. Most books written about jazz by a single person lack perspective because of an absence of personal involvement. With his scholarly and musical background, Dr. Davis has surmounted this problem. Dr. Davis brings together different interpretations, styles, and musical perspectives into one cogent theme. It takes a person with a strong background in scholarship and personal involvement in music to bring together into focus studies of many musical eras and geographical areas.

There are three basic approaches to researching music history:

1. The laboratory method, which involves reading many books, articles, and so on, and then writing a summary or conclusion.
2. The on-site observation, in which the researcher uses the laboratory approach but also is present at some of the musical scenes and performances, making conclusions and summaries through interviews, personal observations, and studies.
3. The comprehensive method, in which the researcher uses the first two approaches and is also a participant. This is the most valid approach. Here, the writer knows his subject from personal experience.

Dr. Davis is one of a few writers who can say "I was there," who gets a lot of material from personal experience. His academic background attests to his scholarly capability. I can personally attest to his personal involvement for I too was there. Nathan Davis has performed with me and the many different bands I have led in the United States and in Europe where I first met him. He has performed with small groups that included Kenny Clarke and Eric Dolphy, with the Parisian big bands that included Lou Bennett, Woody Shaw, and Jimmy Woode, and in groups of pioneering musicians in jazz rock fusion such as the award winning Blackbyrds and 125th St. NYC Band. We were there! In this book, *Writings in Jazz*, Dr. Davis presents his chapters with theoretical as well as methodological materials that arise naturally from such a controversial and historical background. He covers his subject early African music to the contemporary American jazz music scene with intellectual integrity. He brilliantly covers not only the eras and decades of the music but the nuances and dynamics of this unique American phenomenon.

Jazz music is one of many categories of African-American music. Jazz music is often described as a single form of music, yet it is composed of many musical thoughts. Jazz music is like an umbrella with the ribs springing from the major contributors or innovators, covered by a fabric made from the threads of many creative minds. Like a river, jazz has its major sources and tributaries. The music flows unabated, like the Mississippi River, one of the vehicles that transported it. Dr. Davis has charted its course and progression marvelously.

Dr. Donaldson Toussaint L'Ouverture Byrd IV
Educator–Producer–Trumpeter

Acknowledgments

I would like to thank the following people for their contribution to this work: Lois Buterbaugh who typed the first edition of the manuscript, my wife Ursula Davis for editing the original manuscript, Mary Ann Morocco-Perry for typing the final manuscript, and Herbert Jones for helping to compile the original bibliography and discography, Professor Joe Harris, Willie Amoaku, Joyce N. Florida Davis and Pierre Marc Davis for their suggestions, and the number of students at the University of Pittsburgh who made valuable suggestions concerning the presentation of the material. A special thanks to David Baker of the University of Indiana, Bloomington for reviewing the new edition.

A special thanks to (former Provost) Donald Henderson for his contribution; the University of Pittsburgh, for their assistance, and to the following people for their contribution concerning jazz in Europe and the United States: Jack Van Poll (Holland), Walter de Block (Belgium), Elias Gistelinck (Belgium), Niran Jan Jhaveri (Bombay, India), Walter Ojakaar (Tallinn, Estonia), Armando Aflao (Sao Paulo, Brazil), Arnold Bopp (Zollikon, Switzerland), Phillippe Carles (Paris, France), Mike de Ruyter (Amsterdam, Holland), Dr. Francisco Bendezv P. (Lima, Peru), Jurg Solothurmann (Bern, Switzerland), Frank Halfacre (Youngstown, Ohio), Professor Joe Harris (Pittsburgh, PA), Michael Bourne (Bloomingdon, Indiana), John W. Buchanan (Denver, Colorado), Stephen E. Elman (Brookline, Massachusetts), DeRuyter Kemp (Pittsburgh, PA), Robert Paulson (Pittsburgh, PA), Akira Suzuki (Tokyo, Japan), and Maarten Derksen (Zutphen, Holland).

A special thanks to Associate Editor Loretta Riley for her enthusiasm and encouragement, to Jim Crowley of the University of Pittsburgh Book Center, and to Dr. Donald Byrd and Grover Washington Jr. for their remarks. Thanks also to Teaching Fellow Mary Ann Morocco-Perry for the final computerized editing of all musical examples and photo layout, graduate assistants Emmit Price and Ken Prouty for their help in compiling the listening and reading examples, and to Jack Bishop for the transcription of original tapes, and to Dana Och for proofreading the final manuscript.

Introduction

Finally, here is a jazz book written by someone who, in the vernacular, has "been there" and "done that." His credentials for producing an exceptional jazz history book read like the job description which might be created to identify the ideal person to take on such a project.

1. He is a major player who has worked with such highly touted groups as Art Blakely's Jazz Messengers and the Paris Reunion Band and with numerous jazz icons, including Donald Byrd, Kenny Clarke, Johnny Griffin, Eric Dolphy, Woody Shaw, Joe Harris, James Moody, and Grover Washington, Jr.
2. He created and still heads one of the most highly respected and important jazz seminars in the world. Now in its 31st year, the seminar annually presents lectures, clinics, master classes, and performances by the outstanding jazz artists of our time. Throughout the years, a host of great players, including such jazz luminaries as Lee Konitz, Stanley Turrentine, Curtis Fuller, Randy Brecker, Freddie Hubbard, Kirk Lightsey, Thad Jones, Joe Lovano, Jon Faddis, and James Moody have participated in this seminar.
3. He founded and continues to serve as editor of one of the very few refereed journals which exist in the field of jazz.
4. He is a virtuoso instrumentalist who continues to be active worldwide as a performer, clinician, scholar, author, recording artist, and prolific arranger-composer.
5. He is an internationally recognized writer and jazz historian.
6. He has an earned doctorate with high distinction.

7. He has an encyclopedic knowledge of the jazz field and a consuming passion to share that knowledge with the world.
8. He is an articulate and passionate jazz educator.

These credentials belong to Dr. Nathan Davis, who has written one of the most enjoyable and informative jazz history books it has been my privilege to read. Enjoy!!!

David N. Baker
Distinguished Professor of Music and Chairman, Jazz Department
Indiana University

Listening Examples

African and Early African-American Music

Music of the Rain Forest Pygmies—Lyrichord LYRCD 7157

Mbuti Pygmies of the Ituri Rainforest—Smithsonian Folkways CD—SF40401

Heart of the Forest, the Music of the *Baka Forest People of Southeast Cameroon*—
Hannibal Records HNBC 1378

Echoes of the Forest, Music of the *Central African Pygmies*—Ellipsis Arts CD
4020

Central African Republic—Banda Polyphony—Auvidis UNESCO D-8043

Sound of Africa—Sons d'Afrique Series, International Library of African
Music—TR.2

Afro-American Spirituals, Work Songs, and Ballads—edited by Alan Lomax, a
Folk Music of the United States series—Rounder Records CD 1510

Anthology of Music of Black Africa—3 record set—Everest SDBR 3254/3

Music of West Africa—recorded live in Africa by Gilbert Rouget—featuring the
Malinke of coastal Guinea and the Baule (polyphonic sounds) of the
Ivory Coast—Roulette SR 9003

Africa: Ceremonial and Folk Music—recorded in the early 1970s in Uganda,
Kenya, and Tanzania by David Fanshawe—Nonesuch 75-761344

Uganda—Selections include drums, xylophones, flutes, lutes, and lyres

American Negro Slave Songs with Alex Foster and Michel Larue—Tradition/
Everest 75-760042

Negro Work Songs and Calls—edited by B. A. Botkin, a Folk Music of the
United States series—Rounder CD 1517

Wake Up Dead Man: Black Convict Worksongs from Texas Prisons, recorded in the middle 1960s—booklet with lyrics and glossary—Rounder CD 2013

Wade in the Water: African-American Sacred Music Traditions—A Smithsonian Folkways 4 CD set

Sweet Honey in the Rock—All for Freedom: a celebration of the roots, history and future of African-American culture—Music for Little People 9 42505-2

Sweet Honey in the Rock—Still on the Journey: The 20th Anniversary Album— Earthbeat 9 42536-2

Sweet Honey in the Rock—I Got Shoes—Music for Little People 9 42534-2

Cross-fertilization: The Caribbean

Jump Up Carnival—Mardi Gras Carnival in Port of Spain, Trinidad, Steelband Pageant—Delos DE 4014

Steelbands of Trinidad and Tobago—Caribbean Carnival Series—Delos DE 4011

Caribbean Revels, Haitian Rara and Dominican Gaga—A Smithsonian Folkways CD—SF40402

Caribbean Island Music, Songs and Dances of Haiti, the Dominican Republic and Jamaica—Nonesuch H 72047

Steel Drums: the Native Steel Drum Band—Tradition TR 2064

Sparrow Calypso Carnival—Slinger Francisco/"The Mighty Sparrow"

West Indian Spirituals and Folk Songs—Musical Heritage Society MHS 1515

New Orleans as a Focal Point

Jazz Odyssey, Volume I: The Sound of New Orleans (1917–1947)—Columbia Special Products

Jazz Funeral at New Orleans—George Lewis' Ragtime Band—Tradition TCD 1049

Authentic New Orleans Jazz Funeral—Magnificent Seventh's Brass Band— Mardi Gras MG1012

Silver Leaf Jazz Band—Great Composers of New Orleans Jazz—Fantasy GTJCD 15005-2

New Orleans Jazz—Edward "Kid" Ory and Jimmy Noone—Olympic 73-762994

Early Dixieland Bands—with The Original Dixieland Jazz Band and Ladd's Black Aces and featuring Nick La Rocca, Larry Shields, Phil Napoleon, and Miff Mole—Archive of Jazz, Volume 37—BYG 529087

King Oliver—"Papa Joe", 1926–1928—King Oliver and His Dixie Syncopators—Decca 79246

King Oliver: The Great 1923 Gennetts—King Oliver's Creole Jazz Band—Herwin H 106

Louis Armstrong: An Early Portrait—Classic 1920s performances with Ma Rainey, Trixie Smith, Fletcher Henderson, and Sidney Bechet—Milestone MLP 2010

Louis Armstrong's All Time Greatest Hits—MCA MCAD 11032

Louis Armstrong: The Great Chicago Concert—Columbia/Legacy C2K 65119

Louis Armstrong Story—The Complete RCA Victor Recordings—BMG Classics 09026-68682-2

Louis Armstrong Plays W. C. Handy—Columbia CK64925

Louis Armstrong: The Complete Decca Studio Recordings of Louis Armstrong and the All Stars—Mosaic MD6-146

Dixieland—New Orleans: with Jack Teagarden, Pee Wee Russell, George Brunis, Edmond Hall, Max Kaminsky, Eddie Condon, Wild Bill Davison, George Wettling, Ernie Caceres, Brad Gowans, Pops Foster, and Tony Spargo—Mainstream 56003

The Roots of Dixieland Jazz, featuring the original artists—Everest Records Archive of Folk and Jazz Records—73-763004

King Oliver Creole Jazz band, 1923—featuring Louis Armstrong—Olympic OL7133

King Oliver, Louis Armstrong, Bessie Smith: The Blues Heritage—TKO Magnum Limited CJSCD846

Louis Armstrong, 1924–1925 with Fletcher Henderson and His Orchestra—

Louis and the Dukes of Dixieland—Audio Fidelity AFLP 1923

Louis Armstrong, July 4, 1900/July 6, 1971—RCA Victor VPM 6044

Young Louis, "The Side Man," 1924–1927—Decca DL 79233

Louis Armstrong and Al Hirt Play Dixieland Trumpet—4 record set—Murray Hill

The Louis Armstrong Story—4-volume record set—Columbia Masterworks ML54383

New Orleans Vol. IV: Preservation Hall Jazz Band—CBS FM44856

Ragtime as a Jazz Form

The Jelly Roll Morton Centennial, His Complete Victor Recordings: 1926–30—Bluebird 2361-2-RB A

Jelly Roll Morton—The Pearls—Featuring Morton's Red-Hot Peppers—BMG 6588-2 RB

Jelly Roll Morton Vol. 1: The Pianist and Composer—Smithsonian RD 043

Scott Joplin (1868–1917)—Piano Rags—Joshua Rifkin on Piano—Elektra/Nonesuch 79159-2

Scott Joplin: His Complete Works—Richard Zimmerman, Piano—Bescol BSCD 4/4

A Century of Ragtime, 1897–1997, 2 CD set; CD#1: Piano Solos with Eubie Blake, Dick Hyman, Richard Zimmerman, Joshua Rifkin and others; CD#2: Ragtime Orchestras—Vanguard 167/8-2

James Dapogny's Chicago Jazz Band—Original Jelly Roll Blues—Discovery 74008

Jelly Roll Morton—(Ferdinand Joseph La Menthe) recorded from piano rolls in 1924—Everest Records Archive of Folk and Jazz Music FS-267

Ragime Entertainment, a Folkways record with several artists compiled and annotated by David A. Jasen—73-750970

Americana, Volume IV, The Age of Ragtime—Roger Shields, Piano—Turnabout TV-S 34579

Joseph Lamb: A Study in Classic Ragtime—Folkways FG 3562

New Ragtime Guitar—David Laibman and Eric Schoenberg, created and recorded by Sam Charters—Asch AHS 3528

Scott Joplin: The Red Back Book—New England Conservatory Ragtime Ensemble conducted by Gunther Schuller—Musical Heritage Society 513737K

Jelly Roll Morton Plays Jelly Roll Morton—Olympic OL 7131

Black & White Piano—Biograph 72-750268

Rip-Roarin' Ragtime with Dave Jasen on the piano—Folkways FG 3561

Essay in Ragtime, Ragtime Piano Classics played by Ann Charters—Folkways FG3563

The Blues

Reverend Gary Davis: Pure Religion and Bad Company—Folkways SF 40035

Chicago/The Blues/Today!—with Junior Well Chicago Blues Band with Buddy Guy, J.B. Hutto and His Hawks, and Otis Spann's South Side Piano—Vanguard 172/74-2

The Real Blues: John Lee Hooker—Tradition/Everest STR 2089

John Lee Hooker: Plays and Sings the Blues—Chess/MCA CHD-9199

John Lee Hooker: The Ultimate Collection: 1948–1990—Rhino R2 70572

Country Blues Classics, Volume 1—"down home blues"—Blues Classics BC 5

Young Big Bill Broonzy, 1928–1935—Yazoo 1011

Story of the Blues, from the origins of the blues through WWII and beyond—Columbia 30008

John Lee Hooker—Everest Records Archive of Folk and Jazz Music

Negro Prison Songs from the Mississippi State Penitentiary—Tradition TLP 1020

Wake Up Dead Man: Black Convict Worksongs from Texas Prisons, recorded in the middle 1960s—booklet with lyrics and glossary—Rounder CD 2013

Robert Johnson: King of the Delta Blues Singers, 2 volumes—Columbia WCK 30034

Leadbelly: Shout On—Folkways FT 30130S

Lead Belly's Last Sessions—Folkways SF CD 40068-40071

Leadbelly—Take This Hammer—Verve Folkways FV-9001

The Blues Tradition, 1927–1932—Milestone MLP 2016

B.B. King: B.B. King—King Biscuit Flour Hour Records 70710-88038-2

Bessie Smith: The Collection—Columbia CK 44441

Mamie Smith: Complete Recorded Works in Chronological Order—Document DOCD-5357

Clara Smith: Complete Recorded Works in Chronological Order—Document DOCD-5364

Minstrelsy and Its Effects on Jazz

Songs of Stephen Foster: Roger Wagner Chorale—Angel 74-750092

Songs by Stephen Foster: Jan DeGaetani/Leslie Guinn/Gilbert Kalish—Nonesuch H-71268

Americana, Volume V: Stephen Foster Songs with the Gregg Smith Singers and the New York Vocal Arts Ensemble—Turnabout TV-S 34609

Beloved Melodies of Stephen Foster, with The Eric Rogers Chorale and Orchestra—London SP 44050

The Early Minstrel Show—New World Records NW 338

Religious Influences on Jazz

Sing Praises Unto the Lord: Doris Akers with the Simmons-Akers Singers—RCA Victor LPM 1481

Mahalia Jackson: Gospels, Spirituals, and Hymns—Columbia/Legacy C2K 47083

Mahalia Jackson: Amazing Grace—CBS P 14358

Wade in the Water: African-American Sacred Music Traditions—A Smithsonian Folkways 4 CD set

Negro Spirituals: with the Tell Tale Singers and The Goldenaires Choir—Vox STPL 513.110

Afro-American Spirituals, Work Songs, and Ballads—edited by Alan Lomax, a Folk Music of the United States series—Rounder Records CD 1510

Negro Church Music, Southern Folk Heritage Series—Atlantic SD 1351

Anthology of Black Gospel Music—Legacy LEG 114

Marian Anderson: He's Got the Whole World in His Hands and 18 other Spirituals with Franz Rupp on piano—RCA Victor 09026-61960-2

An Introduction to Gospel Song—RBF RF 5

Country Gospel Song, Compiled and Annotated by Samuel Charters—Folkways RBF 19

Spirituals: A Way of Survival—Sounds of Heritage SOH 5001

West Indian Spirituals and Folk Songs—Musical Heritage Society MHS 1515

Caribbean Revels, Haitian Rara and Dominican Gaga—A Smithsonian Folkways CD—SF40402

Voodoo Ceremony in Haiti, recorded live on location—Olympic 75-761540
Voodoo Trance Music: Ritual Drums of Haiti—Lyrichord LLST 7279
Church Songs played on the piano and sung by Little Brother Montgomery
(Eurreal Wilford Montgomery)—Folkways FTS 31042

Chicago in the 1920s—
includes Piano Blues and Boogie Woogie

Jazz Odyssey, Volume II: The Sound of Chicago (1923-1940)—Columbia C3L
32
Boogie Woogie: Volume I—Piano Soloists (Clarence "Pine Top" Smith,
Montana Taylor, Speckled Red (Rufus Perryman), Romeo Nelson, Charles
"Cow Cow" Davenport, Jimmy Yancey, "Clipple" Clarence Lofton, Albert
Ammons, Meade Lux Lewis, Pete Johnson, and Art Hodes)—Jasmine
JASMCD 2538
Jelly Roll Morton, Volume 2—Chicago: The Red Hot Peppers—Smithsonian RD
044
Jazz, Volume 5: Chicago 1—Folkways F-2805
Meade "Lux" Lewis: Barrel House Piano—Tops L 1533
Jazz Piano Anthology—Columbia 74-760079
Cuttin' the Boogie, Piano Blues and Boogie Woogie, 1926-1941—New World
Records NW 259
Bix Beiderbecke, 1924—Olympic OL7130
Chicago South Side, 1927-1929, Volume 2—Historical Records HLP-30
Chicago Jazz, 1923-1929—Biograph BLP 12007
New York to Chicago, 1923-28—Biograph BLP 12007
Chicago Jazz, 1925-1929, Volume 2—Biograph 12043
Master of Boogie: Albert Ammons—BMG 7313835628-2

New York in the 1920s—
The Harlem Renaissance

Jazz Odyssey, Volume III: The Sound of Harlem—Columbia C3L 33
Fletcher Henderson and His Orchestra, 1927-1931—Classics 572

Territory Band Period

Jammin for the Jackpot: Big Bands and Territory Bands of the 1930s—New World NW 217

Swing Era

Benny Rides Again: Benny Goodman Orchestra—Chess/MCA CHD-31264
Benny Goodman Live at Carnegie Hall—Columbia Jazz Masterpieces J2C 40244
Benny Goodman—The Birth of Swing (1935–1936)—Bluebird 60138-2
A Salute to Glenn Miller conducted by Billy May—GNP GNPD 76
Big Bands Greatest Hits, Volume 2—Columbia CGT 31213
Artie Shaw: The Classic Tracks—The Big Bands—Kaz CD 305
Those Swingin' Days of the Big Bands—featuring 36 different well-known Big Bands—Showcase SH 3301
BBC Big Band—The Age of Swing, Volume 1—Bainbridge BCD 2511
Jimmy Dorsey: Big Bands with Bob Eberly and Helen O'Connell with Ray McKinley and June Richmond—Time-Life 4TBB-10
Tommy Dorsey and His Orchestra—Pavilion CD 9740
Les Brown and His Orchestra, Vocals by Doris Day: Sentimental Journey—Encore/CBS P 14361
Woody Herman: The Classic Tracks—The Big Bands—Kaz CD 306
Tommy Dorsey and His Orchestra: The Seventeen #1s—RCA 9973-2-R
Paul Whiteman and His Orchestra: The Best of the Big Bands—CSP P 16784
Coleman Hawkins: The Essential Coleman Hawkins—Verve V6-8568
Coleman Hawkins—In a Mellow Tone—Prestige OJCCD-6001-2
Coleman Hawkins—The Genius of Coleman Hawkins—Verve 314 539 065-2
Big Band Renaissance (5 vols.)—Smithsonian RD 108
Big Band Jazz: From the Beginnings to the 1950s (6 LPs)—Smithsonian RD030

The Dixieland Revival

At the Darktown Strutters Ball: Leonard Gaskin—Prestige/Swingville SVLP 2033
Spreadin' Joy: the Music of Sidney Bechet—interpreted by Bob Wilber Quintet/Septet—Classic Editions CJ-5
Sidney Bechet 1923–1936—Classics 583
Sidney Bechet: The Best of Sidney Bechet—Blue Note

Sidney Bechet: The Complete Sidney Bechet, Volume 1 & 2 (1932–1941)—RCA
    07863 66498-2
Dixieland Jazz in the Forties—Folkways 02853

Bebop

Charlie Christian: Jazz Immortal—Esoteric ES-548
The Essential Charlie Parker—Verve 314 517 173-2
Charlie Parker: Yardbird Suite: The Ultimate Charlie Parker Collection—Rhino
    R2 72260
Charlie Parker: The Charlie Parker Story, A Savoy Jazz Recording—Savoy SV0105
Dizzy Gillespie: The Greatest of Dizzy Gillespie—RCA Victor LPM 2398
Dizzy Gillespie: "Groovin' High" with Dizzy (John Birks) Gillespie (and
    various musicians including Charlie Parker)—Savoy SV-0152
Dizzy Gillespie: Stan Getz—Diz and Getz—Verve 833 559-2
Dizzy Gillespie: Bird Songs, the Final Recordings—Telarc CD-83421
Bebop: Recorded Anthology of American Music—New World NW 270
Charlie Christian—Everest FS 219
Thelonius Monk: Underground—Columbia CK 40785
Thelonius Monk: The Complete Blue Note Recordings—Blue Note CDP 7243 8
    30363 2 5
Thelonius Monk: The Composer—Columbia CK 44297
Miles Davis & Thelonius Monk: Live at Newport 1958 (Davis) & 1963
    (Monk)—Columbia Legacy C2K53585
Bop Begins—Topaz Jazz TPZ 1051
Jazz in Revolution: Big Bands of the 1940s—New World Records NW 284
Bud Powell: Jazz Giant—Norgran/Verve MGN

Progressive Era

Stan Kenton: Artistry in Rhythm—Capitol T-167
Stan Kenton: New Concepts of Artistry in Rhythm—Capitol Jazz CPD 7 92865 2
Boyd Raeburn and Orchestra, 1944-1946—First Time Records FTR 1515
Boyd Raeburn and Orchestra: Boyd Meets Stravinksy—with Dizzy Gillespie and
    other artists—Savoy SV 0185

Stan Kenton: Lush Interlude—Creative World 1005

Stan Kenton: One Night Stand with Stan Kenton at The Commodore—Joyce LP-1030

Stan Kenton: Adventures in Jazz, arranged by Bill Holman, Dee Barton, and Gene Roland—Creative World ST-1010

Stan Kenton: Adventures in Time, A Concerto for Orchestra, composed/conducted by Johnny Richards—Creative World ST-1011

Sauter/Finnegan: The Sound of the Sauter-Finnegan Orchestra—RCA Victor LPM 1009

Claude Thornhill: The 1948 Transcription Performances—Hep Records CD 17

West Coast/Cool Jazz, Third Stream, and Modal Jazz

The Birth of the Third Stream—Columbia Legacy CK64929

Mirage: Avant-Garde and Third-Stream Jazz—New World Records NW 216

Modern Jazz Quartet—Fontessa—Atlantic 1231-2

Modern Jazz Quartet—MJQ: Patterns—United Artists UAL 4072

Modern Jazz Quartet—Best of the Modern Jazz Quartet—Pablo 2521804323

Modern Jazz Quartet—MJQ 40: A 40th Anniversary Compilation—Atlantic 82330-2

Miles Davis: Birth of the Cool—Capitol CPD 7 92862-2

Miles Davis: Kind of Blue—Columbia Legacy CK 64935

Miles Davis: The Ballad Artistry of Miles Davis—SEMA S21-56710

Joao (Meirelles) and His Bossa Kings—Cool Samba: Joao and His Bossa Kings—Getz/Bilberto: Verve 314 521 414-2

Dave Brubeck Quartet: Time Out—Columbia CK8192

Dave Brubeck Quartet: Brubeck Time—Columbia CK 67524

Sonny Criss: Sonny's Dream, Birth of the New Cool—Prestige/Fantasy OJCCD 707

Stan Getz—The Greatest of Stan Getz—Roulette RCD 59027

Stan Getz—East of the Sun: The West Coast Sessions Stan Getz—Verve 314 531 935-2

Stan Getz & Kenny Barron—People Time—Verve 314 510 823-2

Quintessence, Vol. 2—Stan Getz Quartet with Chet Baker—Concord CCD 4858-2

Hard Bop

Sonny Rollins: Alfie—Original Music from the Score with Sonny Rollins and
Orchestra, conducted by Oliver Nelson—Impulse A-9111

Sonny Rollins: Way Out West—Contemporary OJCCD 337-2

Sonny Rollins: Sonny Rollins On Impulse!—MCA Impulse IMPD-223

Art Blakey and The Jazz Messengers: Feeling Good—D/CD 4007

Art Blakey and The Jazz Messengers: A Night in Tunisia—Blue Note CDP 7
84049 2

Art Blakey and The Jazz Messengers: The Best of Art Blakey and The Jazz
Messengers, The Blue Note Years—Blue Note CDP 2 93205 7

Art Blakey Quintet: A Night at Birdland—Blue Note CDP 7 46519 2

Julian "Cannonball" Adderly Quintet: Mercy, Mercy, Mercy!—Capitol Jazz CDP
7243 8 29915 2 6

Julian "Cannonball" Adderly: Discoveries—Savoy SV-0251

Cannonball Adderly Quintet: Plus—Riverside OJCCD 306-2

Jimmy Smith: Respect—Verve V6-8705

Jimmy Smith: Livin' It Up—Verve V6-8750

The Jazz Messengers: featuring Donald Byrd, Hank Mobley, Horace Silver,
Doug Watkins, and Art Blakey—Columbia CL897

Lee Morgan: The Genius of Lee Morgan—Tradition

Blue Mitchell: Graffiti Blues—Sony/Legacy JK 57120

Small Jazz Groups of the 50s and 60s—featuring The Modern Jazz Quartet, Lee
Konitz with Wayne Marsh, The Jazz Messengers, Art Farmer-Benny
Golson Jazztet, Sonny Rollins, George Russell Sextet, and Charles Mingus
Jazz Workshop—New World NW 242

John Coltrane: Giant Steps—Atlantic 1311-2

John Coltrane: The Ultimate Blue Train—Blue Note CDP 7243 8 53428 0 6

John Coltrane: The Art of John Coltrane—Blue Note CDP 0777 7 99175 2 5

Clifford Brown: Clifford Brown and Max Roach—Verve 314 543 306-2

Listen Up: Les McCann—MusicMasters Jazz 01612-65139-2

Straight Up: Jimmy McGriff—Milestone MCD 9285-2

Unity: Larry Young (with Woody Shaw and Joe Henderson)—Blue Note BLP
4221

James Moody: Moody's Mood for Love—Chessmates GRD 823

Free Jazz

John Coltrane: Major Works of John Coltrane—OM, Ascension, Kulu De
    Mama and Selflessness—with McCoy Tyner, Jimmy Garrison, and Elvin
    Jones, and other artists—Impulse GRD-2-113
John Coltrane: The John Coltrane Gold Collection—Dejavu 5-119-2
John Coltrane: A Love Supreme—Impulse GRD-155
John Coltrane: My Favorite Things—Atlantic 1361-2
Miles Davis: ESP—Columbia CK 65683
Eric Dolphy: Out to Lunch—Blue Note CDP 7 46524 2
Eric Dolphy: Outward Bound—New Jazz OJCCD 022-2
Archie Shepp: Four for Trane—Impulse IMPD-218
Don Ellis: Electric Bath—Columbia CS 9585
Ornette Coleman: The Shape of Jazz to Come—Atlantic A2 1317
Ornette Coleman: Change of the Century—Atlantic 81341-2
Ornette Coleman: Free Jazz, a Collective Improvisation by the Ornette
    Coleman Double Quartet—with Eric Dolphy, Donald Cherry, Freddie
    Hubbard, Scott LaFaro, Charles Haden, Billy Higgins and Ed Blackwell—
    Atlantic 1364-2
Cecil Taylor: Unit Structures—Blue Note CDP 7 84237 2
Cecil Taylor: Live! at the Cafe Montmartre—Arista Freedom
Don Cherry: "Mu" First Part—BYG 529.301

Pittsburgh Greats

Billy Eckstine: Everything I Have Is Yours: The Best of the M-G-M Years—Verve
    819 442-2
Errol Garner: Moon Glow—Tradition TCD 1010
Earl Hines: The Essential Earl "Fatha" Hines—Olympic OL 7125
Roy Eldridge: Roy and Diz—Verve 314 521 647-2
Ray Brown: Live at Starbuck's—Telarc CD-83502
Kenny Clarke: Our Man in Paris—Blue Note BST 84146
Absolute Benson: George Benson—Verve 314 543 586-2
Stanley Turrentine: Joy Rode—Blue Note BST 84201
Amhad Jamal: The Awakening—Impulse AS 9194

Women In Jazz

Bessie Smith: The Collection—Columbia CK 44441

Ella Fitzgerald: The Songbooks, The Silver Collection—Verve 4046

Ella Fitzgerald: Newport Jazz Festival Live at Carnegie Hall—Columbia KG 32557

June Christy and the Stan Kenton Orchestra: Road Show—Capitol STBO 1327

Sarah Vaughan: Sarah Vaughan—Everest FS-250

Sarah Vaughan and Lester Young: One Night Stand—Blue Note CDP 7243 8 32139 2 4

Billie Holiday: The Complete Commodore Recordings—Commodore CMD 2-401

Billie Holiday: God Bless the Child—MCA MCAD 20254

Dinah Washington: American Legends: Dinah Washington—Delta 12 749

Patti Page: A Golden Celebration—Mercury 314 534 720-2

Teresa Brewer and Count Basie: The Songs of Bessie Smith—Flying Dutchman 10161

Teresa Brewer: American Music Box, The Songs of Irving Berlin—Doctor Jazz Records FW-40231

Great Jazz Vocalists: featuring Billie Holiday, Ella Fitzgerald, Billy Eckstine, Mel Torme, Sarah Vaughan, Dinah Washington, and Anita O'Day—Polygram 314 520 266-4

Mamie Smith: Complete Recorded Works in Chronological Order—Document DOCD-5357

Clara Smith: Complete Recorded Works in Chronological Order, Volume 2, 1924—Document DOCD-5364

Betty Carter: The Audience with Betty Carter—Vervce 835 684-2

The Gathering: Geri Allen—Verve 314 557 614-2

Just Friends: Marian McPartland—Concord CCD 4805-2

Emily Remler: Transitions—Concord CCD-4236

Patrice Rushen: Signature—Discovery 77065

International Sweethearts of Rhythm—Rosetta RC 1312

Toshiko Akiyoshi—RCA Victor AFL 1-2678

Fusion and Jazz Rock

Miles Davis: Bitches Brew—Columbia C4K 65570
Miles Davis: You're Under Arrest—Columbia CK 40023
Pat Metheny: As Falls Wichita, So Wichita Falls—ECM 821-416-4
Pat Metheny: First Circle—ECM 4-25008
Headhunters: Herbie Hancock—Columbia/Legacy CK 65123
Chick Corea and Return to Forever: Return to Forever—MBG 78118-21022-2
Chick Corea and Return to Forever: Sundance Groove Merchant—GM-530
Weather Report: Black Market—Columbia PC 34099
Weather Report: Mysterious Traveller—Columbia KC 34294
Weather Report: Heavy Weather—Columbia CK 34418
Mahavishnu Orchestra: Between Nothingness and Eternity—Columbia CK
    32766
Steps Ahead: Steps Ahead—Elektra 9-60168-2
Blood, Sweat and Tears: Blood, Sweat and Tears—Columbia CK 63986
Blood, Sweat and Tears: Brand New Day—ABC Records AB-1015

1980s and Beyond

Wynton Marsalis: Standard Time—Columbia CK 47346
Wynton Marsalis with the Lincoln Center Jazz Orchestra: Big Train—Columbia
    69860
Christopher Hollyday: The Natural Moment—Novus 3118-2-N
Nicholas Payton: Gumbo Nouveau—Verve 314 531 199-2
Danilo Perez: Danilo Perez—Novus 1241 63148-2
Marcus Roberts: Time and Circumstance—Columbia CK 67567
Roy Hargrove's Crisol: Habana—Verve 314 537 563-2
Terence Blanchard: Terence Blanchard—Columbia 468388 2
Michael Brecker: Time is of the Essence—Verve 314 547 844-2
Branford Marsalis: Requiem Quartet—Columbia CK 69655
Wallace Roney: Wallace Roney Quintet—9 45914-2
Joshua Redman: Wish—Warner Brothers 9 45365
Benny Green: These Are Soulful Days (with Russell Malone and Christian
    McBride)—Blue Note 7243 4 99527 2 0

Live Jazz at Pitt "The 25th Anniversary Concert"—Pitt 1001
Big Band Treasures, Live—Smithsonian Jazz Masterworks Orchestra—
      Smithsonian RJ 0044
Grover Washington Jr.: Aria—Sony Classical SK61864
Jon Faddis: Remembrances—Chesky Records JO166

CHAPTER 1

What Is Jazz?

Jazz: A World Music

Since Jazz is now an accepted art form in almost every corner of the world, in trying to identify it we are forced to consider many different cultures. Japan, one of the leading industrial nations of the world, has emerged as one of the most important countries for touring jazz musicians. Japan has not only provided a lucrative marketplace for touring jazz musicians from the United States and other Western nations but has contributed new innovations in jazz (see chapter 16 on World Music). The small Caribbean island of Surinam is another country that has emerged as an important contributor to the already overflowing world of the professional jazz musician. Surinam born flutist and multiinstrumentalist Ronald Schnider is one of the freshest voices on the jazz scene. But one thing is certain: jazz is uniquely American. Most historians and scholars agree that jazz was not only born in America, but it was the African-American, sons and daughters of African slaves, who gave birth to jazz.

Further proof concerning the uniqueness of this contribution can be found in the fact that after the passing of the Segregation Act of 1894, Creole musicians found that they had to learn the art of "true Jazz improvisation" from their African-American brothers and sisters.

The list of countries both large and small that have contributed to the development of jazz in the past several years is enormous. I am certain that given the present climate in jazz and a continued development, we will witness a tremendous outpouring of new young jazz musicians from various countries throughout the world. It is safe to say that these new young artists will emerge from places such as Australia, Japan, Russia, India, China, Ghana, Nigeria, Senegal, Brazil, Argentina, etc., as well as North America and Europe. Perhaps the one thing that has kept the art of jazz primarily in the hands of the so-called industrial nations like the United States, Germany, Great Britain, France, etc., is the fact that they own the mechanisms for presenting the music to the general public. By this I mean that if given the same amount of technological assistance in the producing and manufacturing of jazz recordings, videos, etc., and the ability to market these products, I am more than certain that we would learn about jazz musicians, from some of the above mentioned countries, who had not previously been heard. In order for such a product as world jazz to emerge, it would also be necessary for the development of a strong economic base in those areas where the music would be marketed. In other words, if that music is not marketed to people who can afford to pay for it then it would lie dormant. This, in many ways, is a sad commentary on our so-called advanced, cultural society in that economics still dictate the course of history.

Great Britain can be given much credit for having introduced to the world, in a commercialized vein, the music of such artists as reggae artist Bob Marley, jazz musician Courtney Pine, and several other artists from the Caribbean, who had a limited amount of success in the commercial world of music. In the case of Courtney Pine, the young British-born Jamaican saxophonist, we have seen a tremendous amount of interest in his work throughout most of the world, except in the United States. In many ways this is typical of the young, gifted jazz artist who is not a member of one of the advanced technological countries in that they suffer by not having the economic and political clout necessary to make them as successful as their American counterparts. Because he is British, Courtney is able to take advantage of Britain's economic and technological expertise in launching his career. This does not in any way diminish his ability or the ability of the young artists from one of the more "favored" countries from producing genuine jazz, however it does give us an insight into why certain types of music succeed on the world market as opposed to others. The development of sophisticated recording and listening devices has greatly reduced the difficulty of learning jazz firsthand from a master. Thus learning the art of Jazz improvisation is available to anyone who wishes to learn it. As we move into the 1990s, I would venture to say that jazz is truly a world music.

What Is Jazz?

When I first arrived at the University of Pittsburgh to begin teaching jazz courses, I quite naturally inquired where I might hear some good jazz. I was referred to a local motel lounge where I discovered a cocktail lounge act. Musically, the group was very professional. But the person who sent me to see the group considered the band a jazz group. This insignificant incident illustrates the confusion most people experience when identifying jazz. Because of the fusion crossover movement in jazz (the playing of rhythm and blues melodies and rock rhythms by jazz musicians and vice versa) and the fusion of Latin, gospel, country, classical, and various ethnic music, many of us aren't quite sure what jazz is.

Is the music of George Benson, Grover Washington, Donald Byrd, and Spyro Gyra jazz? Many jazz purists say "no." But the musicians who play this music say that it is indeed jazz. Today it is almost impossible to listen to a jazz talk show or interview without hearing someone ask the question, what is or is not jazz?

If the musicians themselves aren't sure, what about the listener? Is the average jazz listener capable of distinguishing true jazz? How many jazz record buyers are, in fact, trained musicians? If "pure" jazz is going to survive the great influx of commercialized fusion, the "pure" artist must find a way to gear his or her music toward a broader, more general audience.

The answer to whether the jazz enthusiast has to be a trained musician to understand jazz is "no." The jazz enthusiast does not have to be a trained musician, or even understand music, any more than the classical music lover has to understand classical music.

This form of snobbery in jazz has hurt the jazz artist more than anything else. Jazz is and should be a music for all people. Music should be felt or experienced. The only true criterion for "judging" the music should be the individual's personal feeling and not some overstated intellectual treatise on the music. Simply put the recording on and listen to it. If you like it (for whatever reason), then it is good music for you. This is not to say that people should not try to improve their knowledge of music, but the individual listener should be the ultimate judge.

What is so exotic about watching a jazz performer in action is the realization that the artist is actually composing and creating new works right before our own eyes. The performer or jazz soloist is the creator, composer, arranger, interpreter and conductor at the same time. This rare display of creative, multifaceted wizardry is often taken for granted by those who are not familiar with jazz, thus making it impossible for them to truly understand the intricacies involved in creating a good jazz solo.

In trying to determine just what is jazz and what is not jazz, I like to refer to what I call the *hipness factor*. That is, jazz for the average jazz fan represents a type of music that is intellectually stimulating and is esthetically rewarding. In other words, he or she feels good and it presents a challenge. Most jazz musicians and fans like to think that they are a notch above the average person that one encounters in society. This is what I mean when I refer to the hipness factor. Unfortunately, the hipness factor can be blamed for isolating jazz from a larger public. The fact that jazz is often presented in such a manner so that those who do not really understand it immediately feel left out, causes a number of potential jazz fans to defect to a more readily acceptable music, namely pop music. Without doubt the over-hip jazz lover or jazz fan does more disservice to the music in the eyes of those who make a living playing this music, of which they are unaware. Whether or not a certain phrase played by a particular musician is in fact more intellectually or esthetically rewarding than that played by another, is a matter of personal taste. What sounds like and is referred to as a great solo line may in fact be a mediocre presentation when viewed by a musician from a different culture. Without doubt, the most important ingredient in deciding what is and what is not jazz, is what I call the *blues factor*. Does it have a blues-like feeling or a blues presentation? I am fully aware that there are those critics, not necessarily writers but musicians also, who will not agree with me on this. For them, any type of improvisation, whether it stems from a blues base or not, is considered jazz. This is incorrect and is at the base of the mass confusion which surrounds the question of what is and what is not jazz. If in fact improvisation alone was responsible for what we call jazz then we would have to accept all the music that we would find in such remote areas as the Outback in Australia, or the improvisational music found in Haiti, or the improvisational music found in the folk music of the Hungarian gypsy. While these musics are indeed stimulating and rewarding and, surely, are based on pure folk ethnic improvisation—they are not jazz. What makes improvisation jazz is its blues base, not the mere fact that it is improvisational. Another point that comes to mind is that many historians and scholars of jazz have stated that the greatest thing about jazz is its spontaneity. Although it is true that true jazz, in its embryonic stages, is entirely spontaneous, the same can be said of many other forms of music including the embryonic states of western European art music before the composer pins it to the score. It is true that a great musician is spontaneous and there is a kind of artistic, esthetic electricity that develops as the artist begins to improvise in a spontaneous manner. Without these elements jazz would not be the dynamic music that it is, but again, we must look at the source and the source is blues.

Listening to Jazz

What should the untrained jazz fan listen for in a recording? The major difference between music and noise is that music is pleasing to the ear and noise is irritating or unpleasant. In recent years the standards for what is considered pleasing to the ear have changed. Those artists whose music was unfortunately labeled "space music" or "outside" in the 1960s have, in many instances, reeducated the public so that many of their works are now accepted. This shows that what music we like or don't like is often determined by our level of exposure to it.

> It is the mass media, with all of its vast resources and power, that often influences what we like and don't like.
>
> *Ursala Broschke Davis*

How can you learn to like a particular form of music if you are not exposed to it? Humans are capable of adjusting to whatever is necessary. If our very survival depended on liking noise, we would all embrace the banging of a tire iron as readily as we now buy a Miles Davis album. If we are tired and irritable, we perhaps prefer to listen to something soothing rather than a highly-charged jazz/rock recording. As you can see, many factors are involved in the music we call jazz. Our taste in music varies according to how we feel at a given moment.

In the 1990s, there is another factor that plays an important role in how we listen to music, and that is the development of ultra sophisticated listening devices. I once remember talking to a Japanese promoter about the possibility of having one of my tapes released in Japan. He informed me that he was interested, but that he would have to hear the quality of the tape since most Japanese have more sophisticated listening equipment than do Americans and therefore would be more critical. I am sure that if, in fact, such a gap in the development of the recorders and tape players did exist, it was only temporary because most of the technologically developed countries have, in the 1990s, merged together to produce what we call multi-national corporations. These corporations produce not only CD players, tape recorders, Digital Audio Tape machines, etc., but almost everything else that we use. So, it is important, as I had mentioned earlier, that the music is produced so that it is not only appealing to its targeted audience but that a number of people can afford to listen to the music.

Listening to jazz is an art form within itself. One of the first things that I remember when I heard my first jazz record was that it sounded somewhat confusing to me. It was not until I learned to distinguish the sound of the various instruments, and to some degree determine the role that each instrument played, that I felt comfortable in listening to the music. First and foremost the majority of the people who listen to jazz tend to listen for a melody. Regardless of how elementary this may sound, the melody of a song is one of its most important ingredients. There are those who would argue that the rhythm of a song is the most important ingredient, but there are many songs that have the same rhythm. Very few songs have the same melody. In fact, if the song has the exact same melody it becomes a legal case and the perpetrator is punished accordingly. The melody is the composer's idea of a particular sound picture. This sound picture consists of scales, melodic motifs, intervals, arpeggios, etc., which according to how they are placed together produce a particular melody. The idea of the melody is to evoke a particular feeling. Without doubt, the melody should be singled out and its role clarified for the listener. The rhythm, in many cases, is the backbone of the composition. As I have stated earlier, rhythm is perhaps the most important ingredient that holds the world together. Without rhythm, there could be no days, there could be no time, there could be no universe, there could be no sound. Sound is vibration and vibration is the continued sequential placement of beats. Thus, if one beat does not follow the next beat in a rapid succession, we have no vibration, therefore no sound. So we must have a distinct and, we hope, effective rhythmic pattern in order for the song to be successful. The rhythm should adequately support the melody. The harmonic scheme of the song is equally important. It serves to support the melody and to give it form and distinction, and plays an effective role in working together with the rhythm to produce an overall structural base on the sound picture. If all of this sounds complicated, it is to the uninformed person. But what is important is that the listener, upon first hearing a piece, distinguish each of the above-mentioned items: melody, rhythm, harmony, etc. One must discern the role that each plays and the significance of that role.

Sound

Sound is the first thing we hear when we listen to music. In his book the *Mysticism of Sound*, Hazrat Inayat Khan states that music is the ultimate art form. He explains that "in the beginning there was the word and the word was sound, therefore all things emanate from sound." Whether or not we accept this philosophy, the fact is that when we listen to music, the first thing we hear is sound. Therefore, in order for a recording to be considered a first-rate musical offering it must sound good. It must sound good both technically and musically. Many excellent musicians have suffered because of poor reproduction of their music. You, as a music buyer, should demand the best in reproductive quality. During the 1940s and 50s, it was common practice for record stores to furnish listening booths for prospective record buyers. This service has all but disappeared.

Aside from the technical side of reproducing the music, the musicians should be highly skillful in producing a sound that is not only pleasing to the ear but complementary to their music. The sound that a musician produces is his or her signature. In jazz there are those artists who produce what we call big robust sounds like tenor saxophonists: Coleman Hawkins, Don Byas and Sonny Rollins, the younger players like Kenny Garrett and Joshua Redman. There were also trombone players who produced what we call big, lush sounds such as J.J. Johnson and Slide Hampton. On the trumpet, we immediately think of Clifford Brown who produced a kind of big, lush, but cutting sound. Then there were those who produced a more mellow sound on their instruments like Miles Davis, Art Farmer, Wallace Roney, John Coltrane, James Moody and Stan Getz. The same can be said about the touch of the piano. There are those pianists, like McCoy Tyner and Monty Alexander, who produced a heavier percussive sound. On the other end of the spectrum, musicians like George Cables and Herbie Hancock produce a more subtle and lighter touch and a mellower sound. There are pianists like Geri Allen who tend to have a cross between a classical and jazz sound and are able to bridge the gap between being percussive and melodic in their approach to sound. As jazz listeners, we are interested not in whether a certain performer has a classical sound on his or her instrument but in whether the sound fits the musical idea. If the artist is a blues-based player, shouldn't the sound have a bluesy effect? One of the major faults of so many jazz artists is that they try to imitate classical musicians on their instruments when in fact they should try to produce a sound that is complementary to their own music.

One of the most impressive examples of the versatility of younger jazz artists is young trumpeter Wynton Marsalis' performance at the 1984 Grammy Awards on national television. After brilliantly performing a classical piece with symphony orchestra, Marsalis adjusted to a more jazz-oriented trumpet sound and performed a jazz composition.

During my many years as a professional jazz musician, whenever I approached symphony musicians for help in producing a "good" sound, I found that they were just as interested in learning to produce a jazz sound on their instruments. Sound is relevant to whatever it is that you are trying to accomplish musically.

Rhythm

According to some musicians the most important ingredient in music is rhythm. Jazz in particular is a rhythmic music. Even in the slow, melodic-harmonic ballad playing of pianist Bill Evans, there is a subtle but definite rhythmic flow that holds everything together. On the other hand, the highly pronounced rhythm strains that flow through the up-tempo music of saxophonist Sonny Rollins, or pianist McCoy Tyner, illustrate a very different approach to improvisation. The very way that a jazz musician attacks a phrase or musical idea differs from the way that his or her symphony counterpart attacks it. To say that a jazz musician plays syncopated rhythms oversimplifies what is a highly sensitive approach to emphasizing a particular melodic phrase. A melodic pattern or phrase can be altered so much by a change in rhythmic approach that it would take a trained ear to recognize the similarities between the two approaches. This can also be said of certain European art musical forms, but the emphasis is not quite as important to the success or failure of a musical idea. Among the more rhythmic players in jazz are artists like saxophonists Charlie Parker, Sonny Rollins, Joe Henderson, Bent Jadik, and Dexter Gordon; trumpeters Louis Armstrong, Dizzy Gillespie, Roy Eldridge, Don Cherry, Clifford Brown, and Benny Bailey; pianists Horace Silver, Mal Waldron, John Lewis, McCoy Tyner, Kenny Drew, Monty Alexander and Marcus Roberts; and trombonists J.J. Johnson and Slide Hampton.

Just what determines whether someone is considered a predominantly rhythmic player or a melodic player? If the musician in question tends consistently to prefer shorter, more syncopated lines over smoother, longer, choppier phrases, we classify him or her as a rhythmic player. For example, compare the music of John Coltrane to that of Sonny Rollins. To say that Rollins is only a rhythmic player and not a melodic player is, of course, incorrect. Such original compositions as "Oleo," "Pent-up-House," "Doxy," and "St. Thomas," show Rollins to be a highly sensitive melodic composer as well as a rhythmic player. But taking a close look at his improvisations in these same compositions, we find that the string that ties together his musical ideas is without doubt rhythm. On the other hand, listening to Coltrane's *Giant Steps* album or the *Cresent* album shows us that Coltrane was more melodic than rhythmic. All music is good music. If the music does not move you to be happy, sad, sentimental, angry, relaxed, and so on, something is wrong. Good jazz music is no different from any other form of music in this respect. The jazz expert who condemns music as being too simple and commercial when it moves someone in a particular way is not facing reality. Each of us has different tastes and different backgrounds and therefore responds to the music in different ways. I was once asked if I was insulted if people danced to my music. My answer was of course, no; I considered it an honor. Music that is danced to is music that is reaching someone.

Example 1

Form and Structure

To state simply that music must have a complex form to be valid is wrong. Form in music exists in various degrees. The overall form of a jazz composition or an improvised solo may consist of various rhythms or only one particularly rhythmic motive or idea. The form of a piece may consist of sixteen measures or of two measures repeated over and over at varying melodic and harmonic levels. Form in some jazz compositions may be an intricate part of the improvisation, whereas in other compositions the form may depend solely on the improvisation to hold it together.

During the 1960s, some jazz composers experimented with presenting certain musical ideas or short musical motifs to a group of talented improvisers with the idea that they would use their collective talents to establish a form. Depending on the versatility of the participating musicians, the composition sometimes took on a form and structure that bordered on brilliance, while at other times the results were disastrous. It is virtually impossible to separate structure from form in Jazz improvisation.

Form is necessary for order. The question then becomes, is it necessary to have order in jazz? The answer to that question is yes. There must be order in jazz just as there is order in other forms of music. That order, which eventually results into a type of form, exists in life, and music is a representation of life. What is often viewed as a music that has little or no order is in fact misleading. During the 1960s period in jazz, which was often referred to as the avant-garde, we find that there was a lot of what we call free improvisation. But in fact this freedom did have a type of order that existed within the work itself. This we call *implied form*. The structure or the form was a result of its own musical breeding. Within the improvisation we find certain cues that were placed at particular sections in the music by the improviser that in fact dictate to the accompanying musicians what the direction was, and in many instances decided whether or not the music would go faster, slower, higher or lower, etc. Thus, we find there is a form that existed in what appeared to be a formless type of music.

Improvisation in Jazz

Just what is improvisation in jazz? Is jazz possible without improvisation? If we define jazz as an improvised music that produces a bluesy feeling, then any improvised music that uses constant lowered thirds, sevenths, or fifths qualifies as jazz. We must identify and associate this jazz feeling with the improvisation we hear in a jazz recording.

Some jazz improvisations are limited while others are rich in both notation and rhythmic figures. Some artists are more classically-oriented (European art music) rather than blues-oriented. A good example would be artists like Bobby Timmons, Horace Silver, and Herbie Hancock. Many artists make such a drastic change in their approach to playing that it is almost impossible to believe that one is listening to the same artist. Compare the improvisations of John Coltrane during his late 1950s period, with Miles Davis and his later, more avant-garde period during the 1960s, when he played with younger players like Archie Shepp, Albert Ayler, and Pharoah Sanders. Coltrane changed not only his approach to improvisation but his approach to playing the saxophone. Instead of continuing with what had become one of the sweetest sounds ever produced on the tenor saxophone, he adopted a more robust and rugged sound. Perhaps he was attempting to adjust his sound to the more robust and rugged phrases of the avant-garde period in general. On the other hand, alto saxophonist Ornette Coleman, after having asserted himself as one of the leaders of the new movement, adopted a more traditional sound. His improvisations became more traditional and he assumed a more Birdlike (Charlie "Bird" Parker) concept. Improvisation, regardless of the traditional genre, is the life blood of jazz and without it jazz in its purist form does not exist. By improvisation I am referring to the free, spontaneous ideas created by the improvising artist and the prearranged or precomposed ideas found in many of the big band charts of the groups of Count Basie, Duke Ellington, Lionel Hampton, Buddy Rich, and Woody Herman. For music to be called jazz it does not first have to be written down. What counts is the style or manner in which the music is performed, the interpretation. When a jazz musician in Lionel Hampton's band reads a chart, he uses both his eyes and ears. The printed notes are mere guides to what the composer is looking for. The composition must be interpreted in an improvisational manner and not merely read note for note.

When we talk about improvisation in jazz we are talking about one of the most important ingredients, the glue that holds the whole fabric together. One of the most important things that must be considered is the fact that simply because an album states that the musician is playing jazz does not necessarily mean that he or she is playing original ideas or is even improvising. Perhaps one of the most disturbing things about many of the players that one hears in jazz is that they are actually repeating what they have copied from other musicians. In other words they learn by copying John Coltrane's licks, Charlie Parker's licks or Clifford Brown's licks. And they tend to become famous and get signed by major record companies because they sound like Charlie Parker, or another particular musician. What is important here is that we must recognize whether or not the musician is playing verbatim what he or she has copied from the artist, or has learned the style of that particular musician, using it as a means to create his or her own improvisation. To merely repeat or reiterate a phrase that another musician has played does not represent "true jazz." It is actually playing somebody else's music, the same as if I would play the music of Haydn or Beethoven. The truly improvisational musician really creates his or her own music from nothing or from a musical idea that has been put forth. Improvisation, originality, creativity—these are the things that make jazz the important music that it is. In order for the music to continue to grow we must have new creators and creations. In order to preserve the music that has already been created we need transcribers; there is a difference. Unfortunately in recent times, due to the ineptness of many of those who produce recordings and run the major labels, we have found carbon copies of the musicians who actually create music being hurled high and far above those musicians who are trying to create something from scratch. Perhaps the reason for this is that it is actually easier and safer to associate oneself with the known rather than the unknown. It is, without doubt, important for musicians learning to play jazz to respect the accomplishments of those who have gone before them and it is definitely important to respect those accomplishments when we consider their historical value. But at the same time, in order to nourish the creativity of the younger musicians and to keep the art alive, it is necessary for us to respect and encourage the unknown creative efforts of the purely spontaneous creative musician.

The Many Styles of Jazz

One of the most obvious and historically significant facts about the music we call jazz is that there are different styles or types of jazz that appeal to different types of people. For the most sophisticated, classically oriented listener, there is *third stream*—a blending of European art music and improvised jazz. For the more blues-oriented jazz buff there is *hard bop* or *jazz fusion*. There is even a style called *free jazz* for the free-spirited person. The jazz listener has a variety of types from which to choose.

Ever since the beginning of jazz, musicians and jazz lovers have been at a loss to describe the various types of music called jazz. During the 1960s, many musicians, especially the African-American artists, began to call their music American contemporary music, revolutionary music, avant-garde, free jazz, and so on. Some jazz musicians even said that their music was beyond being labeled and should be referred to as simply music. To fully understand the various styles of jazz, we must first understand the period that gave birth to each style. Each style was a result of the various social and political conditions as well as musical elements.

During the early New Orleans period, jazz music was contrapuntal and predominantly improvisational in structure. Very few musicians could read or write music. Each musician played whatever seemed to fit or seemed appropriate. The freewheeling style was a reflection of the way people of early New Orleans (early 1900s) dressed, danced, and behaved in general. The lifestyle of Storyville, with its permissive policy toward gambling, prostitution, etc., had as much to do with the development of jazz as did the theoretical and technical training received by the Creoles.

During the 1920s, jazz musicals, even in Harlem, took on a more classical approach. The compromise between jazz and semiclassical music produced a sophisticated dance band style. The elegant harmonies of Duke Ellington, James Reese Europe, and Paul Whiteman were admired as much by the symphony musician as by the jazz artist. The fact that blacks were relegated to the role of servant, and that musicians (especially dance band musicians who performed for high society) were considered subservient, in part accounts for why black musicians were able to get so much work during the 1920s. A recent survey conducted of older jazz musicians in Pittsburgh brought out the fact that in Pittsburgh during the 1920s, black musicians and entertainers were able to get a considerable amount of work at all-white functions. Jazz vocalist Maxine Sullivan once told me that she used to stand on the corner in the Hill District of Pittsburgh and talk to her fellow musicians and wait for perspective club owners and ballroom owners to drive by and ask her to provide them with musicians. As crude as it may have seemed, this was one of the major ways that African-American musicians in Pittsburgh during this particular period got work. It was not until much later, after the triumphs of Whiteman and Goodman in jazz and the upgrading of the musician's image, that black musicians and entertainers began to lose their domination of work in all-white clubs.

Despite this, white musicians who wanted to learn jazz from a black artist would seek out that artist and jam with him regardless of public pressure. In fact, at that time it was chic to be associated with a black artist. The entertainment world has always led the way in the fight for racial equality and does so today.

In spite of the recent outcry concerning racism in the 1990s, it is still the jazz musician who continues to lead the way in social integration. Articles by historian Gene Lees and a March 1995 issue of *Jazztimes* magazine shed much light on the racial problems found in jazz. Perhaps at the center of this is trumpeter Wynton Marsalis, who has been perceived by some as being a controversial figure when it comes to hiring musicians of various races. The fact that Marsalis or any other African-American musician hires musicians who are black or white cannot be seen as an act of racism and must be looked at in a more thorough and understanding manner. Perhaps one of the main reasons for this outcry is the lack of jobs that exist for both black and white musicians in the U.S. At the root of all such accusations is the lack of employment opportunities.

Definitions and Origins

There have been many attempts by scholars, laymen, and critics to define the term *jazz*. Questions of its origins, authenticity, and originality seem to have puzzled our finest academicians. To further complicate matters, many jazz musicians, if asked the question "What is jazz?" have simply responded, "If you don't know what it is, you'll never understand even if I try to explain it—so why bother?" Other musicians simply choose to ignore the question rather than submit to the confrontations of the "scholar." Regardless of the many complicated questions presented by both practitioner and scholar, if we are to give a much deserved place to jazz in academia, we must be able to define and recognize it.

Jazz is a music resulting from years of acculturation, adaptation, and assimilation of both West African and West European cultures in the United States. It is important for us to limit our definition of jazz only to include the United States simply because jazz as we know it developed in the United States, and not in the other numerous European, Latin American and South American colonies. We must also recognize that jazz also includes all the various forms of music resulting from this cultural exchange. The African influence on this cross-fertilization of cultures is called *Africanization*. Africanization occurred everywhere. Latin Catholic countries like Spain and Portugal had already been culturally integrated by various African countries, and so their music was already partially Africanized.

The more contact slaves had with the slave owner the less they were able to preserve their original culture. To please their slave masters, many slaves tried to imitate the ways of their slave owners. The slave knew that the owner would be more pleased with a slave who "spoke his language" and who acted as and imitated the owners in every way possible. Thus in many instances, the African slaves were not only forced to relinquish many of their traditional cultural habits but purposely rejected them in favor of the more acceptable habits of the slave owner.

"During a trip to Brazil, I learned that during slavery Brazilian slave owners were fond of showing off their 'well-groomed, eloquently trained' slaves. A well-dressed slave was a tribute to his or her master. According to many sources, these 'dressing contests' often took place in church. This suggests that in Brazil, especially whenever these 'dressing contests' were held, slave and slave owner enjoyed a special kind of close relationship, contradicting the original idea that there was little or no contact in Brazil between slave and master. This suggests the possibility of similar relationships in other areas of South America."

Without a doubt, many of the African religious songs, worksongs, etc., accompanied the African slaves to the plantations in the United States, and the Americas. What is important about these songs is, and what we fail to realize is, that there was a great deal of transformation that took place within the music itself before a particular group or tribe arrived in the America; thus we have cross-fertilization within cross-fertilization. Attempts to trace the origins of particular songs have proven to be, in many instances, almost impossible since there was a great deal of trading that occurred before the slaves arrived in the Americas. Once they were in the Americas this cross-fertilization was further complicated by yet another transformation of music that took place with various slaves from various tribes throughout the western coasts of Africa. Yet another transformation took place when these songs, which now appear in about their third or fourth mutation, were further changed when they integrated with the music of the western Europeans.

For a culture to survive, that culture has to maintain a certain amount of isolation from an equally strong or stronger neighboring culture. In the United States, African slaves were constantly being exposed to the European cultures of their captors. The degree of cultural exposure was definitely more unilateral than that found in South America. This is not to say that house slaves did not exist in South America, but in general there was considerably less contact.

It is often thought that the slaves imported into the Americas were the outcasts of unwanted members of African tribes. Nothing could be further from the truth. Throughout Africa, natives and tradesmen had been engaged in the traffic of human lives long before the Europeans even thought about supplying their colonies with African slaves. Those most often sought for the slave market were prisoners of tribal wars, which often included chiefs, musicians, historians, and the physically strong. As an analogy, during World II many German prisoners of war were taken to Texas and other American states to work as forced laborers on highway construction, as field hands, and in many other menial jobs. No doubt some of these prisoners of war were from a high social-economic class within the societies from which they came. The same was true of the African slave. The aim of the slave traders was to make as much money as possible; they did not care if a prisoner was of royal descent. (See *The African Slave Trade*, by Basil Davidson.)

The European colonists believed they were doing the African captives a favor by selling them into a more civilized society—a Christian one. That the slaves may have had a religion of their own never came to mind. Slaves were considered to be barbaric and could be saved by introducing them to Christianity by means of slavery.

The African Slave in North America

The long, sometimes fatal voyage to the plantations of North and South America must have seemed like the very end of existence to the captured slaves. Forced labor, inconceivable acts of brutality, and the separation of families and loved ones were the least of their worries. Immediate survival was the urgent matter.

What kind of music might we have had if African slaves had been taken to China or Japan or any other part of Asia instead of to the Americas? On the other hand, what would have been the results if the Africans had been the captors and supplied various African territories with European slaves? Would we have a form of music similar to the music we now call jazz? These and similar questions arise when we try to solve the mystery of jazz. That jazz did develop in the United States is proof that the secret of greatness lies in the coming together of peoples and not in their separation or isolation.

Some people feel that the music of Brazil or Cuba is as strong as the blues or other jazz forms found in North America. All music is as great as the culture in which it exists. We in the United States are lucky that the music we call jazz is of such high spiritual quality that it is now regarded as one of the most dynamic cultural contributions to the world. For the moment let's take a look at the African slave's contribution to jazz. Most African-American music goes much further than the commonly recognized contribution of rhythm. African harmony and melody played a major role in establishing the meaningful tonalities that constitute jazz. For the most part, the African slave's way of looking at music was entirely different from that of his European master. The slave viewed music as something functional. Music served a purpose. This is not to say that the slaves did not entertain themselves with songs, but for the most part music was something that helped them to more easily perform their various chores. One of the tragic facts of dealing with the earlier forms of African-American music is that many of the original songs, such as songs of the motherland, songs of courage, songs to prepare for battle (and what culture does not have such a song?) were soon lost in the long, cruel journey to the Americas and during slavery.

The transformation from African to African-American, as LeRoi Jones points out in his book *Blues People*, must have occurred rather quickly after the first generation of slaves died out. One thing is certain: the slave believed this state of existence to be a temporary one. The number of escape attempts, small revolutions, and uprisings proves this. This state of mind may also account for the easy manner in which some slaves accepted and adapted to the ways and habits of their slave masters. Another reason for the apparent docility of some slaves is that many of them believed that if an enemy was so blessed as to be able to capture them, the gods must indeed be on the side of the captor. If so, the duty of the slave was to obey the wishes of the gods and accept the situation until the gods chose to reverse things. These attitudes account for the image of the sweet, old, humble "Uncle Tom." Perhaps one of the results of this Uncle Tom image is that many African-Americans, in refuting this stereotype, have become openly hostile toward members of other ethnic groups.

"As a part of the 1976 Bicentennial celebration, I was invited to be a guest panelist at the Smithsonian institute to discuss America's contribution to world culture. Jazz critics and historians from all over the world (China, Japan, Germany, France, England, Africa etc.) attended the meeting. As the conference progressed, the one unanimous conclusion was that jazz was indeed America's most original contribution to world culture. Considering such a bold statement from so prestigious a group, one would think that Americans would have welcomed this information with overwhelming pride. But to my knowledge not one major American journal carried a story concerning this report."

Without doubt the Africans brought to the New World were confused and afraid. Being unable to speak the language and to understand what was happening was enough to make them doubt their abilities as warriors. History books are filled with stories of rebellion, bloodshed, and escape attempts, some successful and others ending in sorrow and pain. One thing is certain: the slave was not concerned with creating a new music.

In many instances, music not only helped the slave get through the day's work but served to signal revolts and escapes. African-American percussionist Max Roach, a frequent guest lecturer at numerous universities, including the University of Pittsburgh's Annual Seminar on Jazz, stated that the Negro spiritual "Steal Away Jesus" was an example of the type of song used by the slaves to alert fellow slaves that it was their turn to strike out for freedom and the Underground Railroad. Numerous other gospels, spirituals, and other forms of Afro-American folk music were used for a similar purpose. If indeed African-American folk music did serve a functional role in the total existence of the slave, what, if any, other functions did it have in the life of the new American?

Plantation life, as cruel as it was, offered the African-Americans a chance to develop their musical as well as higher industrial talents. Even the slave masters were delighted in the informal gathering of the slaves. Dancing, singing, handclapping (the simultaneous rhythmic clapping of the hands was a highly developed art form among the plantation slaves), mime acts, banjo playing, and other forms of instrumental music were very common. Many of these seemingly trivial forms of entertainment were the basis of America's earliest cultural forms. For example, the American musical theater owes much to the minstrel show that had its humble beginnings on the plantation.

In addition to the everyday "fun" music found on the plantation, religious music of various sorts also existed. The *song sermon*, which was the spontaneous songlike preaching of the fiery country preacher, gave birth to what was later termed African-American religious music. (The various forms of African-American religious music will be discussed in a later chapter.) The slaves did not preserve their own African religions as one might have expected. Instead, they accepted the religion of their slave masters at an astounding rate. The constant fear of being punished or of being labeled a troublemaker shaped the psyche of the captured slave. One thing is certain, the slaves did not bring Christianity with them.

Religion and plantation musical life were the factors which shaped the African-American's music during the early seventeenth century. Here then are

Dexter Gordon, Woody Shaw and Nathan Davis at the Pittsburgh Jazz Seminar

the real origins of the music we later called jazz—on the plantations and wherever West African and West European cultures came together. As I have stated before, this process we shall call "cross-fertilization." For cross-fertilization to occur, two or more cultures must equally share in the process of cross-fertilizing, otherwise one culture will simply be assimilated into the more dominant one. In the case of African-American music, the domination of the West European culture was neutralized by the process of Africanization. To explain the process of Africanization, first imagine what one might conceivably call the "Midas touch," that is, someone who is able to change the appearance or character of an object merely by touching that object. In the case of Africanization, the person with the Midas touch can change the entire character of the various cultures he or she comes into contact with simply by "touching" them. This process of Africanization is an often overlooked ingredient in the development of jazz. An even more important omission is what I call the process of *African-Americanization*—the further transformation of the results of cross-fertilization and Africanization by the African-Americans. To accurately define the music we call jazz, we must consider all of the elements involved. It is impossible to simply start with New Orleans, thus overlooking the early "cultural zones" that formulated the foundation of the music. Perhaps one of the reasons many writers choose to start the history of jazz with New Orleans is that it is comfortable for them. To take a serious sociological and anthropological look at the origins of jazz presents many problems and necessitates a lot of hard decisions—decisions that revolve around the interpretation of anthropological and sociological data. The cultural examination of the music we call jazz must consider such problems as the African's lack of knowledge of theory as well as his or her lack of knowledge of western European instruments considering, too, his or her innate ability to create intricate yet simple rhythms that lend themselves to what we now call swing. The ability to swing is at the heart of jazz, yet many scholars tend to write about only the western European theoretical approach to playing correct notes and the interpretations of harmonic and melodic data. These theoretical aspects of music are indeed necessary for us to appreciate good jazz performance in the nineties, but had very little to do with the actual creation of the music. Therefore, we should reserve those kinds of critical thinking for the periods in which they are needed to explain and enhance the understanding of the music we now call jazz. The process of African-Americanization is one of the last and most important processes in the development of the music we now call jazz.

Major Differences Between West European Music and West African Music in North America

The fact that jazz did not exist in Africa nor in Western Europe before the advent of slavery in America is strong evidence that jazz was born outside those areas. There is also no evidence that jazz of any form existed in South America or any other country. What then were the major differences between West European and West African music as found in North America? First of all, West European music was for the most part monorhythmic, as opposed to the more polyrhythmic West African music in which as many as seven or eight kinds of rhythms exist at one time.

Example 2

One may argue that polyrhythms also occur in various forms of European music, such as the music found in the Mediterranean area. This can be explained by remembering that most of the music of the Mediterranean area was deeply influenced by the migration of warring and nomadic African and North African tribes. The flamenco of Spain and the fado of Portugal are examples of polyrhythmic music that was affected by such migrations. Much of the so-called "syncopation" in jazz music can also be found in these original and secondary rhythms. Accidental harmony is another musical trait commonly associated with West African music in North America. The harmony most often associated with West African music is accidental harmony—that is, harmony that moves horizontally rather than vertically. However we must remember that there were also some African tribes that actually sang in harmony somewhat similar to that found in Western cultures.

Accidental Harmony

Example 3

If we accept the theory that accidental harmony resulted from the fact that most of the early slave songs were sung in fourths and fifths, we must also accept the idea that many of the early slaves' songs, marking the beginning of jazz, were taken directly or indirectly from the music of the European slave masters. Many of these European folk songs were immediately transformed and in many instances were hardly recognizable. Supporting this theory is the fact that many of the earliest slave songs were sung using intervals of fourths and fifths and occasionally thirds. Also, most forms of music in Africa and on the plantations were functional, that is, they served a definite purpose. It is often said that European music is, or was at one time, completely opposite in character from the music of Africa. Nothing could be further from the truth. It is possible to find certain similarities in the music of such different nationalities as the Irish and the Ghanaians. Once during a discussion session at Wesleyan University concerning ethnic music, I was surprised to learn that many other elements found in African-American work songs (rhythm, melodic contour, color) could also be found in certain Irish work songs, specifically the songs sung by Irish washer women. Thus, it is important for us to realize that both Africa and Europe had functional music.

A number of studies have been made proving or disproving the connection between West African and West European music. One of the finest of these works is Paul Oliver's *Savannah Syncopators*. Another good source book in this area is Gunther Schuller's *Early Jazz*. Both authors do an excellent job of tracing African-American music back to its African sources. The blue note, misunderstood more often than any other original musician element found in jazz, is the bastardizing of certain notes, most likely the lowering or flatting of the third, fifth, and eventually seventh degree of the West European diatonic scale.

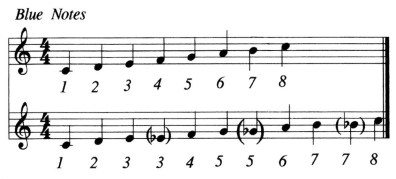

Example 4

It is incorrect to label blue notes as flats. This superimposes European musical terminology on a basically non-European musical element. A more correct way of describing these notes is that the note is simply lowered to a certain degree. Why am I being so meticulous about the labeling of one small musical sound? Because since the inception of jazz and the packaging and commercialization of its contents for world distribution, jazz has been denied an existence of its own. Critics, historians, and lay-people alike have been guilty of referring to jazz in the only musical context with which they are familiar—western European music. Intentional or not, this has prejudiced the recognition of jazz as an original musical form.

During the 1960s, many of the so-called avant-garde composers of that period were actually on the right track when they developed special symbols to represent musical effects that they wanted. Many of these effects actually enhance the music by permitting the composer to extract sounds from the instruments that were not normally associated with western European notation. Ethnomusicologists also use a similar system in developing special notations to produce sounds not normally associated with western European notation. The jazz musician has failed to take full advantage of many of these musical opportunities that were introduced by the avant-garde composers of western European art music during the 1960s. The closest that jazz came to this form of enhancement was the use of various symbols to shorten or elongate a note or to punctuate a particular rhythm; but they did not take full advantage of developing a completely new notation system.

How can we correct this? New theoretical terms and concepts must be developed.

Now that jazz has entered into the arena of academia, it is necessary for us to do more than merely interview the few innovators who are still alive. In addition, we must now undertake the difficult task of analyzing and deciphering this information.

Early Names for Jazz

Throughout the history of popular music, jazz and its related musical forms have been called by a number of different names. These names include blue music, march music, novelty music, juke music, ragged music, folk music, sin music, and so on. (By ragged music we mean that the music was looser or freer than other forms of music common at that time. It does not mean that the music was less artistic in any way. The term ragged was frequently used to describe the music now called jazz.) In recent times, jazz has been labeled swing, progressive, bebop, cool, rhythm and blues, soft rock, hard rock, country rock, avant-garde, American contemporary music, and so on.

One theory for this seemingly random labeling of jazz music is that the industry, in order to survive, must find new ways of presenting the music to the public. Another theory supported by more militant groups in the United States is that jazz is constantly relabeled so that African-Americans will find it impossible to claim the music as their own since it is presented under a different name, repackaged, and sold as a completely different music. Regardless of which theory one accepts, the fact is that jazz and its related musical forms have been sold under an array of different names. (A chapter dealing with the politics of jazz will appear later.)

On a visit to New Orleans to perform at a local nightclub, Lou's and Charlie's, I had the distinct pleasure of meeting banjoist and author Danny Barker who informed me that the early New Orleans musicians did not call their music *dixieland*. Instead, he informed me, they preferred to call their music *traditional New Orleans music*. Unfortunately during my first couple of days of the engagement at Lou's and Charlie's, I had publicly announced that I wanted to play a dixieland number and afterwards several musicians approached me, including

Charlie Bering, the owner of the club, and informed me that they would like to play an example of early traditional New Orleans music that was on the juke box in the club. The music sounded completely different than what we know as dixieland although, I must admit, there was some resemblance. Instead of the traditional dixieland with its many contrapuntal lines played by the various instruments; the trombone, the clarinet, the cornet etc., I was privy to a music that more resembled the music of the French Caribbean. The music had an almost pseudo-Latin feel that resembled, in many ways, a kind of Africanized version of samba but with a jazz feel to it. Later, I learned from several other of the older New Orleans musicians that the dixieland term was primarily reserved for the music that had been made by the earlier white jazz musicians and that the black jazz musicians preferred that their music be called *traditional* since they felt it was, in many ways, quite different than the music played by their white counterparts.

Work Songs

A number of different song types or forms go into the general makeup of the music we now call jazz. One of the most well-known of these forms is the *work song*. The work song can be traced to Africa as well as to Europe and other continents, but it is the African version of the work song that has contributed to the development of jazz. Work songs of various sorts were imported into the Americas from Africa. Students of African-American music commonly assume that work songs were basically the same throughout the Americas. In fact, they varied with the climate, type of work being performed, and the geographical location of the originator. Areas where picking cotton was the major type of work produced a different type of work song than did areas where railroading was the primary type of work. Work songs, regardless of type, usually carried a special rhythm designed to stimulate and support the labor groups performing the task at hand. According to musicologist Eileen Southern in her book *The Music of Black Americans*, "the role of the song leader should not be underestimated in the African call and response form. It was he, the work song leader, who chose the song to be sung, who embellished the basic melody and improvised appropriate verses to fit the occasion and who brought the performance to an end."[1] The veteran African-American blues folk singer, Huddie Ledbetter, better known as "Leadbelly," was said to have been one of the best work song leaders. He was especially known for his consistent rhythm and his ability to lead his fellow workers in song. So powerful was he as a work song leader that according to legend he was one of the most sought after work song leaders in the country. Various types of work songs existed in both North and South America. The sea shanty was a type of work song found along coastal areas. African slaves whose main type of labor was to row large cargo barges invented songs to aid their work. Many of these songs have found their way into the modern blues of the 1960s and 70s. Many early work songs were built around a single phrase repeated over and over. The entire melody was held together by a continuous or repeated basslike figure called a drone.

It is common knowledge that Leadbelly's music, even in his later years, always made use of the drone. John Storm Roberts, in *Black Music of Two Worlds*, states "The laying of railroad track, for example, was not a technique brought with the slaves, but the use of song for an extremely restricted purpose—instructing track-layers in what to do next—is indeed African."

The Drone

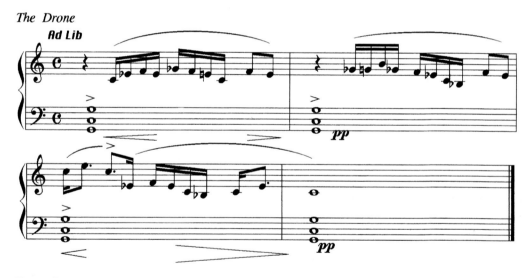

Example 5

"Walk to the car, steady yourself,
Head high!
Throw it away
That's just right
Go back and get another one,
You got the wrong one that time...
Walk humble and don't you stumble,
And don't you hurt nobody
Walk to the car and steady yourself."[2]

Example 6

To further explain the importance of rhythm in the work song, let's look at a popular work song recorded by Leadbelly, "Looky Yonder, Where de Sun Done Gone." This particular song was often accompanied by a grunt or moan that was used primarily to aid or reinforce the rhythm.

Looky, looky yonder, (huh)! Looky, looky yonder (huh)!
Looky, looky yonder, (huh)! Where de sun done gone.

Example 7

The ever-popular call-and-response form, the deliverance of a musical statement and the answering of that statement, is also a vital part of the work song's effectiveness. Without the response, there may not have been an effective physical exchange between leader and worker. The field holler and street cry are miniature forms of the work song. A good example of the street cry as a type of work song can be seen in jazz pianist Herbie Hancock's "Watermelon Man." The humble figure pushing the watermelon cart has but one object in mind and that is to sell as many watermelons as possible. By singing or crying "watermelon man," he is advertising his wares and at the same time easing the burden of pushing the cart filled with watermelons. The field holler is similar. The weary slave who lifts his or her voice in agony and cries "Lawd hope us oba com dis hea buddon" is also using a form of the work song. That the holler or call is not complete does not diminish its effectiveness in helping complete a task.

Signifying Songs

Signifying songs can also be traced back to Africa where they were songs of ridicule. Members of a tribe who had committed a particular crime were often punished by being subjected to impromptu songs being sung by their fellow tribesmen about the nature of the crime. Signifying songs in the U.S. had their beginnings on the plantation. In fact, it is safe to say that without the signifying songs, the blues we know today would not exist. One would have to look for quite some time to find an authentic blues that does not use the form. Signifying songs were also a vital part of the minstrel show and other slave gatherings during the 1800s. During and after slavery, signifying songs were used as a form of "blackmail" by various African-American entertainers. Good signifying song leaders could, if the occasion presented itself, get "rich." In many ways, the Afro-American signifying song can be compared to the West Indian calypso in that both designed to carry a message of social significance.

The West African *circle dance*, which is often found in concert with the more popular call-and-response form, and the *ring shout* are other important examples of West African forms found in African-American culture. Even today it is possible to find the purest form of the circle dance accompanied by the ring shout and call-and-response pattern in what we African-Americans call the "Holy Roller Church." This term usually refers to the sanctified or spiritualist churches found in the black ghetto in many urban areas. During a visit to Bahia, in the northern part of Brazil, my wife and I witnessed an authentic condomble worship ceremony (a religious worship service somewhat resembling the voodoo services associated with Haiti). The "African Circle" dancing found in the Holiness Churches of Kansas City was performed also in exactly the same manner thousands of miles away in Brazil. The worshippers, mostly elderly women, moved counterclockwise in a circular motion, slowly shuffling their feet to the hypnotic sound of the polyrhythmic drum beats. A year later, we made a trip to Trinidad, West Indies, and were invited to attend an original Shango service high in the mountains overlooking Port of Spain. There we found exactly the same circle dance being performed. The beautiful, elderly African-American women danced the same shuffle to the sounds of African drum rhythms. Although the language was different (a mixture of Yoruba, English, French, and Spanish), the concept was the same.

The Instruments of Jazz

The Drum

The *drum* was one of the earliest instruments played by humans. (The first musical instrument was the human voice.) Throughout the world are different types of drums: the footed drum from East Africa, the tubular drums made from tree trunks, goblet drums, hourglass drums, and finally the well-known trap drum set used by jazz drummers. The trap set, or full set of drums as we know it today, was not used by the earlier New Orleans marching bands. Instead they used the separate parade snare drum together with the crash cymbals and bass drum, etc. During the early years, because each of the percussion instruments was played separately, more than one percussionist was necessary. However, with the consolidation of the percussion instruments only one person is needed to play all these instruments,

Drum Set. Photo by Ralph Echols.

namely the bass drums, the snare drum, the cymbal, and later the side, or sock, cymbal. (According to jazz drummers Art Blakey and Kenny Clarke, the side, or sock, cymbal was invented by Ethel Minor in Pittsburgh. Ethel Minor took two aluminum tops, tied one top to her foot and struck the second top, which was already positioned on the floor. This simple invention revolutionized jazz drumming.)

One of the most popular instruments used in jazz since its early beginnings is the drum set, or multi-percussion ensemble, as it was referred to by jazz drummer Freddy Waits. The first use of the drum in early jazz centered around the parade drum, or bass drum, used in marching bands, the forerunner of the later New Orleans jazz combo. After the introduction of the trap set, the drummer was expected to do more than just keep time. Although according to Professor Joe Harris, retired percussion instructor at the University of Pittsburgh, the modern drummer's main job is simply to keep time, recent developments have seen the drum expand to a melodic as well as percussive instrument. Drummers such as Tony Williams, Alex Acuna, Jack DeJohnette, Idris Muhammad, Ed Thigpen, Billy Brooks, and Winard Harper not only keep time but contribute melodically to the music being performed. During the 1960s the drummer was expected to contribute to the overall melodic concept of the piece. In fact, some drummers like the legendary Elvin Jones, Billy Brooks, and J.C. Moses were so involved in the melodic concept of the music that traditionalists sometimes felt that they were not "keeping the beat." To this, the new drummers replied that they were indeed keeping the beat but were using what was termed "implied time." During the 1970s, jazz saw a return to the more traditional concept of keeping a steady, swinging beat.

Keeping a steady beat is so important to the commercial success of a recording that many recording studios provide what is called a click track, to help the drummer maintain a steady pulse. The drum machine is an electronic metronome-like instrument used to provide accurate rhythm. The click track is recorded on a separate track and is erased once the session drummer has accurately recorded the drum track. The result is a steady, constant rhythm that rarely changes.

Many of the top drummers in jazz like Kenny Clarke, Max Roach, Shelly Manne, Joe Morello, Ed Thigpen, Idris Muhammad, and Elvin Jones not only played accurate rhythms but played the melody and sometimes even harmony on the drums. By properly tuning each drum (thirds, fifths, and sometimes even sevenths are possible on the drum set), the drummer is able to play within the harmony.

The Trumpet

The *trumpet* is one of the most popular instruments in jazz. Louis Armstrong, considered the "father" of the jazz trumpet, was

Trumpet. Photo by Ralph Echols.

responsible for making the trumpet popular in jazz. According to Curt Sachs in his book, *The History of Musical Instruments*, the earliest trumpets did not utilize a mouthpiece and had no bell. They were cylindrical and were hollowed from logs or cane. All the player did was sing, speak, or simply blow through the object. During a field trip to Haiti in 1971, I was presented such a hollowed trumpet by a group of traditional musicians. Earlier that day I witnessed a concert by an all-trumpet "orchestra." Each musician played on an instrument capable of sounding only one note. Each was responsible for sounding the right note at the right time and in the correct sequence of notes.

Because of its early use in the French military bands, the cornet found its way into the jazz bands of early New Orleans music. Trumpet and cornet players like Armstrong, Buddy Bolden, Bix Beiderbecke, Dizzy Gillespie, Clark Terry, Miles Davis, and later Clifford Brown, Donald Byrd, Maynard Ferguson, Benny Bailey, Woody Shaw, and Wynton Marsalis are all important contributors to the development of the trumpet in jazz. One reason for the trumpet's early appeal was its loud, brassy sound. According to legend, "King" Buddy Bolden often advertised his upcoming concerts and dances by standing in the middle of town and blowing his trumpet loud and clear. Though the trumpet is most often as-

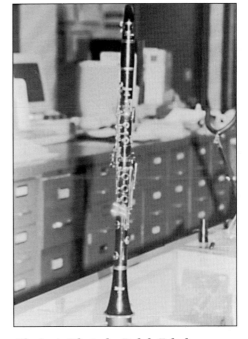

sociated with brassy, penetrating sounds, it is also capable of creating soft, round, plush, romantic sounds. Trumpeters like Miles Davis, Art Farmer, Bobby Hackett, Carmell Jones, Wallace Roney, Terence Blanchard, Wynton Marsalis, Chet Baker and Chuck Mangione represent the softer, more romantic approach to the instrument.

The Clarinet

The *clarinet* in jazz reached its high point in popularity during the 1930s. One of the most popular clarinetists during this period was Benny Goodman. Before Goodman, Johnny Dodds was an important contributor to the clarinet in jazz. Because of Goodman's popularity as a bandleader

Clarinet. Photo by Ralph Echols.

and innovator, along with the undeniable contributions of fellow clarinetists Artie Shaw, Jimmy Hamilton, Woody Herman, Sidney Bechet, and Lester Young (Young was one of the most original and most underrated clarinetists in jazz), the clarinet took its place alongside the trumpet as a major jazz instrument. Earlier contributions were made by Johnny Dodds, Jimmy Noone, Albert Nicholas, Buster Bailey, and later by Buddy DeFranco, Ron Odrich, Eric Dolphy, Alvin Batiste, and Eddie Daniels.

In recent years, largely due to the efforts of Eddie Daniels, the clarinet has seen a rise in popularity. Because of its difficult fingering and often shrill sound, many musicians have decided to use the clarinet only as a double rather than as a major instrument.

The Alto Saxophone

The *alto saxophone* in jazz reached its peak in popularity during the 1940s with Charlie Parker. Parker's handling of the alto saxophone was akin to Armstrong's performance on trumpet. Both were creative, innovative, and relentless in their

search for musical excellence. Both were responsible for introducing new sounds and ideas to jazz and new approaches to playing their instruments. According to jazz veteran drummer Kenny Clarke, during one of his European tours, Charlie Parker attended one of the weekly informal workshops sponsored by the Selmer Instrument Co. in Paris, France. Master classical saxophonist Marcel Mule attempted to correct the way Parker was fingering a particular phrase. Parker assured Mule that it was possible to play the passage with his personalized fingering: "I know it's possible because I just played it." Marcel Mule was at a loss for words.

At first, the saxophone, with its combination brassy-reed sound, provided a new voice for the aspiring jazz artist. With the popularity of the alto saxophone, the clar-

Alto Saxophone. Photo by Ralph Echols.

inet drifted into the background. Instead of the clarinet, the alto sax now took the lead. Artists like Don Redman, Johnny Hodges, Benny Carter, Pete Brown, Lee Konitz, James Moody, Sonny Stitt, Phil Woods, Julian "Cannonball" Adderley, Jackie McLean, Peter King, Ornette Coleman, and the late Eric Dolphy have introduced some of the most innovative sounds in jazz on the saxophone. During the 1950s "Cool Period," the alto saxophone assumed an almost classical sound. The pure straight sound of "cool," with little vibrato, by artists like Lee Konitz and Paul Desmond was a fresh concept.

More recently, artists like Grover Washington Jr., Kenny Garrett, David Sanborn, Gerald Albright, and Arthur Blythe have extended the range of the saxophone in general, especially as a result of Grover Washington's penetrating and dynamic use of overtures.

The Tenor Saxophone

The B♭ *tenor saxophone* in jazz, in contrast to the higher pitched E♭ alto saxophone, has become, next to the guitar and the drum, the most frequently played instrument in jazz. Many of jazz's most popular tenor saxophonists are converted alto saxophonists. According to tenor saxophonists Sonny Stitt and John Coltrane, after hearing Charlie Parker, many alto saxophonists conceded that there was nothing left to play on alto, so many of them adopted the tenor saxophone. Whether this is true or not, the fact is that immediately after the arrival of Parker (1940s), alto saxophonists declined in number and the tenor saxophone gained in popularity.

The tenor saxophone, with its soft subtones, plush low and middle register tones, and the high shrill, piercing sound of the upper register is still one of the most frequently chosen instruments by young aspiring jazz musicians. Some of the most innovative tenor saxophonists in the history of jazz include Coleman Hawkins, Lester

Tenor Saxophone. Photo by Ralph Echols.

Young, Dexter Gordon, Ben Webster, Chu Berry, Stan Getz, Zoot Sims, James Moody, Jimmy Heath, Sonny Rollins, John Coltrane, George Coleman, Grover Washington Jr., Ronnie Scott, Benny Wallace, and Wayne Shorter. In recent years, veteran tenor saxophonist Dexter Gordon returned from Europe to the New York scene to provide new life to the current jazz scene.

The Soprano Sax

The *soprano saxophone* as a solo instrument is one of the most difficult of the saxophone family to play in tune. The first jazz soloist to dominate the jazz scene by playing the high-pitched, shrill sound of the soprano sax was Sidney Bechet. Alto saxophonist Johnny Hodges, a stabilizing force with the Duke Ellington Orchestra, was one of the major forces behind the development of the soprano saxophone during the 1930s and 40s. The next great contribution on the instrument came from tenor saxophonist Eli (Lucky) Thompson, a veteran of the Lionel Hampton and Billy Eckstine orchestras. Without a doubt, the major breakthrough on the soprano saxophone took place in the 1960s when John Coltrane used the instrument on his recording of "My Favorite Things." Steve Lacy and Dave

Soprano Saxophone. Photo by Ralph Echols.

Leibman are among the few jazz artists who concentrated mainly on the soprano. In Europe, Bechet disciple Claude Luther and French saxophonist Barney Wilen, together with English baritone saxophonist John Surman, have made important contributions on the soprano saxophone.

When I started playing the soprano saxophone with Eric Dolphy's group, in 1964, his advice to me was, "Only play it if you feel it. It has to be an extension of your present instrument. Don't play it the same way you play the tenor because it is not a tenor but another voice." Presently, two of the most innovative soprano saxophonists, who seem to do just that, are Wayne Shorter and Grover Washington, Jr.

The sensitivity involved in playing the soprano saxophone, especially when it comes to tuning, is a problem that most soprano saxophonists find difficult to deal with. Throughout history, the soprano saxophone served a vital role as the lead solo voice in the saxophone section, somewhat similar to the role played by the primadona soprano voice in the Italian opera. Without a doubt, Coltrane's use of the instrument helped to restore the high visibility and important role played by the saxophone in Jazz, during the 1960s. Perhaps more than anyone else in modern times, it was Grover Washington Jr. who popularized the instrument by playing it so well in tune and with such control, that the "bad boy" image of the soprano in the sax section was eliminated. This image came about because of the difficulty of playing the instrument in tune. Because of the pioneering efforts of the above mentioned artists, we see and hear more saxophonists adopting the soprano as their primary instrument.

The Baritone Saxophone

The *baritone saxophone* is the "root" or bottom of the reed section. Its deep rich dominant texture adds fullness and depth to the harmonies in a reed section. Although both a bass and contrabass saxophone exist, of the lower sounding saxophones, the baritone sax is most commonly used. One of the most popular sounds from the baritone saxophones was that of Ellingtonian Harry Carney. His soft, rich, haunting sound is said to have greatly influenced the writing style of Duke Ellington. Other great baritone saxophonists include Serge Chaloff, Gerry Mulligan, Pepper Adams, Leo Parker, Cecil Payne, and Sonny Stitt. During my brief sojourn in Chicago from 1953 to 1957, I recall Chicago musicians buzzing about the fluency of Sonny Stitt on baritone. Many of his contemporaries considered him one of the major innovators on the instrument. In Europe, John Surman and Ronnie Ross are among the major contributors. American baritone saxophonist Sahib Shihab, who lived in Europe for a number of years, was

Baritone Saxophone. Photo by Ralph Echols.

more responsible than any other baritone saxophonist for stimulating interest in that instrument in Europe, as a solo instrument.

During a recent concert in Pittsburgh at Heinz Hall, I was privileged to hear Grover Washington Jr. play an unaccompanied solo on baritone saxophone. His tone was rich, warm, and vibrant, and was reminiscent of the sound that Harry Carney produced during his period with the Duke Ellington Orchestra. I'm more than positive that if he chose to, he could become a leading spokesperson on this instrument. Another younger musician, James Carter, a multi-reed player, also shows considerable promise on the baritone saxophone. During the 1960s, English baritone saxophonist John Surman and Americans Nick Brignola, Grover Washington Jr., Howard Johnson, and Charles Davis were, without doubt, the most impressive voices on this instrument. The premiere sound on baritone saxophone to emulate is still Harry Carney.

The Piano

The rhythm instruments in jazz include the piano, drum, and bass, in some instances the guitar, vibraharp, and various percussion instruments, and recently an assortment of synthesizers. Traditionally, the role of the piano was to keep rhythm. Early piano players assumed the role of the banjo by keeping time and occasionally suggesting the harmonic scheme of the piece by playing chords. Later during the Ragtime era (1900s) and the Boogie-Woogie era of the 1920s, the piano also played the bass line. This practice was discontinued during the Kansas City period when the bass became more prominent. At this point the pianist began limiting much of what the left hand previously played so that the walking bass could be heard. During the 1920s, Earl "Fatha" Hines introduced a style of piano playing that was later called "trumpet style" because of his concentration of playing single note octaves with the right hand. This was an im-

Piano. Photo by Ralph Echols.

portant innovation because it placed the piano in the same solo category as other single-note instruments such as the trumpet, clarinet, and saxophone. Prior to this, most pianists played what was known as a pianistic style, which consisted of playing both hands in more harmonic style. Bud Powell carried this concept further with his Parker-like improvisation during the 1950s and 1960s.

Throughout the years, the piano has served a very important role in helping to change the concept in improvisation and jazz. Some of those pianists responsible include: Jelly Roll Morton, James P. Johnson, Teddy Wilson with his great stride style, Art Tatum, Milt Buckner and George Shearing who popularized the block chord solo style, Horace Silver, Hank Jones, Bud Powell, Bill Evans, Kenny Drew Sr., Wynton Kelly, and more recently, Mulgrew Miller, Cedar Walton, Herbie Hancock, George Cables, Geri Allen and Benny Green.

The Bass

The *bass* in jazz made its first appearance during slavery as a single string plucked over a square, pegged instrument. Its sole function was to provide rhythm or to keep the beat along with other makeshift instruments like washboards, jugs, musical saws, wagon wheels, and cylindrical trumpets. On these instruments, the slaves played the first examples of what later developed into the music we now call jazz.

During the late 1800s and earlier 1900s, New Orleans marching bands preferred the tuba or contra-bass for keeping time. As soon as jazz began to make its appearance in the saloons and cathouses of the red-light districts, the bass was again adopted. The first major modern soloist on the instrument was Jimmy Blanton. His technical mastery of the instrument enabled him to perform hornlike improvisations on the instrument. Oscar Pettiford and Ray Brown were two important American bassists who extended both its technical and harmonic possibilities. In recent years, the

Bass. Photo by Ralph Echols.

electric bass has become a favorite substitute in some groups for the upright bass. Such players as Monk Montgomery, Bob Cranshaw, Stanley Clarke, Jaco Pastorious, Abe Laboriel, John Patitucci, and Bob Magnusson have proven to be quite capable of providing a true bass sound on the instrument. Bass players such as Ray Brown, Leroy Vinnegar, Jimmy Garrison, Red Mitchell, Niels Henning-Orsted Pederson, from Denmark, Peter Trunk from Germany, Buster Williams and Jimmy Woode have all contributed to the development and freedom of the bass in Jazz.

The Guitar

The *guitar* is probably one of the world's oldest instruments. However, as a jazz instrument the guitar was not used as a solo instrument until the 1920s. During the 1800s the banjo was the primary string instrument used in jazz groups. Around 1900 blues guitarists often played boogie-woogie lines on the guitar in roadside bars and taverns, creating a new concept of guitar playing. Such styles as "bottlenecking" (a style created in the Delta by guitar players who used broken bottle tops on their fingertips to produce a sliding, blues effect) gave the blues guitarist a certain commercialism that elevated the guitar in popularity. Perhaps the most important development of the guitar was the introduction of the amplified guitar, or electric guitar. Although most historians agree that Charlie Christian was the first to play the electric guitar,

Guitar. Photo by Ralph Echols.

guitarist Eddie Durham says he played the instrument first and introduced it to Christian. Belgium-born gypsy guitarist Django Reinhardt later extended the technical capability of the instrument by introducing fast, free-flowing, and unusual scalelike patterns. Guitarists such as Kenny Burrell, Joe Pass, Jim Hall, Wes Montgomery, Grant Green, Ted Dunbar and George Benson, and more recently, John McLaughlin, Pat Martino, Larry Coryell, John Scofield, Pat Metheny, Vic

Juris, Russell Malone, and Mark Whitfield have done much to extend the range of the guitar in jazz.

The Trombone

The *trombone* in jazz had its official begin-ning in the marching bands of New Or-leans. Although there are numerous examples of slaves playing trombones along with other homemade instruments at gath-erings, it was not until after the Civil War that the trombone was first widely used in jazz groups. Kid Ory of New Orleans was among the first prominent soloists on the instrument capable of matching musical innovations with artists such as Louis Arm-strong. Another trombonist, who intro-duced unusual sounds to jazz, especially "animal" noises, was Joseph "Tricky Sam" Nanton, a member of the Duke Ellington orchestra. From its early beginning as a rhythm instrument, the trombone grew into a first-rate solo instrument with the help of Jimmy Harrison, "Miff" Mole, and J.C. Higginbotham, and later J.J. Johnson, Slide Hampton, Kai Winding, Curtis Fuller, Albert Mangelsdorf and Robin Eubanks.

Trombone. Photo by Ralph Echols.

The Flute

The *flute* as a solo jazz instrument dates back to the early recordings of Wayman Carver during the 1930s. Before that time, and even afterward, the flute was used primarily as a second instrument by saxophonists. Rare photographs of early jazz groups during the 1920s show big bands with flutes, gong bells, and numerous other "unusual" instruments. According to Leonard Feather in *The Book of Jazz*, the flute was not used on a full scale until 1953–54 by artists like Frank Wess, Herbie Mann, and Bud Shank. Herbie Mann was the first to make a name for himself solely as a flutist. One of the reasons it took so long for the flute to be accepted as a solo instrument was its "light" sound. Most bandleaders were looking for an instrument that could compete with the trumpet or saxophone in volume. With the introduction of amplified instruments pioneered by Selmer, King, and independent Bill Smith, and recently the Frapp Co., the flute, clarinet, and other "lighter" sounding instruments could be heard.

Other flutists who have made outstanding contributions on the instrument are James Moody (considered by many musicians to be the premier flutist in jazz), Yusef Lateef, Frank Wess, Buddy Collette, Herb Geller, Rahsaan Roland Kirk, Joe Farrell, and two of the most technically proficient of all, Hubert Laws and Dave Valentin.

Flute. Photo by Ralph Echols.

The Vibraphone

The *vibraphone* in jazz owes its existence to the African xylophone or balaphone. The early African instrument was often made by carving out a large wood log. Long wooden bars were then shaped into various sizes so that their length, width, and thickness determined the type and quality of sound produced. In some instances, the "bars" were struck while suspended over a body of water housed in the bottom of the hollow log, thus producing a mellow, ringing type of sound.

During the 1920s, society dance bands used various marimbas, bells, etc. in an attempt to produce a more European classical sound. However, it was not until the 1930s that the

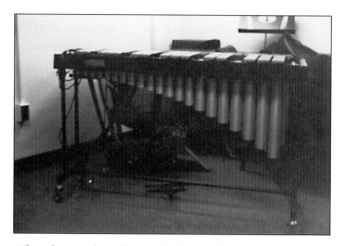

Vibraphone. Photo by Ralph Echols.

vibraphone began to emerge as a major solo instrument in jazz. One of the first great soloists on the instrument was Lionel Hampton. During the late 1930s drummer Kenny Clarke also developed a promising technique on the instrument. The 1940s saw vibraphonist Milt Jackson emerge as a major soloist with Dizzy Gillespie's various groups. As opposed to Hampton's more percussive approach to playing the instrument, Jackson's approach was a more melodic one. As a member of the M.J.Q. (Modern Jazz Quartet), Jackson was able to perfect his soft melodic style. It was his experience with this group that contributed greatly to the acceptance of the vibraphone as a major solo instrument in jazz.

Terry Pollard was one of the first female jazz musicians to concentrate on the vibraphone as a major instrument. She possessed one of the most remarkable techniques associated with the instrument. Her touch, although not as soft as that of Jackson's, was a combination of Hampton's percussive approach and Jackson's more soft, melodic approach. Other vibraphonists who have contributed greatly to the development of the instrument in jazz include Red Norvo, Terry Gibbs, Dave Pike, Teddy Charles, Vic Feldman, 'Lem' Winchester and Mike Mainieri. During the 1970–80s, Gary Burton, Bobby Hutcherson, Dave Friedman, Roy Ayers, and Stephon Harris have all made significant contributions to the development of the vibraphone as a major solo instrument in jazz.

Conclusion

The word *culture* usually refers to the learned behavioral patterns of a particular group of people, which reflect the total aesthetic values of the society. African-American culture in its infant stages was a reflection of two main broad groups—namely West Africans and West Europeans. The process of cross-fertilization, Africanization, and Afro-Americanization is further complicated by the number of subgroups (hundreds of African tribes, both East and West Africans) and many predominantly West Europeans that were represented both as indentured slaves and as colonists, and by the much over-looked contribution of America's first inhabitants, the American Indian. Many jazz greats, like Oscar Pettiford and Charlie Mingus, proudly proclaimed their American Indian heritage long before it was considered chic to do so. There are many documented accounts of runaway slaves being sheltered by neighboring Indian tribes; many of the slaves even rose to the level of chief. Almost every African-American family I know acknowledges the presence of American Indian blood.

Music, as a form of culture, is a means of aesthetic expression through the medium of sound. During slavery, music was one of the most reliable forms of culture available to the African slaves. It served them in many ways: the easing of pain, relieving the burden of forced labor, as escape songs, as a means of education, and as a means of "funnin" around.

Suggested Readings and Listening

Books
Davidson, Basil. *The African Slave Trade (Precolonial History 1450-1850)*. Boston-Toronto: Little, Brown and Co., 1961.

Hahn, Janheinz. *Muntu the New African Culture*. New York: Grove Press, Inc.

Herskovits, Melville J. *The Myth of the Negro Past*. Boston: Beacon Press, 1958.

Jones, LeRoi. *Blues People*. New York: William Morrow and Co., 1963.

Nketia, J.H. Kwabena. *The Music of Africa*. New York: W.W. Norton and Co., 1974.

Oliver, Paul. *Savannah Syncopators: African Retentions in the Blues*. New York: Stein & Day Publishers, 1970.

Roach, Hildred. *Black American Music: Past and Present*. Boston: Crescendo Publishing Co., 1973.

Roberts, John Storm. *Black Music of Two Worlds*. New York: William Morrow and Co., 1974.

Southern, Eileen. *The Music of Black Americans: A History*. New York: W.W. Norton, 1971.

Records
American Negro Slave Songs (Alex Foster and Michel Larue). Tradition Records by Everest Records, #2108.

Anthology of Music of Black Africa. Everest Records, Everest #3254-3.

Negro Prison Songs (Alan Lomax). Tradition Records by Everest Records, TPL #1220.

Niger la Musique des Griots. Ocora Records, Ocr #15-20.

Olatunji Drurns of Passion. Columbia Records, CS #8210.

Songs of the Watutsi Folkways. Folkways Records, Fe#4428.

Profile

LOUIS ARMSTRONG • If there was one figure in the history of Jazz that most historians agree was the first great improvisor, it was Louis (Satchmo/Pops) Armstrong. Armstrong, born Louis Daniel Armstrong (1901–1971), was born in New Orleans into humble beginnings. He developed into one of the most important cultural icons in world history. The controversy concerning the actual date of Armstrong's birth and place of birth has often been attributed to the inflated mystical imagination of over-zealous fans. The facts concerning the actual date of birth, according to histori-

ans Paul O. Tanner, David W. Megill and Maurice Gerow, is that Armstrong was in fact born on August 4, 1901, in New Orleans, LA. "The myth has always been that Daniel Louis Armstrong was born on July 4, 1900. However, extensive research has uncovered his baptism papers at the Sacred Heart of Jesus Church in New Orleans stating that he was actually born August 4, 1901."[3] The fact that the 4th of July is one of the U.S.'s most popular holidays is probably why Armstrong's birth was associated with that date.

As a child, Armstrong is reported to have been rather adventurous, often getting into minor scuffles and other juvenile escapades. One such event, the shooting of a pistol into the sky to celebrate New Year's Eve, landed him in the Colored Waifs Home in New Orleans. It was here that he learned to play the cornet. Armstrong, in a documentary film, stated that he excelled in learning the cornet because he was a natural. He was soon promoted to the leader of the group. Armstrong's predication towards leadership qualities influenced the directors of the home to appoint young Armstrong as the leader of the band. It also served him later in his career as he rose to the top of the Jazz world.

Like the majority of the New Orleans jazz musicians of his time, Armstrong worked as a part-time musician at various odd jobs to earn a living. During this period his playing was limited to performing in various marching bands and in the numerous clubs in the Storyville section of New Orleans. His career as a major jazz performer began when he joined the orchestra of trumpeter King Joe Oliver. In the Oliver orchestra he developed the lyrical style of improvising that would influence the direction of jazz on all instruments. When Oliver left New Orleans for Chicago in 1917, Armstrong inherited the honor of being the most popular trumpeter in New Orleans. During this period he also began performing with the orchestra of Fate Marable who played on the many riverboats along the Mississippi River. Between 1924 and 1925 Armstrong joined the orchestra of Fletcher Henderson in New York. In his role as the resident "hot" man, he began to exert his influence on musicians such as tenor saxophonist Coleman Hawkins and saxophonist-arranger Don Redman. In 1926 he formed the "Hot Five" group (later known as the "Hot Seven") which produced some of his most memorable music.

Perhaps his most important break came in 1929 when Armstrong was invited by his mentor, trumpeter King Joe Oliver, to join Oliver's band in Chicago. It was in Chicago that young Armstrong began to gain as a musician. He could not only play anything but he was an exceptional entertainer as well as a brilliant musician. Because Chicago was one of the most important major cities for jazz, as well as a major economic hub, Armstrong secured a permanent place in Jazz history by gaining a reputation there. As his reputation grew so did the opportunities for him to play. Everybody wanted Louis Armstrong to perform.

His triumphant tours of Europe and the United States in 1934, 1942 and 1952, propelled Armstrong to what is now regarded as "superstar" status. His recordings of popular standards such as "Wrap Your Troubles in Dreams," "On the Sunny Side of the Street," "Sleepy Time Down South," and "Mack the Knife," coupled with his appearances in numerous films such as "High Society" and "The Glenn Miller Story," made Armstrong one of the most popular jazz artists in history. During his career Armstrong received numerous awards and often toured with his groups for the U.S. State Department.

Armstrong suffered a series of illnesses during the 1960s and was hospitalized over a period of months. In 1969, he filmed "Hello Dolly" with Barbara Streisand. In 1971, after an appearance at the Waldorf-Astoria Hotel in New York City, he suffered a heart attack. Louis Armstrong died July 6, 1971 at his home in Long Island, New York.

CHAPTER 2

New Orleans

New Orleans as a Focal Point

Jazz is the result of years and years of cross-fertilization and the Africanization (and African-Americanization) of West African and West European culture in North America. It was born not only in New Orleans, as many historians would have us believe, but on the plantations in the north and south of the United States during the late 1600s, 1700s, and early 1800s. Numerous studies of the birth of jazz pay special tribute to New Orleans as the one and only birthplace of jazz. The truth is that jazz developed more openly in New Orleans due to the money and traffic generated from having one of the biggest seaports in the country. The booming economic climate of New Orleans provided a base for the entertainment business to grow. Entertainers from New Orleans as well as the surrounding areas all settled in the Crescent City to find work.

During the early 1800s, the city of New Orleans was dominated mainly by the French and Spanish. The general mood of the city was French, but "the additional presence of Italians, Englishmen, some Germans, a few Slavs, some Scots and Irishmen, along with the African population provided a unique cultural setting for the new music." The style of music that emerged from within this melting pot was closely aligned to the music found in other Latin Catholic areas such as the Caribbean and parts of Central and Latin America. The mixture of French military marches, French quadrilles, Spanish folk songs, British folk songs, and indigenous African music was soon to develop into hot-tempered jazz. In addition, as Marshall Stearns states in *The Story of Jazz*, many runaway slaves from neighboring islands found their way to New Orleans, bringing with them the various cultural forms acquired on their plantations.

Creoles

More than any other group, the Creoles of Color were responsible for bringing together these various cultural entities and traits. (The term Creole of Color as used in this work refers to offspring of mixed French, Spanish and African descent.) I can well remember how astonished I was to learn on a field trip to Martinique French West Indies that many of the 'White' or European (French) Caribbeans considered themselves to be Creoles. In fact, one French lady was so surprised that most of those in our party had not initially considered her a Creole that she briefly stopped our tour of the island to explain in detail the history of the Euro-Caribbean. In many instances these sons and daughters of plantation owners inherited the entire fortunes of their European fathers. (As a child, I heard stories about slave owners using European prostitutes or indentured slaves for breeding purposes.)

Some Creoles of Color became wealthy slave owners in their own right. Many were well-educated, often studying in Europe to become musicians, lawyers, doctors, and so on. Some remained abroad. Yet others returned to their families, bringing with them their newly-acquired culture and education. Creoles were accorded certain rights in the city of New Orleans that even poor whites did not enjoy. Many were deemed untouchable. Because of this quasi-freedom, Creoles developed a society of their own. Creole musicians performed in as European a manner as possible. Association with African slaves or white freedmen was at a minimum. According to Roger Bastide in his book *African Civilizations in the New World*, the Creoles, out of necessity, were forced to develop a separate culture to adjust their lifestyle to the environment in which they found themselves.

The Black Codes, or Code Noir, was established during the late eighteenth and nineteenth century to govern the interaction between slave and slave owner. For the most part, these laws were designed to protect the rights of the slave owner and to ensure the continued enslavement of the African. The Black Codes varied from state to state (see John Hope Franklin, *From Slavery to Freedom*). In addition, the Black Codes provided for the freeing of many Creoles—mainly the women and children. Events such as the Quadroon Balls (grand dance galas open only to some Black African women, Creole men and women, and whites, but closed to Black African men) were common. The Creoles in many instances had the best of two worlds. They enjoyed the creative spontaneity of the African slave and at the same time acquired the habits and culture of the ruling European class. Many of the Creoles inherited the wealth of their French and Spanish fathers. Some were educated in Europe as lawyers, doctors, and of course, musicians. Most of them chose to return to their families in the United States. However, a small group preferred to remain in Europe. Those who chose to return brought with them the highly technical training they received in their various fields. In the case of the trained musicians, they brought with them the concept of classical phrasing and a highly polished technique. The fact that the Creole serves as a bridge between the traditional African culture in the New World and western European culture also plays a larger role in the development of jazz than is normally thought.

Most of us are familiar with the fact that the slave owner took at will his pick of female slaves. However, few of us know that many middle class slave owners, or those who could afford it, set up separate households and families with Creole women. Thus, as one can see, there was a special exchange of cultures that took place between 'Black, White and Brown' in New Orleans. This exchange not only altered the music but it also changed the speech, dress, education, politics, and total lifestyle of New Orleans.

Many of our great jazz personalities were Creoles: Alphonse Picou, Sidney Bechet, Barney Bigard, Albert Nicholas, Buddy Petit, Freddie Keppard, Kid Ory[2]. In fact, it is safe to say that most of the recorded musical examples of early New Orleans jazz is Creole. Possibly the real jazz, the early music of the Black African, was never really presented in its purest form but only in a much watered-down version. For it was not until the passing of the Segregation act of 1894 that the Creoles found themselves in the humiliating position of being on the same social level as their alienated Black African brothers. The Segregation Act declared that all people descended from one or more African parents would be classified as Negro or Black, eliminating the well-protected social structure of the Creoles. Many of the Creole musicians found themselves forced to learn to play the very blues music that many of them had previously rejected. Marshall Stearns states in *The Story of* Jazz that:

> "The Creoles of Color had much to learn about Jazz which their academic training could not give them. This account of Picou's attempt at making the change from Creole music to Jazz is interesting. He states: 'When I was very young, I took lessons from the flute player at the French Opera House. He made me practice fingering for six months before I was permitted to play a note.' While still in his teens Picou was invited to play in the Jazz orchestra of his friend, the trombone player Boubol Augustat. Picou was shocked when he discovered that they had no written music. He was expected to improvise. Boubol told me, 'Just listen,' and I sat there not knowing what to do. After awhile, I caught on and started playing two or three notes for one."[3]

Was Creole music jazz or was it completely different music altogether? According to various reports coming out of New Orleans during the early 1800s, the music sounded more Latin than it did jazz or quasi-jazz. This distinctively Latin flavor can be attributed to the Spanish and Caribbean influence found in New Orleans during this period.

Language

The influence language has on the development of various ethnic music is indeed interesting. It is my belief that language is very influential in shaping the concept of all music. It is highly conceivable that the Creole language played a significant role in shaping the overall sound of early New Orelans music. If the human voice is, as is often said, the original musical instrument and all other mechanical instruments fashioned after its sonority, it seems only logical that one's concept of music is, to a great degree, shaped by the sounds one hears from birth. The human voice is, in many instances, the first and most important sound we hear. The Creole language must have been an important factor in shaping Creole music just as African and then African-American dialects were, and still are, important in shaping that music. In the following example, the pronunciation of the words has a tendency to cause a slight variation in the pitches indicated.

Language in music, whether instrumental or vocal, should be one of the first subjects learned if one is to fully appreciate the aesthetics of the music to

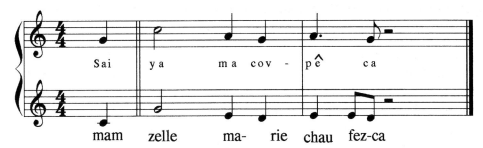

Example 6

be studied. The difference in the pronunciation of a word can alter the entire feeling of the work. A blues singer who sings "Ain't nobody's bisness" would sound completely out of context if he or she sang "It isn't anyone's business." The original feeling is gone in the latter version. As a kid growing up in Kansas City, I, along with the other "hip dudes" in my neighborhood, made fun of the kids who spoke with a thick African-American "accent." This was long before the 1960s "Black Is Beautiful" era. Though we made fun of the kids who spoke this "foreign" tongue, we never ceased to grow ecstatic whenever we heard Dinah Washington or Ray Charles sing the blues with exactly the same "accent." This self-hating mockery went even further when we went to school. Instead of teaching us about the origins or possible value of studying this "home-grown language," the teacher constantly lectured us on the stupidity of people who spoke in such a manner. The tonal inflections, rhythmic structures, and the rejection of and injection of totally original vocal sounds all contributed to the development of the music we now call jazz.

Congo Square and Cross-Fertilization

If not directly responsible for the birth of jazz, the city of New Orleans provided the proper environment for its early development. Many of the great musicians, often associated with the New Orleans movement in jazz, learned their craft in the Crescent City. In 1817, as a result of the frequent slave uprisings and the increasing fear of vodun (voodoo), a group of slave owners and city officials got together and declared a vacant lot known as Congo Square an official "recreation" area for the slaves.[4] Providing a meeting ground for the slaves to gather and exchange cultures was not the intent of the slave owners. They were simply taking precautions against further slave unrest, which had intensified with the banning of all African slave religious worship services, the playing of drums, and certain dances.

Congo Square was one of the most important points of cross-fertilization between West European and West African cultures. Sunday afternoons found Africans from several tribes dancing, singing, and communicating in ways that may not have been possible if there had never been a place like Congo Square. Such dances as the Conga, the Juba, and the Havana were performed. Various African drums and other African-derived instruments like wooden trumpets, quills, and other forms of African flutes, as well as the newly-acquired plantation-made instruments, rhythm sticks, rattlers, bones, and metal rhythm instruments were among the first instruments to be used in jazz.

The theory that jazz may have begun in Congo Square may provoke an argument from those who believe that jazz started with Dixieland in New Orleans, but the evidence I have mentioned cannot be ignored.

Voodoo

It is almost impossible to discuss any form of African-American culture without discussing its religion. Voodoo, or vodun as it was first called, was originally an African religion. African slaves accepted Christianity mainly because of the European colonists' domination of their lives. Many of the slaves who readily embraced the Christian religion did so only to please their masters. Others actually believed that they would be saved from the cruelties of slavery by accepting the religion of the slave master.

"If we accept the theory that jazz, as it was played on the plantations in the United States during slavery, started by using these simple instruments, we must say that the music called jazz, which was played in New Orleans during the late 1800s and early 1900s, is in fact a different music. The original music was probably a purely improvisational, Latin-type of free or collective improvisation so common during the late 1960s."

During the early 1800s both slave and master were involved in the all-powerful mysticism of voodoo. Even today a number of active jazz musicians believe in the mystical powers of voodoo.

"Drummer Arthur Taylor once told me a story in Paris about a fellow drummer, Philly Joe Jones. Taylor was having trouble with his neighbors across the hall in his Paris apartment. The neighbors, two young American girls, complained that Taylor practiced his drums at ungodly hours of the night, making it impossible for them to sleep. After several warnings from his landlord, Taylor decided to look for another apartment but first sought the advice of his friends, including Philly Joe Jones. Jones advised Taylor to sprinkle a certain powder outside the girls' door, stating that if he did so in the proper manner, he wouldn't have any more trouble with the girls. According to Taylor, he followed Jones's advice and sprinkled the powder around the girls' door. After a few weeks, Taylor noticed that he hadn't heard any more complaints from the girls or the landlord. The elated Taylor decided to tell Jones, his "spiritual advisor," about his success. When he did, Jones responded with an astonished, "You mean that stuff really works?"

Whether or not voodoo really works is not important. It is one part of the African-American's religion that still exists today, and it did play a major role in the lives of certain musicians. It is reported that Jelly Roll Morton and other early jazz musicians were true believers in voodoo as a religion. One of the major faults of studies done on jazz and other forms of African-American music is that the scholars and historians have failed to penetrate the psyche of the artist and understand the time in which he lived. The traditional music of the voodoo services affected the music of these musicians. The strong spirituality often associated with the true voodoo worshipper is present in the spiritual improvisational solos of the true jazz musician.

"Voodoo is one of the most misunderstood religions in the world. According to many legends, it started among the Quida, or Whydah, peoples of West Africa. This serpent-worshipping cult proved to be so spiritually superior to the warring Dahomians that the Dahomians embraced vodun as their own religion. Arriving in the Americas as slaves and finding the same serpents that were used in vodun worship in Africa, Dahomian slaves supposedly decided that the gods favored vodun as the right religion for their peoples. Thus vodun, later called voodo-voodoo, found its way into the religious practices of the early African-American slaves."

Major Innovators

Throughout the history of jazz a number of major innovators and popular figures have been given a historical status equal to that of heroes. I once asked a sociologist about this elevation of musical personalities. His answer was that people constantly need a godlike figure. Sometimes this figure is a political personality and at other times a movie star or jazz musician. The profession of the elevated person is not important. The only criterion for being idolized is that the person projects an image of greatness.

As far as jazz musicians and jazz historians are concerned, "King" Buddy Bolden was one of the first jazz musicians to achieve this high status. Bolden was a cornetist who played in New Orleans during the latter part of the 1800s. According to many of his peers, Buddy was one of the loudest cornet players in New Orleans. To advertise an upcoming concert, he would simply get up in the middle of town and begin to blow as loud as he could. His sound was so powerful that it could be heard for miles around the city. He also had a reputation for being a "lady's man." He was fond of having his young, women admirers carry his cornet to engagements, and during his hot improvisations he could often be seen flirting with the women in the audience.His smooth manner and bold approach may have cost him his freedom. It was not easy for a Negro to assert an air of independence during this period in New Orleans. Bolden's direct approach and somewhat unusual manner got him committed to a Louisiana mental institution. At that time, it was impossible for blacks to assert any independence or authority. Many of Bolden's friends and associates pointed out that had Boldlen been a white musician reacting in the same bizarre manner, he would probably not have been arrested and placed in a mental institution. Some of the stories surrounding his commital were as bizarre as his acts of "insanity." Many of his followers claim that he "blew" his brains out, while others stated that had he been white he would not have been committed—that he was only temporarily insane and should have been freed immediately. Regardless, he was committed to the East Louisiana State Hospital and remained there, off and on, until his death in 1931.

Buddy Bolden was not only an intelligent musician but worked at many other jobs like most of the other musicians around New Orleans. (There were few, if any, full-time musicians at that time.) Bolden worked both as an editor of a local scandal sheet, "The Cricket," and as a barber.[5] During the early years of jazz in New Orleans, it was very common for musicians to work at any job they could find. Being a jazz musician was not yet considered a profession worthy of one's full attention. Jazz was just a "fun" music to be played only for amusement. Many musicians worked as shoe repairmen, farm laborers, parade musicians, waiters, and so on. Buddy Bolden was, despite reports to the contrary, an astute businessman who was one of the first jazzmen to actually book several bands under his own name.[6]

Among the many other early New Orleans musicians were ragtime pianist Jelly Roll Morton and cornetist Freddie Keppard. Keppard, who was originally a string player (violin, mandolin, and later accordian) was, according to many of early New Orleans jazz musicians, one of the best bluesmen around.[7] According to Jelly Roll Morton, "I never heard of a man that could beat Keppard—his reach was so exceptional, high and low, with all degrees of power, great imagination and more tones than anybody."[8] He later went on to work with such prestigious groups as the Olympia Orchestra and The Original Creole Orchestra. The importance of Keppard as an outstanding soloist is often overlooked and played down by most writers. However, if one seriously considers the tremendous compliement paid him by none other than Jelly Roll Morton himself, we must reevaluate his importance in the development of early New Orleans traditional music.

'King' Joe Oliver was one of the great New Orleans bluesmen responsible for taking jazz north to Chicago. During his early years in New Orleans, he worked with some of the top jazz bands, including The Olympia Jazz Band, The Onward Brass band and Kid Ory's. Oliver was considered to have been a talented businessman, often working with two, sometimes three, different bands during the same period. Later, in Chicago, he is said to have worked with both the Bill Johnson Band at the Royal Gardens, on 31st and State Street, and in clarinetist Lawrence Duke's band at Bill Bottoms Dreamland Cafe.[9]

In order to really understand the importance of music in New Orleans during the late 1800s–early 1900s, one must first consider the source of that music— its people. The southern-dominated* culture that prevailed in New Orleans was destined to produce lively music. Music was a part of the everyday lives of the numerous West African, Italian, Spanish and French natives. When they found

---

*Southern-dominated refers to the numerous Italian, Spanish, West African, and French cultures that dominated the area.

themselves in the New World, this genuine love for music as an integral part of their existence did not stop.

In New Orleans, music was heard continuously in the home, on the streets, in the dance halls and concert halls. The contribution of the many Latin immigrants from neighboring Latin and Caribbean islands, such as Cuba, Santo Domingo, Haiti, Mexico, etc. (along with the music of the native Indians), played a much understated role in the development of the music that came out of New Orleans. When one takes this fact into consideration, it seems ironic that the concept of fusion was not investigated in more detail.

The fusing together of the music of the southern cultures and that of the western European colonists (English, French, Italians, Scots, Germans) produced a transformed version of the mazurkas, polkas, waltzes, etc.

The emergence of the New Orleans (Jazz) Brass band was in fact an outgrowth of the French presence in New Orleans. One of the reasons for the popularity of the brass bands was the role such bands played in the parade marches. In addition to parades, they also performed at funerals and concerts. In fact, brass bands, just as other European customs, reflected an attempt by the West European colonist to duplicate European lifestyles in the New World. Surely there was no brass tradition in Africa prior to 1619.

Keppard was, according to historians, the first jazz musician to be asked to record, but he turned down the offer because he feared others would copy his style from the recording. As a result of Keppard's refusal, the Original Dixieland Jass Band (in the early days of jazz, the word *jazz* was written *jass*) made the first jazz recording. The one fact that many scholars tend to overlook is that whenever we hear a recording of what is supposed to be true New Orleans Dixieland, we forget that the majority of these musicians were not recorded until they had already left New Orleans. By this time, many of them had already changed their style to a more commercialized, in some instances watered-down, version of the jazz they had played earlier. In fact, many of the early great improvisers were not recorded until much later in their careers. Alto saxophonist Captain John Handy, one of the Crescent City's top alto sax players, was not recorded until the 1960s. Saxophonist and clarinetist Sidney Bechet, trumpeter Louis Armstrong, drummer Baby Dodds and his brother, clarinetist Johnny Dodds, drummer Papa Jack Laine, clarinetist Alphonse Picou, cornetist Nick La Rocca, and violinist Paul Dominguez were among the first professional jazz musicians.

Dixieland

The music played in New Orleans during the late 1800s and the early 1900s is referred to as *Dixieland*. Just how the music got this name is unclear. Some critics say that it was named after the popular ten-note bill (the Dix piece) used under the French colonial rule. It was the custom to name anything coming out of that particular geographical area *Dix*. Thus the music was said to have come from Dix-land. Others attribute the name to the fact that the music came from below the Mason-Dixon line. Regardless of the etymology, the music was not called jazz at that time. Most people agree that it was not until around 1917 that the name jass (jazz) was commonly associated with this music. Leroy Ostransky states in his book *The Anatomy of* Jazz that the word jazz, or jass, was probably used long before 1914. Ostransky cites cornetist Nick LaRocca, who claimed that the Original Dixieland Jazz Band was first to be publicly called a jazz band.

The popularity of the name was soon capitalized on by such bands as the Original Creole Jass Band, the Olympic Jass Band, and so on. For commercial purposes, various bands were called "the original jass band" and every musician named "King." For example, Paul Whiteman was the "King of Jazz" (1920), and Benny Goodman was the "King of Swing" (1930).

Dixieland

Example 7

The Preservation Hall Jazz Band represents the typical traditional New Orleans "Dixieland" jazz band.

For the most part, Dixieland music was more improvised than its ragtime counterpart. Dixieland players usually played from memory a kind of variation on march themes, which gave the music a more improvisational rather than compositional flavor.

The most common instrumentation in Dixieland bands during the early New Orleans period was cornet (later the trumpet was used instead of the softer sounding cornet), clarinet, trombone, violin, banjo (later replaced by the trap set). The earliest forms of Dixieland were usually played at parades and for outside functions, mainly picnics. Therefore, some of the first instruments used in jazz were the parade drum (instead of the later, more popular trap set), the tuba (which was used for parades in place of the string bass, which was used later), flutes, lower brass instruments, and so on. The French military march, more than any other European type of music, served as a vehicle for the improvisational prowess of the early jazz musician. When questioned about the type of music they played, many New Orleans musicians simply said they were playing "march music."

Secret Societies

Secret societies played a major role in the development of jazz during the early years of New Orleans. Secret societies not only provided work for New Orleans jazz musicians but served as social clubs for them. Many secret societies sponsored such activities as picnics, social parties, balls, dinners, and, more than anything else, they provided insurance and burial plans. The thought of an "undignified" death—a death without an adequate funeral—prompted many New Orleanians to join the ever popular secret societies. During an interview, New Orleans jazz great Danny Barker explained that there were many different types of secret societies. Blacks had their own societies. There were Creole societies, quadroon societies, octoroon societies, white societies, and so on. Each society hired musicians of its own "race" to perform. Many Creole musicians would not play black society functions for fear of being ridiculed for associating with lower-class musicians.

Many blacks probably were attracted to join secret societies out of fear of loneliness. One theory is that Blacks could no longer find consolation in their original African tribes; they created a "tribe" away from home. According to Marshall Stearns, Louis Armstrong mentions as many as twenty-two different secret societies in his book *Satchmo*.[10] This gives some indication of the importance of the secret societies within New Orleans society: A good example of the African-American's fear of death in poverty can be seen in the motion picture *The Liberation of Lord Byron Jones*. In the movie, a black funeral director skillfully tries to sell a packaged funeral to a poor, black innkeeper. The fact that the innkeeper has suffered a life of hardships and humiliation makes her a prime target for the smooth sales pitch of the business-minded funeral director. This fear of death was accompanied by the desire for a "mighty fine" funeral so that one's friends could see one depart in "style." Brass bands were often employed to play funeral marches. In fact, the funeral marching band has a long tradition in the development of jazz. The long, drawn-out tempos of the band, as it mournfully played its way to the cemetery, was no doubt a prime contributor to the refined mournful sound one finds in New Orleans music. Although other cultures have used funeral marching bands, the New Orleans funeral band was unique in that it played jazz. According to most Jazz historians, it was in the return march from the cemetery that the jazz contribution to the funeral band was born. The drummer was responsible for setting the pace. The role of the master drummer as conductor can be traced back to Africa. During a concert tour of North Africa in 1966, drummer Kenny Clarke and I witnessed an Egyptian ballet performance in the city of Carthage (Tunisia) where the drummer served as both percussionist and conductor. At first there appeared to be no conductor directing the orchestra, which was composed of violins and other western instruments. But on closer look, we found that the drummer was directing the entire performance. His position to the rear of the other musicians did not seem to affect their ability to follow his direction.

The early African-American accepted death as a time to celebrate rather than a time for sorrow. During slavery, many slave mothers would kill their newborn to spare them from the horrors of slavery. Celebrating death as the moment of final liberation is understandable when one considers the inhuman treatment received by many slaves.

Storyville

The Storyville section of New Orleans with its grandeur and elegance was one of the city's most important contributions to jazz. The seaport of New Orleans was developing into an international trading center, and this along with the influx of tourism attracted not only musicians from neighboring communities but such unwanted businesses as prostitution, gambling, and so on. To control this growing menace to the "respectable citizens," a group of businessmen, local politicians, and interested citizens got together with Alderman Sidney Story to discuss ways in which the situation might be stopped. Story proposed Section I of

Ordinance 13,032 C.S., through which the political establishment of New Orleans could contain all the illegal activities within a thirty-eight block area.[11] Prostitutes were registered and other measures taken in an attempt to control the threatening situation. It was in the Storyville section that many musicians, both black and white, learned to play jazz. Such clubs as Tom Anderson's Cafe, the 101 Ranch Club, LuLu White's, and the Tin Type Hall served as "jazz academies" for those musicians who otherwise could not find the occasion to play jazz. The 101 Ranch is said to have been one of the clubs where the Original Dixieland Jazz Band learned to play jazz by listening to African-American and Creole musicians. There were no recordings during this time so the only way a musician could learn to play jazz was by playing with those musicians who already understood the language. Of course, many Creole musicians found work at the more respectable dance halls and private dances.

Undoubtedly, the atmosphere in Storyville during the early years of jazz was one of excitement. According to soprano saxophonist Sidney Bechet, "music was in the air." It must have been similar to the feeling one gets when walking through the heart of Rio de Janeiro, Brazil during Carnival—everywhere there is always someone singing, strumming a guitar, or dancing. This festive atmosphere gave the musicians (semi-professionals and amateurs) a foundation and prepared the "audience" for the music that followed.

Another important contribution to this festive atmosphere created by the musicians was the New Orleans bordellos. According to David Dexter, Jr. in his book, *The Jazz Story*, bordellos played a very important role in the development of jazz in New Orleans. Many fine musicians played the bordellos, but Spencer Williams (unrelated to Clarence but a close friend and associate) is probably one of the few musicians reared in one! There was, at times, fierce competition between bordellos, and many owners would use whatever methods of advertising they felt would attract business. According to Dexter, Antonia Gonzales, a bordello mistress, "would dress in her most appealing robe and entertain between 'tricks' with spectactular trumpet solos." However, most research on musicians in New Orleans bordellos indicates that the majority of them employed a single piano player. In some cases, the more elegant houses used classically-oriented violinists and in some cases small string ensembles. Because of racial segregation between blacks and whites and further division between blacks themselves, many houses refused to hire certain musicians. For instance, many bordellos and clubs refused to hire "pure" black musicians and would hire only "octoroons" (one who is one-eighth black or colored) or those who looked white or Spanish. This is important when uncovering why certain musicians were talked or written about and why they appeared in the forefront of a particular movement. Some musicians were chosen simply because they had been hired for the "right" color and not because they were major musicians or creative innovators. Discrimination in the hiring of musicians found its way into every other facet of New Orleans life.

The closing of the Storyville section brought an end to one of the most productive periods in jazz history. Many musicians were forced to leave and seek employment in less musically-productive northern cities. According to Buerkle and Barker in their book *Bourbon Street Black*, the Storyville section was closed because four sailors were killed in the district. This, along with the wartime effort and the constant political hassles over the very existence of the illegal activities conducted in Storyville, forced local and federal authorities to place the Storyville district off-limits to all military personnel. Later, after much protest from the district's businessmen, an ordinance was passed that forbade all such activities as prostitution, gambling, and so on, within the district. This forced an end to the flouishing jazz scene and eventually an end to Storyville as a haven for jazz.

The migration of large numbers of black Americans to the urban areas of Chicago, New York, Detroit, and other cities between 1910–1920 forced many musicians to leave along with their audiences. Thus, Dixieland found its way into the urban areas of the north. The Original Dixieland Jazz Band, the first jazz band to record, was responsible for popularizing the name *jazz* in the north. The name *jazz* began to appear in print through the publicizing of the group's many appearances in northern areas. The origin of the word *jazz* is worthy of some investigation. One of the theories is that it was first used in connection with a jazz musician by the name of Jassbo Brown. Jassbo, according to early reports, was a player of brass instruments who so excited his fans that they often chanted "We want Jassbo." This gave way to the shorter "We want Jass." Another theory is that the name was often used in the Storyville district to describe something "immoral." (According to many of the older New Orleans traditional musicians, the term usually referred to sexual relations.) Yet another theory is that the name *jass* was brought over with the slaves from Africa. Regardless of its origin, the word was used to describe the music that developed, during the early 1900s, in New Orleans.

Conclusion

Although jazz as we know it during the New Orleans period (late 1800s–early 1900s) did develop in areas other than in New Orleans, it settled there and "adopted" the city of New Orleans as one of its bases. The large migrations of people along the Allegheny mountain area and to other parts of the country provided a nucleus for the soon-to-be jazz enthusiast. Among the various nationalities living in New Orleans at this time were Italians, French, Englishmen, Germans, Slavs, Scots, Irishmen, and a large black and African slave population. Creoles of Color were also a vital part of the New Orleans scene.

The music that emerged from this melting pot somewhat resembled the music found on the Caribbean island of Martinique and other French colonies. The French quadrille and military march, and various other folk songs, came together with original African melodies and were transformed through a process called Africanization. One thing is certain and that is that the process of Africanization was responsible for the transforming of European and African music into what is now known as jazz. Such a statement is bound to elicit disagreement. Jazz, in its purest sense, is a form of African-American folk music. But the fact that jazz is now played and enjoyed by people all over the world, regardless of race or creed, is proof that the music is a result of a particular environment and not a result of color.

Perhaps the most important contribution of the city of New Orleans to the development of jazz was its Storyville section. Storyville was the section of town that housed the city's illegal activities—gambling, prostitution, and so on. It was here, many historians have claimed, that real jazz developed. However, many older New Orleans musicians, including Danny Barker, claim that Storyville was just one of the sections in town where jazz was played. Before the advent of Storyville, Congo Square played an important role in the early development of jazz. It was here that one of the most important cross-fertilizations of West African and West European cultures took place. This old vacant lot "given" to the slaves to let off the frustrations of work soon developed into a major tourist attraction. People came to Congo Square from all over the world to watch and listen to slaves who, because of their varied cultural backgrounds, couldn't even understand each other.

This then, along with the plantation, was one of the areas where the real jazz developed. New Orleans and its hustling city life came much later. Musicians like Buddy Bolden, Freddie Keppard, Joe Oliver, Jack Laine, and Jelly Roll Morton performed in the cathouses, river boats, picnics, society balls, and at other social functions to give jazz its first real boost. Its economic prosperity helped establish the tradition of New Orleans as the "home of jazz."

Suggested Readings and Listening

Books

Bastide, Roger. *African Civilizations in the New World*. New York: Harper & Row Publishers, 1971.

Buerkle, Jacke V., and Barker, Nancy. *Bourbon Street Black*. London: Oxford University Press, 1973.

Dexter, Dave. *The Jazz Story*. Englewood Cliffs, New Jersey: Prentice-Hall, 1964.

Franklin, John Hope. *From Slavery to Freedom*. New York: Alfred Knopf, 1974.

Ostransky, Leroy. *The Anatomy of Jazz*. Seattle: University of Washington Press, 1960.

Steams, Marshall, *The Story of Jazz*. New York: Oxford University Press, 1956.

Records

Smithsonian Collection of Classic Jazz (Smithsonian Institution P611891).

Original Dixieland Jazz Band (World Records Club. SH. 220).

Louis Armstrong at Symphony Hall CMCA.2-4057.

JAZZ III/New Orleans (Folkways FP57).

CHAPTER 3

Ragtime

Profile

"JELLY ROLL" FERDINAND JOSEPH MORTON • was born in New Orleans, Louisiana, September 20, 1885. Earlier in his career he learned to play the guitar, trombone, and later mastered the piano. It was on the piano that he made his most important contribution to jazz. However, we must also take into consideration his numerous compositions and, to a lesser degree, his ability as a blues singer when analyzing his contributions to jazz. Such Morton compositions as the "King Porter Stomp," "Wild Man Blues" and "Chicago Breakdown" became standard repertoire for professional jazz musicians.

During the early years, Jelly Roll worked mainly in the "sporting houses" of New Orleans. Most of his work during this period (1900s) was as a solo pianist. This gave him the musical freedom to explore the rhythmical and structural content of the music. Shortly after his solo performance in New Orleans, Jelly Roll began touring with various instrumental groups, including McCabes Minstrel Troubadors, Bunk Johnson and, later, his own popular "Red Hot Peppers."

Ragtime pianist "Dr." Jelly Roll Morton was one of the most colorful figures in the history of jazz. He was also one of its most innovative pianists and composers. Photo courtesy of Rutgers, the Institute of Jazz Studies.

Around 1915, Morton traveled to St. Louis, Kansas City, then went on to San Francisco and Los Angeles. Perhaps the most productive period of his recording career was between 1926–27, when he recorded for Victor. In

Chicago, around 1922, he "began making player piano rolls and records, among them a series for Gennett Records."[1]

According to John Chilton, the talented Morton also tried his hand at a number of other careers, which included boxing promoting and running a Hotel-Club. Throughout his career Jelly Roll experimented with a variety of businesses, as well as performing as a jazz artist. After settling in California, around 1940, he developed health problems and was subsequently hospitalized and eventually died in 1941.

Structure

One of the most popular forms of jazz during the late 1800s was ragtime. Since ragtime was usually written down and subsequently improvised, some earlier critics doubted that it should even be called jazz.

In its early stages, ragtime was basically written for piano (see example). Pianists like Scott Joplin, Jelly Roll Morton, James Scott, Tom Turpin, Louis Chauvin, Tony Jackson, Eubie Blake, and Joseph Lamb were among the top rag players. Ragtime was "born" in the Midwest and not in New Orleans as most people assume. As the legend goes, Scott Joplin rode into the city of Sedalia, Missouri, playing what local musicians described as "funny" music. This "funny" music (ragtime) consisted of a rhythmic left hand that emphasized the first and third beats and an improvised version of the melodic line in the right hand. Ragtime was basically a composer's music. In most instances, it was up to the improviser to interject his or her melodic improvisations into the precomposed melody. This was in direct contrast to Dixieland, which depended more on the spontaneous improvisations of the performer. Ragtime more resembled the European concept of music in that there was a definite form and structure to the music, whereas Dixieland was basically free. Ragtime had a pseudorondo pattern. According to Marshall Stearns, "If we give each section a letter of the alphabet, they occur in this order: AABBACCDD. (In classical rondo, the first strain returns regularly before each new strain.) The third strain (CC) or trio—a name taken from the march—is often the featured tune, frequently repeated."[2] David R. Baskerville

Example 8

tells us that rags often consisted of five or more sections. The technique of referring to different sections of a composition is definitely European. Baskerville
goes on to explain how some rags started in one key and later dropped to a sub-
dominant key.[3]

Many ragtime composers were concerned about the "legitimacy" of their
music. Scott Joplin's "Maple Leaf Rag" was one of the most important works of
its time. In addition to "Maple Leaf Rag" Joplin is credited with a number of other
compositions such as "Original Rag," a number of waltzes and two operas,
Treemonisha and *A Guest of Honour*. Basically all of these works were based on
European versions of the waltz, march, opera, and so on.

Origins

Ragtime dates back to the early 1800s mining camps of the Midwest where the
music was originally played on the guitar. Guitarists, rather than pianists, were
usually employed because the mining camps were abandoned as soon as they
were completely saturated. It simply did not pay to buy a piano when a guitar
was more mobile and occupied little or no space.

Just why and how did ragtime start in the Midwest? Because of geographical
location, Sedalia, Missouri, became a favorite "stopover" haven for weary, trav-

eling salesmen. Local businessmen, realizing the economic potential of the city, "opened the city" to prostitution and gambling. Again, most of the activities were contained in one main area, Main Street. Soon word began to spread that one could have a fine time in the city. Musicians, including Scott Joplin, were attracted to the Midwest.

Many of the musicians attracted to Sedalia, as well as local talent, found time to study at the local conservatory with a native German music teacher. Although ragtime had begun as a fun music, some musicians found that in order to perform the new complicated melodies, composed by the likes of Joplin, they had to study. Many of these musicians also studied composition. Joplin's long overlooked opera, *Treemonisha*, is considered a classic. The French military march served as a guide for composers writing in the ragtime tradition. Such markings as "In March Tempo" or "Tempo de Marcia" were common on ragtime sheet music during the 1800s. French quadrilles, polkas, and German folk songs also served as bases from which ragtime musicians improvised.

If Scott Joplin is considered the "Father of Ragtime," then "Jelly Roll" (Ferdinand) Morton was without doubt the "King." Morton's colorful character, coupled with his enormous talent, made him one of the most important figures to emerge during the Ragtime Era. Morton worked mainly as a pianist, but is rumored to have been equally talented on the guitar and trombone. Although there is no evidence of his studying privately, as did so many of his contemporaries, Morton was a thorough and creative artist. One of his musical tricks was to invite a visiting pianist to play his best "licks" and then duplicate the same "licks," adding a little "Mortonism" just to liven things up. This musical treat, together with his ability as a blues singer and arranger, earned him the respect of early ragtime jazz men.

According to legend there was a definite trend to the development of rag. The trend appears to have started in Sedalia, moved on to St. Joseph, then to St. Louis, and on to New Orleans. Ragtime music in New Orleans is said to have been more rhythmic. The immediate successors of rag were the Harlem Stride Piano School and the ever-popular Chicago Boogie-Woogie School. Besides the mainstream jazz or rag composers, musicians like John Philip Sousa and Daniel Emmett also composed ragtime melodies. In fact, Sousa was perhaps one of ragtime's most successful ambassadors, since he often performed ragtime pieces in his many travels to Europe areas outside the United States. As mentioned earlier, the general form for ragtime—AA-BB-A-CC-DD structure—is very often found in march music.

Example 9

The basic mood of ragtime was light and happy. This may be attributed to the use of ragtime music as the "official" show music for the minstrel show. Jelly Roll Morton first transcribed his ragtime improvisations for other instruments, making him one of our first jazz arrangers. Morton simply transcribed, note for note, the sounds he played on the piano for sax, clarinet, trombone, and so on. The smoother ragtime was heard at the same locations as its rougher "sister," Dixieland. The name ragtime was first used to describe that "ragged" music ("ragged" because the music was played in a loose fashion and not strictly as it was written) commonly associated with the Midwest. Because the music had an unusually rough quality in its early stages, it was termed "ragged music." Many of the so-called Dixieland pieces referred to on recordings are in fact "rag."

Ragtime and European Classical Music

Ragtime as an art form was revered in both the United States and Europe. Its roving melodies and haunting rhythms directly influenced such prominent composers as Claude Debussy, Erik Satie, Igor Stravinsky, Darius Milhaud, and Paul Hindemith, just as it influenced a generation of American composers beginning with Charles Ives.[4] Immediately after the advent of ragtime, one could hardly hear a classical work written by the above mentioned composers that didn't have some melodic, harmonic, or rhythmic relation to ragtime. Many modern music composers are shocked when I insist that many works of composers like Igor Stravinsky and Charles Ives are almost exact duplications of ragtime pieces that I have heard. But when ragtime hit the scene in the late 1800s, European classical art music never recovered from its impact. The effect of ragtime on Western European music has never been properly examined. In his dissertation, author David Baskerville does an excellent job in giving examples of European composers 'borrowing' from jazz, especially ragtime music. However, given the importance of a music, acknowledged by the composers as having changed their own perspective on music, one would take for granted that the proper study of ragtime and other forms of jazz would constitute a substantial part of every serious music historian's studies. However, we find just the opposite. Often, jazz, is given a brief, token mention (examine the length of material devoted to jazz in your standard music history text), if discussed at all.

Scott Joplin was born in Texarkana, Texas, on December 24, 1868 and died in New York City, on April 11, 1917. Perhaps Joplin's most important contribution was his ability as a composer. He is also given credit for composing the first jazz opera *Treemonisha* and later "A Guest of Honour" (Chilton). He concentrated his efforts mainly around the Kansas City, Sedalia, and St. Louis areas.

The more aggressive composers of European-based art music, like Debussy, Stravinsky, Dvorak, Copeland, and Satie did not hesitate to incorporate these new and inspirational sounds into their own compositions. David Baskerville attributes Europe's attraction to African-American jazz to the general tone or atmosphere set by the leading painters and sculptors of the day (Gauguin, Modigliani, Picasso).[5]

Ragime pianist Eubie Blake was one of the oldest active performers in jazz until his death.

Many European composers during the late nineteenth century were tired of the heavy Wagnerian romanticism that had earlier prevailed and were ready for a change. African-American music, which was so completely different from their own music, inspired them. The fact that many of the early modernists (1920s) were mainly pianists (the piano was one of the main instruments used in ragtime) may account for their acceptance of ragtime.

Many dances reflected the rhythmic punctuations of ragtime. The cakewalk, a dance based on the way blacks imitated the Sunday afternoon strolls of their white plantation masters, and the ragtime dance were the most popular. Traces of the cakewalk can be found in modern dances.

It is safe to say that composers like Scott Joplin were very much aware that their music was European-oriented. In fact, they made it a point to shape their music to sound as European as possible. Both Joplin and James Scott were trained in the music of Chopin, Schumann, and other composers of European piano music. Another pianist not often mentioned as a giant among ragtime performers is Blind Tom Bethune—Blind Thomas, according to Eileen Southern in *The Music of Black Americans*, was born in Columbus, Georgia in 1849. According to historians of African-American music, Blind Thomas was a musical genius who could play from memory anything he heard just once. He was famous for repeating entire symphonies and piano works, as well as animal sounds. An an interpreter of ragtime works, he was one of the best.

Is Ragtime Jazz?

For the moment, I would like to focus on the question of whether or not ragtime is really jazz. To lend credibility to the idea of jazz as an art form, most critics have come out strongly in favor of giving ragtime its rightful place as an integral part of the music we call jazz. Yet others have emphatically denied rag a place in jazz, stating that it is a special kind of music closely related to a popular, semi-classical form of music rather than to jazz. The fact that the music developed in the Midwest and not in New Orleans didn't help in establishing rag as a "legitimate" form of jazz. Another point was that ragtime was a composer's music—it was, in most instances, written down. This gave publishers the upper hand in determining what the music would be called. (Unfortunately, the music industry—the recording companies, publishers, distributors, media—has often dictated the course of jazz history. It is the industry that determines by what name we, the public, shall know the product.) Publishing houses often hired pianists to demonstrate sheet music. One such pianist was Lil' Hardin Armstrong, the wife of trumpeter Louis Armstrong. Many of these pianists were classically trained as both composers and pianists. This appealed to the commercially-minded publishers because it gave a legitimacy to the music being sold. At the other end of the musical scale, ragtime composers like Jelly Roll Morton and Scott Joplin brought a kind of natural African-Americanism to the flow of ragtime. Morton's was more of a stride effect—the kind of swing prominent some years later during the Harlem Renaissance period.

Reactions to Ragtime

For a particular artist's style to succeed there must first be a solid business foundation to support it. In the case of ragtime, F.A. Mill's Tin Pan Alley Publishing Company and John Stark's publishing firm were the most important. Stark eventually became the publisher of such classics as "Maple Leaf Rag" and the "Original Rag."

But Ragtime was not always readily accepted by the American Public. According to author David Ewen in *History of Popular Music*, ragtime became so popular by the end of the nineteenth century that it was attacked in an editorial in the *Musical Courier* in 1899. "A wave of vulgar or filthy and suggestive music has inundated the land.... Nothing but ragtime prevails." Two years later, the American Federation of Musicians passed a resolution to do everything in its power to "suppress and discourage the playing and publishing of such musical trash." These quotations give us a clear picture of the country's reaction to jazz. Recently, a student of jazz history at the University of Pittsburgh conducted a study of the negative reaction of the press toward jazz during the late nineteenth century and early twentieth century and discovered that many daily newspapers, during this period, carried stories that condemned the playing of rag-time and other forms of jazz. In addition, they warned their readers to protect the "weaker sex" (presumably women and children) from dancing to this "devil's music." Some newspapers even went so far as to say that the music caused its listeners to "go into sexual fits" and could cause "lunacy." Given these accusations, it is easy to understand why ragtime, and other forms of jazz, had such a difficult time becoming established.

Ragtime reached its peak in the 1920s. Major touring groups found themselves serving as ambassadors of goodwill both in this country and abroad. Recently ragtime has been rediscovered as a major art form. Classical and semi-classical pianists took to the music as though it had been part of their existence for years, though many of them had earlier rejected the music because it was not "legitimate." Today, modern techniques and the general acceptance of the most forceful forms of the avant-garde have made ragtime music a welcome addition to piano literature. Such recordings as Scott Joplin's "Maple Leaf Rag" (the Smithsonian Collection of Classic Jazz) and Jelly Roll Morton's "Perfect Rag" (History of Classic Jazz—Riverside) indicate the degree of artistry developed during the ragtime era.

One of the controversies often associated with the labeling of the music we call jazz is the usage of the term *ragtime* or *Dixieland*. Most historians agree that the early 'jazz' music, heard in and around New Orleans during the late 1800s and early 1900s, was called traditional music and later Dixieland. However, the term *ragtime* can and has often been used to describe the music of Buddy Bolden during that period. As I stated earlier, ragtime was originally conceived as a keyboard music derived from the early banjo stylings of midwestern entertainers. Later, it found its way into the repertoire of instrumental groups throughout the country. The highly-syncopated feeling produced an atmosphere of celebration. The highly-accented delayed and accelerated rhythms were very typical of West African drum rhythms.

On the keyboard, many of the players only used the black keys, thus giving rise to the theory that black entertainers were forbidden to use white keys. Another theory is that because many of them couldn't read music, early black rag performers limited themselves to only black keys.

The early performers of ragtime developed a formidable technique in spite of the fact that they had little or no training. The fact that most ragtime composition called for complete independence of hands as well as a strict sense of timing and an understanding of musical form (AA BB A CC, etc.) served as natural musical training that was unique. As these performers progressed to the stage of studying privately (as many of them did), this naturalization, coupled with a structured musical education, produced some of the most brilliant, technically-advanced keyboard artists ever. I am more than certain that a thorough investigation into this question would advance the study of keyboard performance technique in both European classical music and jazz.

The intricate polyrhythmic blending of beats also suggests a highly-sophisticated form of counterpoint that would rival many of our great composers. The fact that this independence developed from jazz and is spontaneous is even more formidable. The better ragtime pianists were ambidextrous, or at least very close to it. In order to perform the numerous independent melodies that were a part of the improvisations in both hands, it was necessary for the rag performer to develop such a technique.

Some of the dances associated with early rags were the cakewalk, buck, wind, and the jig. Ragtime music also accompanied "coon" songs (songs associated with blacks).

The American fascination with rag gave birth to the first educational publication devoted to the understanding of ragtime. In 1897, Ben Harvey published a work, entitled *Ragtime Instructor*, which explained how to rag various compositions. Some years later, Axel Christensen developed a series of ragtime programs aimed at educating would-be 'raggers' on how to understand and perform the music.[6]

Perhaps the most important, non-professional performer responsible for the success of rag was publisher John Stark, who started out as the owner of a small music store in Sedalia, and later became one of the most important publishers of rag.

Conclusion

Ragtime developed in the Midwest, mainly around Sedalia, St. Joseph, Joplin and St. Louis, Missouri, during the 1800s. One of ragtime's major figures, Scott Joplin, was the major composer of the music in this region. The fact that Joplin came from Texarkana, Texas, shows that ragtime was not only a product of Sedalia, Missouri, but was played in the entire Midwestern region.

Sedalia, St. Louis, and New Orleans produced different styles of ragtime. In Sedalia, we find a more European type of approach, with smooth but intricate melodic lines. St. Louis, on the other hand, produced a more "jazzy" style, utilizing more syncopation. The New Orleans style of ragtime was more bluesy and rhythmic than the other two styles. The African-Latin rhythms that dominated the music of New Orleans music also influenced rag once it reached New Orleans.

Ragtime music exerted an enormous influence on the classical music of Europe during the 1900s. After the introduction of ragtime to Paris during the early 1900s, many European composers incorporated jazz ideas into their work. Ragtime was, undoubtedly, one of the most Europeanized forms of jazz to emerge. Later, Third Stream and some forms of free jazz also borrowed heavily from European classical music.

Suggested Readings and Listening

Books

Blesh, Rudi and Janis, Harriet. *They All Played Ragtime.* New York: Grove Press, 1966.

Feather, Leonard. *The Book of Jazz.* New York: Dell Publishing Co., 1976.

Ostransky, Leroy. *The Anatomy of Jazz.* Seattle: University of Washington Press, 1960.

Schuller, Gunther. *Early Jazz.* New York: Oxford University Press, 1968.

Stearns, Marshall. *The Story of Jazz.* New York: Oxford University Press, 1956.

Records

Joplin, Scott. "The Cascades." Riverside History of Classic Jazz, SDP 11-RLP 12-112.

Joplin, Scott. "Maple Leaf Rag." Smithsonian Collection of Classic Jazz, side 1, P 11892-AS 11892.

Morton, Jelly Roll. "Maple Leaf Rag." Smithsonian Collection of Classic Jazz, side 1, P 11982-AS 11892.

CHAPTER 4

Religion and Jazz?

The Great Awakening Period

One of the periods in jazz, most often associated with the origins of African-American religious music in the United States, is the Great Awakening Period. Evidence that there would be a Great Awakening emerged as early as the beginning of the 1800s along the eastern seacoast, mainly Massachusetts, Kentucky, and Virginia. But it was on the plantations, mainly in the South, where African-Americans made their first and most significant contributions to religious music. More than any one person, it was the Southern plantation preacher who was responsible for the fiery, bluesy delivery so commonly associated with both blues and religious music (spirituals, gospels). The song sermon, with its strong musical approach to the gospel, gave birth to the now popular, traditional gospel style. Many modernists may claim that it was Thomas A. Dorsey who started what is commonly called gospel music, and Dorsey did, in fact, bring a new sound to gospel. But the African-Americanism, the bending of notes, the swaying of rhythms, the soulful courting of the English language, was a result of the intermixing of various multi-ethnic cultures on the plantation during the early years of slavery. Undoubtedly Dorsey's experience as a blues artist (he was an accompanist for blues artists like Ma Rainey and jazz artist Bunk Johnson) led him to introduce those African-Americanisms that helped make him the "King of Gospel." But the "original" gospel style did not start with Dorsey; it originated on the plantation during slavery.

If the Great Awakening was greatly responsible for the introduction of African-American religious music in the United States, what were the conditions that made such a cultural idiom possible? During the latter part of the 1700s, the country developed a strong feeling of uncertainty and guilt concerning slavery. This feeling of guilt paved the way for the fiery preacher who capitalized on public sentiment by introducing "the only likely solution to their problems"—religion. In many instances, the preachers, both blacks and whites, preached side by side. Their offer to save and to "put in a good word for the doomed sinner" attracted both slave and slave owner. In a typical camp meeting, one could find slave and master holding hands in prayer asking for the forgiveness of their sins. The fact that many of the people attending these camp meetings, especially the slaves, were from a lower economic and social level accounts for their willingness to accept the word of the professional preacher without question. (It was a common practice for poor whites to "rent" or borrow slaves for particular social events to impress their peers. Both poor and wealthy slave owners were among those worshipping together with the African slaves.) After the services, each group returned to its previous social level.

During a religious camp meeting it was not uncommon to see subjects dancing in a kind of crazed frenzy—singing, shouting, crying—all done in the name of God. (This practice of dancing and talking in tongues is still practiced today in what is normally called The Holy Roller Church (sanctified church) by many African-Americans.) In many instances the preachers exerted a kind of hypnotic control over their subjects, prompting the general populace to become alarmed at what might happen if the preacher embraced an antislavery platform. This and other social issues of the day helped bring an end to the religious awakening period.

The idea of entire congregations allowing themselves to go into hypnotic trances can be traced to various African religions—mainly voodun (voodoo), where the idea of becoming totally submerged in the Spirit was part of the ceremony. It is also likely that the ancient concepts of European Christianity prepared the Euro-Americans to accept this new and special brand of African spirituality.

I have witnessed the results of such spirituality in my Aunt Ollie Brown's (Big Mama's) Holy Roller Church. Many Sunday mornings, after I had returned from playing a gig, she would stop me as I tried to pass quietly by her and her congregation (Sunday services were held in her home in Chicago) and call out, "Son, come on down and play some for the Lawd 'cause you done been playing all night for the devil." So I would descend the stairway, take out my sax, and begin improvising with the already hot, flowing rhythms of the church musicians, which usually included an organist, drummer, tambourinist, and so on. Even at that time (1953–54) I could hear no difference between what she called the "devil's music" and the "Lawd's music." I would listen for the key or tonal center, get the mood of the piece, close my eyes and "wail." Another time, a touring musical group was providing the music for a local "tent" meeting in Kansas City. A friend and fellow musician, Henry Smith, approached me excited about the alto saxophonist who was appearing with the "soul minister" at the revival meeting that week. Immediately, we both hurried to hear this weird disciple of "Yard Bird," Charlie Parker. Sure enough, the saxophonist sounded like Charlie Parker and even acted like him. At intermission (when the musicians had taken a short pause in between sermon and music), we approached him and asked how he felt about playing jazz in church and what he considered the main difference between jazz and gospel. To our surprise he answered that there was no difference and that he was playing in the same style as when he played in a nightclub. I had been right. If there was a difference between jazz and gospel-spirituals as performed in the African-American church, it was not in the music itself, but in the lyrics and the interpretation of the printed word. The haunting rhythms, the bending and turning of the notes, and the phrasing were all the same. One of the reasons jazz was associated with the devil was because of its origins on the plantation and in the Storyville section of New Orleans, where prostitution and gambling were a way of life.

Perhaps the most significant musical contribution from the Great Awakening Period was the cross-fertilization of West African and West European religious music. In fact, one can safely say that this was one of the most musically integrated periods in the history of the United States.

Just what is it that makes a song soulful enough to be called a spiritual or gospel? Needless to say, all songs that referred to God were not necessarily gospels or spirituals; a number were mere folk songs. Some of these songs can be found in the vast amount of minstrel music of the 1800s. Slave songs or "coon songs" were songs that referred to the African-American way of life.

One of the most important aspects of African-American church music is its blues-like character. In *The Spirituals and the Blues*, James H. Cone states: "The spiritual, then, is the spirit of the people struggling to be free; it is their religion, their source of strength in a time of trouble. And if one does not know what trouble is, then the spiritual cannot be understood"[1] If one subscribes to Cone's thesis (that it is impossible to understand the spiritual unless one understands trouble), it is easy to understand why there have been so many different interpretations of both the spirituals and the blues.

The psychological effect of the Great Awakening Period also contributed to the development of African-American religious music in the United States. Sermons almost invariably spoke of the hereafter as if nothing could be worse. The high level of intensity of the sermons is believed to have caused many people to suffer strokes. The Reverend Samuel McCorkie noted that "Persons with weak nerves, women, adolescents, and Negroes were most frequently moved to hysteria of an unregulated nature."[2] Perhaps the honorable Reverend McCorkie was not familiar with the religious history of Africans, Indians, or even the early Greeks. This behavior was none other than a form of what the Indian yogis called nirvana, a transplanted state of existence. The early Greeks also participated in ceremonies designed to bring them to a spiritual state of existence.

The religious music produced during this period is often grouped into three categories: spirituals, gospels, and jubilees. All other forms fall into these broader categories. The gospel, which grew out of the song sermon, is usually highly-syncopated in rhythm, spontaneously conceived (except in the case of the later gospel style associated with Thomas A. Dorsey), and praises God. The spiritual usually has a more evenly composed rhythmic structure and is more relaxed in character and was derived from previously composed British protestant hymns.

"There are a number of opinions about the origins of the term gospel. Since we are talking about jazz, we will limit our definition to include only that music which represents the African-American's religious experience in this country. Thomas Dorsey's brand of gospel was definitely blueslike in character. The accented rhythms and blueslike phrasing of Dorsey's music place it in the pop category."

Early Gospels and Spirituals

The religion of hope, often found in the lyrics of the early gospels and spirituals, was a psychological aid to the early slave. The constant referral to Jesus as "He" and the reliance on the protection of "God the Father" shows how the early African-Americans saw religion as a force capable not only of soothing the soul but of providing protection against the evils of slavery.

The early gospels and spirituals served as a social unifying force. The slaves had no one else to turn to, except for an occasional sympathetic owner. Their only recourse was to throw themselves wholeheartedly into their religion. The early slaves preferred the Baptist religion, mainly because the Baptist religion fol-

Rev. Joe Stevens. Early African-American religious music, together with blues, formed the foundation of the music we now call jazz.

lowed the custom of completely submerging the body during baptism. To the African slave who believed in the "holiness of water," more water meant more religion. Since water has always been considered a healing agent and a general life-sustaining agent, this makes sense. Also, many of the slaves tended to imitate the life styles of their masters, and in the United States there simply were more British Protestants than there were Latin Catholics.

Many of the early spirituals were precomposed British Protestant hymns that were Africanized or perfomed in an African-American style. Many other spirituals were composed or created by the slaves themselves. What is important is that it was the Africanizing or Afro-Americanizing of the already existing music that was responsible for how the music sounded. It is highly possible to African-Americanize a Chinese religious piece to such a degree that it could fall into the category of a gospel or spiritual. Again, it is not the song that determines whether

Rev. Joe Stevens. The call and response form can be traced back to early African traditional forms. Here the preacher makes a statement and the congregation responds.

or not a composition can be classified as a spiritual or gospel, but the manner or style in which the piece is performed.

The Fisk Jubilee Singers, founded in 1871 by George White, helped popularize gospel music and spirituals in the United States. One reason for their great success was the image they presented of the African-American as a highly cultivated and talented individual. The early stereotype of the African-American had been as an uneducated but talented "heathen" who could sing and dance. The tremendous success of the Fisk Jubilee Singers drew much attention to Fisk University. In fact, the Fisk University Singers—later known as the Fisk University Jubilee Singers—are often given credit for saving the university from financial disaster. Other African-American groups like the Hampton Singers, formed in 1873 at Hampton Institute in Virginia, the Howard University Gospel Singers, and later, the Tuskegee Choir organized in 1931 by William L. Davison contributed to the development of gospels and spirituals in the United States. Among the great soloists and composers who have contributed to the development of the African-American spirituals and gospels in the United States are vocalists Marian Anderson and Leontyne Price, whose great success as performers of European art music as well as African-American music helped to focus attention on the importance of gospels and spirituals as a major contribution to world music literature. Roland Hayes and Paul Robeson were among the most accomplished male performers of spirituals and gospels.

The Jubilee

The Jubilee was either a sacred or secular piece performed in an African-American style to announce good news. Thus the birth of a newborn (there were times in the history of the African-American when the birth of a newborn was considered bad news and the death of an elder good news) or the marriage of a young couple was celebrated by the singing of a jubilee. One of the most popular jubilee groups in the history of African-American music was the Fisk Jubilee Singers. Through their many tours, the Fisk Jubilee Singers introduced African-American music to the world.

Other Functions of Religious Songs

African-American church music during slavery also had a political role. For example, certain religious songs were used as warning songs for escaping slaves.

During a seminar on jazz at the University of Pittsburgh, African-American percussionist Max Roach gave an example of slaves using the hymn "Steal Away Jesus" as a signal to those whose turn it was to join slaves from other plantations in escaping to the North by way of the Underground Railroad. Using a song as a signal for escape is very old and was used in Africa long before slavery in the United States. Still, many of the older generation of African-Americans strongly deny that gospels and spirituals were ever used for anything other than religious purposes. Religious songs also gave strength to endure the almost impossible conditions existing during slavery. Thoughts of freedom, relief of pain, and reward in heaven constitute the major part of the text of African-American religious music. Dances were also used to prepare and signal the slaves. In Brazil the much danced Copoeira was, in reality, a type of martial art believed to be invented by the Brazilian slaves to help defend themselves during early plantation uprisings in that country. As part of their "kata," or training, the slaves sang and danced warlike movements that looked like part of a harmless dance. The slave owners watched the performance not knowing that the slaves were preparing for a revolution.

Religion and Pop Music

A number of singers have used the church to launch careers in the more lucrative field of American pop music. In recent years, religious performers have been able to demand more and more for their services, belying the cliche that an artist had to be in the area of pop music to make money. Artists like Mahalia Jackson, James Cleveland, and Edwin Hawkins have been able to command as much for a performance as most pop acts. The renowned Staple Singers have not only been able to command top dollar for their performances, but have done much to bridge the gap between secular soul and sacred soul. The church has given us such pop singers as Aretha Franklin, Dionne Warwick, Ray Charles, Sam Cooke, and Della Reese. Almost every African-American jazz musician of any notoriety cut his or her musical teeth in the church.

Conclusion

Jazz, blues, rock, and just about every other form of African-American music had its origins in the Afro-American church. The home of the African-American church was the plantation. It was here that the spirituals, gospels, and jubilees were born. The preacher was the "chief enforcer" of plantation morals. He was responsible for the spiritual, as well as the musical, salvation of his followers.

The black preacher's power over his congregation was enormous. Much of his power can be traced back to the follower's belief in the worship of voodoo and the preacher's role as a procurer of such powers. Many of the followers of the new Christian religion believed that the preacher was not only a "holy" man but that he alone could ask the spirit of God to solve their problems. This unshakable faith in the supernatural powers of the black preacher established him as doctor, lawyer, and medicine man. Thus, the all-powerful black preacher, more than any one person, was responsible for shaping the sound of the music sung by the early slaves.

During the Great Awakening Period (1800s), African-American religious music often came in contact with minstrel and ragtime music. It was here that one of the major phases of cross-fertilization took place. The mixture of these two major forms of jazz (ragtime and minstrel music) provided the extra technical musical elements that were missing in early jazz. Many religious songs were used as signals for escaping slaves. The double meanings of some of these songs have never been deciphered. Songs like "Lord Show Me the Way" and "Steal Away Jesus" were two of the most commonly used songs. There was also a close affinity among the African slaves to the biblical Jews. Slaves found the suffering of the Jews synonymous with their own.

Voodoo was present throughout the beginnings of jazz. Many of our early jazz musicians were believers in voodoo. Jelly Roll Morton, one of the musicians most affected by the voodoo cults of Louisiana, has been placed at the scene of historical voodoo ceremonies. One story is that Jelly Roll, on several occasions, burned up new and expensive suits to rid himself of a particular voodoo curse. The fact that musicians are constantly being called upon to publicly exhibit their personal spirituality may account for why so many became "victims" of voodoo. Both voodoo and jazz improvisation, especially when it is at a high level of intensity, demand total spiritual commitment. Many jazz musicians that I have come in contact with have possessed strong spiritual qualities.

The recent "cross-over" of jazz and gospel is, in part, responsible for the commercial success of many religious groups. Performers like Mahalia Jackson, James Cleveland, Edwin Hawkins, and the Staple Singers doubled their audiences. On the other hand, religious music has provided the musical foundation for artists like Dionne Warwick, Sam Cooke, Della Reese, and Ray Charles. The fusion of religious music and jazz is not new. The real beginnings of the religious cross-over took place sometime during the early 1700s. The rejection and acceptance of various musical forms by new African-Americans played an important role in the development of African-American religious music. Some forms of European religious music were accepted intact, though other forms were totally rejected, either because they were too difficult or because they did not serve a definite purpose. One misconception that has hindered the popular acceptance of African-American music in the world has been the African-American's belief that any popularization of the music was sinful. It was all right to "almost" swing, but it was wrong to really swing.

Suggested Readings and Listening

Books and Articles

Boyer, Horace C. *Gospel Music Comes of Age*. Chicago: Black World—Johnson Publishing Co.

Cone, James H. *The Spirituals and the Blues*. New York: The Seabury Press, 1969.

Heilbut, Tony. *The Gospel Sound*. New York: Simon and Schuster, 1971.

Tanner, Paul, and Gerow, Maurice. *A Study of Jazz*. 5th ed. Dubuque, Iowa: Wm. C. Brown, 1984.

Records

Cleveland, James. *James Cleveland and the Angelic Choir*, vols. 1, 2, 3.

The Staple Singers. *The Best of the Staple Singers*. Buddah, BDS 2009.

CHAPTER 5

Minstrelsy and
Its Effect on Jazz

The Minstrel Show

The minstrel show, with all of its elegance and glory, has often been called the Mother of the American Musical Theater. Considering the various types of music that emerged from that period, the minstrel show obviously did play a large role in introducing certain aspects of African-American music to the general American populace. The minstrel show was divided into three distinct parts: the Show Proper, the Olio, and the Playlet or Parody.[1] The Show Proper introduced individual acts such as comedians and solo singers and usually ended with the cakewalk. The Olio, or second section, consisted mostly of solo dance acts. The third and last section, the Playlet or Parody, was largely devoted to a particular theme, which in most cases was based on a comical situation depicting Negro plantation life. It was in this section that other forms of African-American folk music received attention. Work songs and other plantation songs were used to give an authenticity to the performance.

In many ways, the minstrel show resembled a circus in that it was usually introduced or announced by parading clowns, medicine men, and spasm bands (spasm bands consisted of instrumentalists who played makeshift instruments made from paper, wood and just about anything else they could find). The music was often gay and was not considered "serious." The music used in the minstrel show itself was termed *minstrel music*. The term *minstrel* is believed to have originated from *minister*, evidence of some type of religious relationship. Composers like Stephen Foster (considered by many one of the most authentic of the minstrel composers), James Bland, and Daniel Emmett were responsible for many of the compositions used in the show's format. The accompanying music or background music for the show was ragtime.

During intermission, or between acts, classic blues singers such as Gertrude "Ma" Rainey and Bessie Smith entertained the audiences. Why was the minstrel show so important to the development of jazz in the United States? Most importantly, because it was one of the major sources of employment for early jazz performers. Respected artists like Ma Rainey, Jelly Roll Morton, and Lester Young were all employed by minstrel shows at one time or another.[2]

The minstrel show also launched the Classic Blues Period. The Classic blues Period got its name as a result of Ma Rainey's insistence that audiences give her due respect during her performances. The fact that she was a woman singing the blues led audiences not to take her performances seriously. Ma Rainey responded by threatening to take matters into her own hands if the audience didn't "shutup." She was such a well-endowed woman with such a strong determined voice that the audience responded with "Hey, let's be quiet and listen to Ma—she's got class." Soon, other performers followed in her footsteps—Bessie Smith, Ida Cox, Clara Smith, Trixie Smith, Victoria Spivey, Bertha "Chippie" Hill, Alberta Hunter, Mamie Smith and many others. (Since there was no such thing as a jazz recording during the early inception of the Classic Blues Period, many of the above mentioned singers represented a much later period.)

The T.O.B.A. and Minstrelsy

The T.O.B.A. (Theatre Owners and Booking Agency) was responsible for finding employment for the majority of the black artists during the height of the minstrel movements. Vocalists, comedians, dancers, and instrumental performers were all employed by the T.O.B.A. To imagine the impact of this organization on the entire minstrel period, compare it with modern booking agencies. If accepted by the T.O.B.A., the artist, in most instances, did not ever have to worry about employment. Clubs, hotels, and other places of entertainment were obliged to accept lesser talents if they wanted to have the privilege of booking more talent-ed performers. On the other hand, a performer, no matter how talented, did not get a regular opportunity to work if he or she was not a member of the agency. This same system exists today. Lesser known acts are often suddenly pushed to fame on the heels of more established performers. Those club owners who are strong enough can reject the lesser talent, but the weaker owners are forced to go along with the agency's offers.

If the minstrel shows gave a considerable number of jazz musicians em-ployment, what were the effects of the musical union between minstrel com-poser and jazz performer? For the most part, it was the minstrel composer, regardless of his or her racial origins, who gained the most. The entire basis of the minstrel sound was taken from the lifestyle of the African-American slave. Without the stereotype of the African-American slave, there may never have been any such phenomenon as the minstrel show. The language, mood, thought, con-cepts, manner of walking, and overall gestures were exact imitations of the slave. According to Marshall Stearns in *The Story of* Jazz, Tom Rice (considered by many the undisputed "father" of the minstrel show) got his entire act for one show from watching an old deformed slave, by the name of Jim Crow, hobble and jump around in the stable of his master.[3] This was not an uncommon practice during this period. Promoters combed the countryside listening to "slave melodies," often borrowing and incorporating them directly into their performance. In many cases, little is known of the originators of the melodies. This brings to question Stephen Foster, noted as one of the country's most authentic minstrel composers. Did he borrow many of the melodies atrtributed to his pen, or was he simply in-fluenced by the music of the time? Without taking anything away from Foster, most critics agree that his sound came from the music of the slaves. This, of course, happens in any period. It is, for example, almost impossible to compose a pop song without borrowing, to some degree, from previous songs. Stephen Foster was certainly greatly influenced by the mulatto nurse who cared for him through infancy. Many believe that it was the lullabies and the melodies sung by this nurse that gave Foster such perfect insight into African-American folk music.

An important, overlooked aspect of the minstrel show is that not until after the Civil War were blacks allowed to tour as free agents with the show. Because of the lack of authentic black talent in the minstrel show, the only portrayal of slave life, before the Civil War, was done by whites. All imitations were second-hand. One unfortunate result of this was that immediately after the Civil War, when blacks had a chance to introduce their version of authentic slave life, many of them imitated the great white minstrel actors. Also, many of the dancing contests which pitted such greats as Henry Juba Lane and Sam Lucas against white dancers, were staged. Whether this was done to stimulate interest in the show or to keep down racial tension is not clear, but many of the old minstrel dancers attest that "fixing" the dance contest was routine.

Outside the United States, minstrel shows were best known in England where they were known as "Christies." In the United States, minstrel shows were first popular in Kentucky, Tennessee, and Ohio. Among the most popular minstrel groups were the "Georgia Minstrels," the "Virginia Minstrels," the "Christy Minstrels," the "Rabbit Foot Minstrels," and the "Ohio Minstrels."

No one doubts that the minstrel show was one of the most popular forms of entertainment during the 1800s, but few can account for its popularity. The fact that the minstrel show originated on the sourthern plantation gives us some clue as to why it was a popular form of entertainment in the South. White slave owners were accustomed to and expected to see shows that made fun of the African slave. This was a way to superficially rid themselves of some of their guilt. The minstrel show became almost as popular in the North as in the South. In reality, there was little difference between racial attitude toward blacks in the North and in the South. In many instances, there was no problem getting material, and it was free of charge.

As soon as the minstrel show had risen to become one of America's major forms of entertainment, it began to fall, giving way to other amusements, such as "talking" movies and vaudeville.

The minstrel music of the 1800s was not only gay, but in many ways reflected the culture of the old South. Original slave songs, describing the ways and habits of the slave, often found their way into the concert halls of the upper class. Apparently little or no thought was given to the social conditions described in the songs.

The American minstrel show was, in many ways, an adaptation of the already established European minstrels which were called Christies in England. Minstrel performers have been traced back as far as the early fourteenth century. The development of the black-face minstrels in the United States is credited to Thomas D. Rice, who was dubbed the father of the minstrel show. However, according to Dailey Paskman in his book, *Gentlemen Be Seated*, a German immigrant, billed as Mr. Grawpner, was the first person in the United States to perform as a one-man black-faced minstrel.

The minstrel shows were extremely popular during the late 1800s and early 1900s. Although there were skits depicting other ethnic groups, the main focus of the minstrel show was the African-American. During its early period, the minstrel shows were more comedy routines featuring three or four entertainers. It was not until its later rise in popularity during the late 1800s and early 1900s that it became a full-length show.

If one ethnic group other than African-Americans can be associated with the origins of the minstrel show, it is the Germans. The Germans were so popular as minstrel performers that many non-German performers adopted a German accent. The next most popular non-African-American minstrel entertainers were the Irish.

Conclusion

The minstrel show played a major role in providing employment for jazz musicians. Singers, comedians, instrumental performers, and so on, were all used to furnish music for the show. The minstrel show itself consisted of three major parts: the Show Proper, the Olio, and the Playlet, or Parody. The Playlet, or Parody, was the section that gave rise to the American musical. In addition, many of our early writers used the minstrel show as a setting for their works. During the 1900s, American musical and literary life was full of minstrel ideas and concepts. The country seemed to thrive on its newly-discovererd creative genius.

Minstrel composers like Stephen Foster, James Bland, and Dan Emmettt provided much of the music for the minstrel show. Many times they drew their materials from the songs of the slaves and then published the songs as authentic compositions. This "borrowing" was a common practice among both black and white minstrel composers. Many songs attributed to Stephen Foster were sung to him by his mulatto nurse.

The Classic Blues Period got its start during the Minstrel Show period. Classic blues performers like Ma Rainey, Mamie Smith, and Victoria Spivey were often hired by the minstrel show directors to sing during the intermissions. A number of women performers were hired during this period. Many women could not find other employment solely because they were female. Male performers could, if necessary, travel as a single act or perform in a number of clubs not available to women. Outside the United States, minstrel shows were popular in England, where they were called "Christies." Military band director John Philip Sousa was responsible for introducing the music of American minstrel composers to England.

Suggested Readings and Listening

Books

Jones, LeRoi. *Blues People*. New York: William Morrow and Company, 1963.
Southern, Eileen. *The Music of Black Americans*. New York: W. W. Norton and Company, 1971.
Steams, Marshall. *The Story of Jazz*. New York: Oxford University Press, 1956.

Records

Songs By Stephen Foster. Elektra H-7133.
Dixieland Jazz...Scobey and His Frisco Band Jansco RSLP 5231.

CHAPTER 6

The Blues

The Blues as a separate jazz form has been the subject of much research since its popular acceptance, during the early 1900s. Some critics of jazz, especially those who adhere to the theory that rock and roll is a separate form without any jazz origins, have stated that the Blues is not related in any way to jazz. Some critics have even gone so far as to try to prove that the Blues actually developed in Europe and not in America. They claim that the harmonic structure of the Blues (I_7, IV_7, V_7, I_7) proves that the Blues is definitely not African-American in nature since the early African slaves didn't have harmony as one of their working "musical tools." Such nonsense hinders the much needed "jazz education" of our population.

I can remember hearing the Blues in my early childhood, and I am sure that this is the case with the majority of African-Americans born in the United States. The Blues was always present in the home, whether in the form of a spiritual or a "sin" song. It is impossible to live a typical African-American existence in the United States without some contact with the Blues. The African-American lifestyle is a "Blues lifestyle." To know the Blues is to know hardship.

In the United States, the Blues was always taken for granted by most and hidden by the rest. E. Franklin Frazier mentions, in *The Black Bourgeoisie*, that

B. B. King along with his favorite woman, his guitar Lucille, is one of the most important figures in blues to emerge since the blues revolution of 1960. Photo courtesy of the Institute of Jazz Studies.

during the 1940s most so-called intellectual blacks were actually ashamed to admit that they liked the Blues. Many would go so far as to hide Blues recordings under the bed, if they were expecting visitors who didn't appreciate hearing the Blues. The attitude prevailed until the beginning of the 1960s, when young whites adopted the Blues as the "official" revolutionary music of their time. Thanks to their acceptance, great Blues artists such as B. B. King, Otis Redding, Junior Parker, and Howlin' Wolf began to receive the recognition they deserved. The Beatles, more than any other group, reminded the world of and gave credit to the African-American Blues performers of the past who developed the Blues into an art form. The acceptance of African-American Blues by young whites in America, and eventually in Europe, signaled interest in identifying with the struggles of their oppressed black brothers and sisters. This prompted the people in the music industry to take a serious look at what was then called R & B, or Rhythm and Blues. During this period, the Blues again proved capable of bringing together thousands of people from various cultural backgrounds. Not only did the

Sonny Terry and Brownie McGhee, two of the most respected blues artists to help pioneer the bridge between rural and urban blues. Photo courtesy of Bobby Davis.

Blues physically bring thousands of young Americans together, but it gave insights into the African-American lifestyle.

Where did it all start? There is no official birthdate for the Blues. If one considers that the Blues grew out of the field hollers, street cries, and work songs of the past, then it was born during the early 1700s, on the plantations of the South. The Blues is an African-American creation. The closest thing that we can find resembling the Blues in Africa are the Bantu rain songs and the African "signifying" songs, or songs of "ridicule."[1] Both of these forms, while not exactly Blues in content, do have strong Blues-like features. Both use Blues tonalities that suggest a strong tie to African-American folk Blues. A thorough search for original African elements retained in the Blues suggests that such forms as the call and response, the field holler, the work song, the street cry, the sea shanty, the signifying song, the Bantu rain song, and the ring shout, along with bluenotes and certain types of polyrhythms, can all be traced back to Africa. In fact, many of these forms can also be found in other types of African-American music. If the Blues was born, raised, and developed on the plantations of the South, who nursed it to its present form of maturity, and where did this nursing take place? The Blues can be divided into various schools. (School in this case refers to geographical location rather than academic grouping.) These schools are as follows:

- ◆ The Delta area, which includes Mississippi, Alabama, Louisiana, and most of the Gulf area.
- ◆ The Territories, which include Texas, Louisiana, Arkansas, Oklahoma, and Missouri.
- ◆ The Southeastern seaboard, which includes Georgia and Florida.

In addition to these areas, there are the urban schools of Chicago, Kansas City, and Memphis.

These areas represent the geographical locations most saturated by a particular type of music. Country Blues was born in the rural areas and has no specific geographical boundaries. Later, country Blues migrated to the urban areas of the North, underwent a few changes in character, and became known as urban Blues.

During the early development of Blues it was unheard of to find a professional Blues singer. It was generally understood that anyone could sing the Blues.

The lonely farm hand, the house slave, the cleaning person could all "strike up" a soulful rendition of the Blues on demand. It was the thing to do when one was feeling bad. My aunt, "Big Mama," sang Gospels all day long and would get upset if I even suggested that she was singing "worldly music." (Her Gospels sounded exactly like many of the blues songs typically sung on Chicago's south side.)

There was no definite form in the Blues during its early stages; each person shaped his or her own melody. If you felt like curving a note here or bending a note or word there, you did it without criticism. You didn't have to adhere to any harmonic concepts. The idea of a definite form in Blues did not come until much later in its development, during the early 1900s. Form was introduced in the Blues simply to facilitate the playing of the Blues by more than one or two people. As long as there were only one or two performers singing or playing the Blues, there was no need for form. As soon as more than two performers got together to perform the Blues, things became confused and a unifying element was needed. I personally feel that technique and form have developed to such a point that they have overshadowed the main ingredient in Blues—the feeling. Where is the lonely voice that looks up in the sky and shouts, "Ma Lawd, somebody be done hope me dis moan-nin?"

Example 10

Proof that Blues, at one time, existed without a definite form can be found in statements by early Blues performers such as Memphis Slim and Curtis Jones, both of whom I worked with in Europe. I remember an incident in Paris, during the middle 1960s, when Memphis Slim, Kenny Clarke, dancer Geoffrey Holder, Nancy Holloway, and a number of French musicians were invited to perform the first color TV special in France. As a member of Kenny Clarke's group, we were, in addition to performing our own program, asked to accompany Memphis. As Memphis began to sing chorus after chorus of "Summertime," it became apparent that the band and vocals were in two different places. After several repeats and a heated discussion, it became obvious to me that Memphis was singing in a free Blues style. This was a good example of how the performance of African-American music has changed as a result of the influence of European style and form. Memphis Slim was interpreting the music in an "original" African-American Blues style. We, the "hip" purist jazz musicians, should have automatically given him the freedom to do so, without question. But instead we imposed our newly acquired European theoretical techniques on his style. This is a mistake jazz musicians often make when dealing with pure, authentic forms of the Blues.

Here is an example of the standard, accepted harmonic structure for Blues:

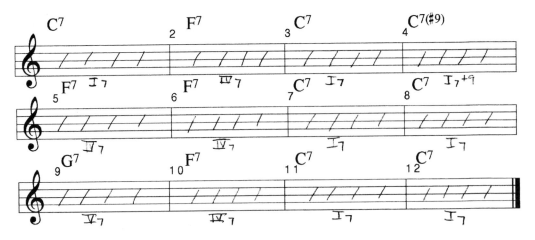

Example 11

Many of the older Blues singers like Brownie McGhee and Sonny Terry often performed earlier blues without regard to the above mentioned harmonic sequences. Sometimes they changed the form because "the words don't fit otherwise," or they just didn't feel like the change should come at that particular point in the music. Earlier singers like "Leadbelly," whose real name was Hudder Ledbetter, and John Lee Hooker used a type of drone when performing the Blues. The drone, described in *The Harvard Dictionary of Music* as "a long sustained note usually in the bass," was used in place of the later, popular harmonic scheme. This led some historians to look for a connection between British folk music and Blues since both forms tended to use the drone as base for melodic movement. On close examination, however, it was discovered that certain African cultures also employed drone-like tonal structures in their music, using bagpipe-like instruments.

The bending of certain notes, namely the third, fifth, and seventh degree, gave Blues its blue, or low-keyed, sound. To say that these notes were flattened is wrong if we are to keep working with the concept of Blues as an original African-American music. To flatten a note is to lower the note one half step. To bend or lower the note, however, suggests lowering the note anywhere from one half step to three or more steps. One of the major problems in interpreting the blues, and other forms of African-American folk music today, is that we have not developed a system for analyzing the music. If we are going to continue to use European terminology in analyzing the music, we cannot expect to preserve its originality.

A technique often used by the Delta area Blues singers was *bottlenecking*. In bottlenecking, the performer slides his or her hand up and down the strings of the guitar, producing a slide effect. This sound was originally produced by placing the broken tips of whiskey bottles on the fingertips and sliding the fingers along the strings.

Another interesting fact about the structure of Blues, is that Blues singers developed the habit of singing a musical statement and immediately repeating that statement before finishing the idea with a closing statement.

> I woke up dis moaning, feeling mighty blue
> I woke up dis moaning, feeling mighty blue
> If I didn't have you, baby, I wouldn't know what to do.

Example 12

Some historians believe that the blues performer repeated the first line of the Blues for two reasons. First, he or she wanted to be sure that the message

Mose Allison is considered by many to be one of the smoothest blues sounds around. Photo courtesy of Bobby Davis.

reached the audience, and second, the performer was improvising the lyrics and the repetition gave him or her time to think of the next phrase. Considering the philosophical content of most Blues lyrics, I am inclined to accept the first theory as the most likely. However, both theories are possibly true. Jazz trumpeter Clark Terry's story of his song "Mumbles," reveals more about the blues. "Mumbles," as Terry explains, came about as a result of his playing clubs in East St. Louis, during his early years as a musician. Clark noticed that the performer and the audience were often so intoxicated that neither one understood the other. Therefore, it didn't matter whether or not the performer sang the right lyrics. This gave Clark the idea of a song based on "mumbling." Throughout the years I have heard Clark, I have never seen "Mumbles" fail to evoke a burst of excitement from an audience.

William Christopher Handy, composer, cornetist, and Blues singer was the undisputed "Father of the Blues." Handy, a well-educated man (he studied music at Huntsville Agricultural and Mechanical College), was the composer of such all-time favorites as "Memphis Blues" and "St. Louis Blues." He was the first person to publish the Blues as a serious form of music. In addition to being a publisher, Handy worked with Harry H. Pace to establish Pace's Swan record label as the first all-black-owned recording company in the United States. According to John Chilton in his book, *Who's Who of Jazz*, Handy, despite suffering from a disease that eventually left him blind, continued to involve himself in the recording and publishing business until his death in 1958. A number of rumors accuse Handy of not being a true "Blues performer" simply because his entrance into jazz circles was as a cornetist and as a member of numerous ragtime bands. This is no argument because jazz is Blues and Blues is jazz. One cannot exist without the other. It was not until jazz began to be generally accepted and achieved box office appeal that the promoters started to divide various forms of the music into separate marketable commodities. Regardless of how economically lucrative this was, it only hurt and confused jazz as a whole.

Urban Blues

Urban Blues with all its "modernization" was still country Blues. The major difference between urban Blues and country Blues was the lyrics. Country Blues tended to be about working habits, love affairs, and general problems of the country. Urban Blues focused on problems in the city. Problems such as love affairs and money were still present, but now they were related to the city. Urban unemployment was a common subject. Singers now sang of working for Ford Motor Company and other industrial giants. In the lyrics, cars replaced mules, assembly line work replaced shucking sugar, apartments replaced farm shacks. There was even a time (during the early 1920s) when shooting replaced stabbing. The entire history of African-American life can be traced by carefully studying the lyrics of Blues performances.

The Blues has taken on several forms throughout the years, which suggests that it is indeed a broad and flexible song form. We have known the Blues as "rhythm and blues," "urban-country blues," "rock and roll," "rock," "acid-country," "folk," "hard," "soft rock," "soul," "pop," and many other names. One of my functions as vice-president for Segue Records in Pittsburgh was to check the charts to see what songs were selling. During that time, most of the top selling songs labeled as "soul" rarely made the overall pop chart. (This situation has changed. Soul music is now regarded as a top money-maker.) During this same period, I read a newspaper article that reported that certain black producers were upset because soul music artists were not receiving top recording industry awards.

According to the article, whenever a soul music artist began to win too many awards the officials simply recategorized the areas and started a new category. While this is true of some industry officials, it is not representative of all recording officials, nor is it purely racial. The industry follows the market, and if the market shifts in a particular direction the industry follows.

Was Charlie Parker, the well-known jazz saxophonist, a Blues artist or not? What about Elvis Presley or Mahalia Jackson? If Blues is jazz and jazz is Blues, how do we classify these artists? We know for sure that artists like Bessie Smith, the "Empress of the Blues," Ma Rainey, the "Mother of the Blues," and Dinah Washington, the "Queen of the Blues," were considered classic Blues performers. These performers were vocalists, which made it easy to identify if they were singing Blues. But what about the instrumentalist who performs the Blues? Is there any way of telling if an instrumentalist is a Blues artist? Yes, if the performer plays in a style that thas those qualities that are normally associated with a Blues vocalist. During the 1940s, saxophonist Big Jay McNeely was considered one of the best Blues saxophonists in the country. Other instrumentalists like Lynn Hope, Earl Bostic, the late King Curtis, Junior Walker and Louis Jordan have also been classified as blues artists. These artists bend, caress, and "Blue" the same notes as their vocal counterparts. The only difference between the two is that the public can more easily identify with the vocalist and hear and understand his or her lyrics, than they can imagine what the instrumentalist is trying to say. This has prompted many hornmen to sing as a part of their regular performance. Imagination is needed for the best possible response from the Blues. Both the performer and the listener have to form mental pictures of the music. If the music, whether it is Blues or not, does not evoke some kind of a mental picture, something is missing.

Race Records

The Blues is the basic foundation for every jazz musician. From Duke Ellington to Miles Davis, jazz musicians have always used the Blues as a foundation for improvising various styles of jazz from the more intricate sounds of bebop, to the "space" music of the 1960s. At times, jazz purists have strayed from the Blues claiming that the Blues does not offer enough of a musical challenge, but those that have made any significant mark in jazz have always found their way back home to the Blues. The two ingredients for a good jazz musician are a thorough

Bessie Smith, dubbed the Empress of Blues, emerged as one of the most innovative and influential voices in blues. Photo courtesy of the Institute of Jazz Studies.

church music background and a solid foundation in the Blues. Musicians who have been successful without these two experiences have acquired them superficially or by playing with other musicians who have had these experiences.

The 1920s is considered, by most historians, the Jazz Age. It was also the beginning of what was later called the Blues Era. While the rest of the country was listening to and supporting big band jazz, a quiet but strong revolution was underway in the black music world. Race records were born. Race records were recordings of black artists directed primarily toward the African-American market. Mamie Smith opened the door for race records with her popular hit "Crazy Blues." Other singers followed. The record companies pursued the market and began recording Blues on a regular basis.

T.O.B.A.

The record industry plays a major part in the success of every artist: As mentioned earlier, the Theatre Owners and Booking Agency was the arm of the music industry, responsible for the success of the majority of Blues acts, during the 1920s. The T.O.B.A. (which to black artists stood for Tough on Black Artists or Tough on Black Acts) booked hundreds of acts. Jazz drummer Kenny Clarke once told me that, during the 1920s, there was very little, if any, interest among white agents for booking black acts; therefore, most of the black acts helped each other by sharing club and ballroom contacts. The T.O.B.A.'s territory extended mainly along the Eastern coast of the United States, namely New York City, Buffalo, Washington, D.C., and Baltimore, and later branched out into Pittsburgh, Chicago, and other areas of the Midwest and South. If a black artist was successful within the T.O.B.A.'s circuit, he or she could count on enough work to get through the year.

Another unjust activity of the music industry was the use of mobile recording units to record Blues singers, during the 1920s. As the race record market began to open up, recording companies started sending mobile units out into the rural areas in search of new material. The units would locate a likely prospect, flash a handful of money, and persuade the performer to "sing into the microphone." In many cases, performers never received any money for their efforts. When one considers that very few artists were aware of such things as copyright laws and royalties, it is easy to understand why many of them were reluctant to have their music recorded. Even academia is guilty. Music libraries are full of

Blues vocalist Dinah Washington was responsible for influencing a new generation of young singers that included Nancy Wilson and Dianne Reeves. Photo by Raymond Ross, courtesy of Rutgers, the Institute of Jazz Studies.

music "collected" in the field—all in the name of scholarship. Many of our early Blues recordings were collected in this way. It is a common fallacy that all Blues are sad. There are happy Blues, sad Blues, melancholy Blues, religious Blues, historical Blues, philosophical Blues, sinful Blues, and just about every other kind of Blues. Throughout the history of blues, white singers like Janis Joplin, Sophie Tucker, and vocalist-pianist Mose Allison joined the ranks of African-American Blues performers like Aretha Franklin, Billy Preston, B. B. King and Ray Charles to give the world a new kind of Blues—a "togetherness" blues. While the new group of Blues singers offers a different side of the Blues, the older pros like Jimmy Witherspoon, Joe Williams, and B. B. King continue to carry on the original African-American tradition with thousands of contented fans.

Suggested Readings and Listening

Books
Hadlock, Richard. *Jazz Masters of the Twenties*. New York: MacMillan, 1965.
Ellington, Duke. *Music is My Mistress*. New York: Doubleday and Co., 1973.
Higgins, Nathan I. *Harlem Renaissance*. New York: Oxford University Press, 1971.
Oliver, Paul. *The Story of the Blues*. Philadelphia: Chilton Book Co., 1969.

Records
Henderson, Fletcher, "Wrappin it up" #7.
Trumbauer, Frankie and His Orchestra #5 "Riverboat Shuffle."
Lewis, Meade "Lux," "Honky Tonk Train Blues" #22.
     (The above are from the Smithsonian Collection.)
The Blues (Folkways Jazz Anthology, vol. 2). Folkways, FJ 2802.

CHAPTER 7

Chicago and New York During the 1920s

Profile

DUKE ELLINGTON • Edward Kennedy "Duke" Ellington is considered, by many, the most important American composer of the twentieth century. Only the fact that his music is jazz and not European classical music has prevented some people from granting him that honor. I was constantly amazed during my tour of Europe and Latin America to find that so many musicians consider Ellington as America's most important composer.

If indeed Ellington was such a great composer, what in his music makes him a "superstar" among composers? Many would answer that it is because Ellington composed music for the individual members of his orchestra rather than merely writing an arrangement like so many other composer-arrangers. We must also keep in mind that Ellington was blessed with some of the most gifted musicians in jazz. The musical union of these great minds was bound to create greatness. Of course, without the creative genius of Ellington, these same musicians might never have achieved so much.

Duke Ellington was born in Washington, D.C., April 29, 1899. His early interest was in art and not music. According to John Chilton in *Who's Who of*

Duke Ellington, in a class by himself, is considered by historians all over the world to be America's most important composer. Photograph by Bob Parent. Courtesy of Don Parent.

Jazz, "Duke" once had his own sign-painting business. His early interest in music began with music lessons from a neighbor. His professional career started when he began substituting for local pianists around Washington. However, it was with the Elmer Snowden band that he got his first big break. Later, Ellington assumed the leadership of the group and began to develop his famous concept of orchestrating each composition to fit the individual performers. Ellington never studied composition with a famous composer, but this was nothing rare for that time. Early jazz bands were the source of every musician's inspiration and musical education. Improvisers learned by imitating the great soloists of the day, and composers also learned by listening to and duplicating the great soloists.

The popularity of the Ellington Orchestra, during the 1920s Harlem Renaissance, centered around its ability to imitate jungle sounds while accompanying musicals. Ellington brilliantly incorporated the highly individualized sound of musicians like trumpeter Bubber Miley, trombonist Joe Nanton (Tricky Sam), and baritone saxophonist Harry Carney, into his compositions. According to music historians, one of the most important jazz events of the 1920s was Ellington's opening at the then popular Cotton Club. It was at the Cotton Club that the band and Ellington gained their international reputation as one of the best jazz orchestras in the world.

A number of great soloists have emerged from the Ellington orchestra, but one of the most influential was alto saxophonist Johnny Hodges. So great was his alto saxophone sound that Ellington declared, when Hodges died, that the band would never sound the same. His style and sound were so unique that it was impossible to find a replacement for him without getting a secondhand "carbon copy." In many ways, the same was true of Harry Carney. Ellington, with his keen awareness, noticed the uniqueness of this baritone sound and on many occasions used the baritone instead of the alto to lead the section.

Another characteristic of Ellington was his dedication to sacred music, which dated back to his childhood and the tremendous influence of his mother. Later when he was in the position to contribute to the abundance of sacred music, he decided to compose something religious.

One of the most important contributors to Ellington's musical career was Billy Strayhorn. Strayhorn's musical concept was so closely allied to Ellington's that many of the compositions often attributed to Ellington by his fans were actually Strayhorn compositions. "Take the A Train," which later became Ellington's theme song, and the very lovely ballad "Lush Life" were written by Strayhorn. The musical bond between these two great musicians was unsurpassed. Ellington often said that whenever he came to a standstill while composing a piece, he would call "Sweetpea," as Strayhorn was known, and, sure enough, Strayhorn would come up with the answers. Once when Ellington was composing a piece, he called Strayhorn to write an introduction for the work. Strayhorn composed the introduction while miles away in another town, using the same beginning tones and the same ending as Ellington. Ellington had indeed found his life's partner.

One of the traits that made Ellington so popular was his grace and elegance, which, according to him, he inherited from his father. So graceful and diplomatic was Duke that he was dubbed America's "official diplomat" at large. The U.S. State Department used him to represent the country on foreign trips. Even when not serving in this official capacity, he represented the country in a manner no other person could. In the view of many, he was the elder statesman of jazz, a world figure.

There have been several periods of large migrations in which blacks from rural areas of the South moved to the industrial areas of the North. One of these periods was between 1910 and 1920. With the closing of the seaport in New Orleans, hundreds of musicians flocked to the northern cities in search of work. The cities most affected by this large migration were New York City, Buffalo, Detroit, Chicago, and Los Angeles. As jazz moved up the river from New Orleans, record companies like Black Swan, Gennett and Okeh Records soon began recording blues vocalists, while Decca, MCA, and several of the larger companies began recording the newly-imported sound of New Orleans music.

Chicago

During the 1920s, Chicago was home for various types of jazz—specifically New Orleans traditional music. During an engagement at a New Orleans jazz club "Lu and Charlie's," I interviewed several leading New Orleans musicians. One was banjoist Danny Barker. Danny told me that there was a distinct difference between what is commonly called Dixieland and what is known as traditional New Orleans music. Dixieland, Barker said, referred to the type of music played by the non-black musicians, while traditional New Orleans music referred to the music played by the black musicians. During the intermission someone played a song on the jukebox that was supposed to be typical, New Orleans traditional music. This music sounded similar to music I had previously heard in Martinique, French West Indies.

"Art Blakey once told me a story concerning the Japanese jazz group that opened the concert tour that he and the Messengers were conducting. According to Art, he and the other members of his group were talking backstage prior to their performance. As the time approached for them to go on stage, Art turned to his men and asked them to stop talking so that they would be ready to go on stage immediately after one of their preconcert recordings had finished playing. As the curtain opened, they were all very surprised to find the young Japanese group taking a curtain call. Art and the Messengers had actually thought they were listening to a recording of themselves."

The Jazz Age, as the 1920s was named, offered much encouragement to the aspiring jazzman. There was work for almost everyone. The popularity of phonograph recordings, radio, sound tracks for movies, and the thriving business of the nightclub industry during Prohibition, all provided work for the jazz musician. During the 1920s, there was hardly a speakeasy that didn't employ a jazz band. Even the word *jass*, later spelled *jazz*, caught on. For jazz, the most important thing about the 1920s was the growing popularity of the phonograph record. Recordings made it possible for a future jazz musician in Deepwater, New York, to reproduce the best recorded efforts of the veteran New Orleans professional. This revolutionized the entire music industry. Even today, as I travel throughout the world, I am surprised to hear jazz musicians in Europe, Africa, South America, and Japan play some of the most stimulating jazz that I have ever heard. It is true that, in some instances, the foreign musician learns by copying, but what a copy! Even now, phonograph recordings are the most important source of information for young musicians who are learning to play jazz.

Boogie-Woogie

Boogie-woogie was the name of one style of piano music played in Chicago during the 1920s. The boogie-woogie style consists of the constant repetition of an ostinato-like bass line with the left hand. This supported an improvised melody or melodies performed with the right hand.

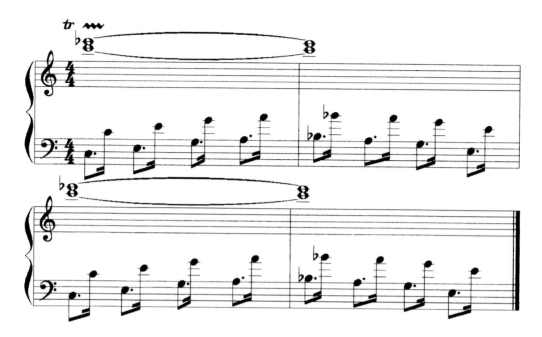

Example 13

Among the leading boogie-woogie pianists, during the 1920s, were CowCow Davenport, Clarence "Pine Top" Smith, Meade "Lux" Lewis, Albert Ammons, and the incomparable Pete Johnson.

Many of the boogie-woogie piano players were victims of their own inadequate handling of the business side of music. CowCow Davenport and Pete Johnson were good examples. Davenport changed jobs often and eventually tried his hand at operating a music store, and later, his own cafe in Cleveland. Both ventures were unsuccessful. Despite a seemingly successful, colorful career, Pete Johnson suffered intermittent periods of unemployment as a pianist and often had to accept day jobs to sustain himself.

During this particular period in Chicago and New York, the art of piano playing was a matter of social pride. It was thought that if a musician could afford a piano he or she must be financially stable. The poorer musicians settled for less expensive instruments like the guitar. During the 1920s in Chicago, the most vigorous jazz was performed at "house rent" parties. House rent parties were given by tenants to raise enough money to pay their rent. Only those musicians considered to be good performers were invited without having to pay. As a youngster growing up in Kansas City, I attended a number of house rent parties. The only difference in the modern-day parties was that they were called "tax" parties and recorded music was used. To a lesser degree this practice still exists today.

The boogie-woogie style owes much to the mining areas of the Midwest. For it was in the Midwest that boogie-woogie got its start. Boogie-woogie was first performed on the guitar and not on the piano as most people believe. In the mining camps of the Midwest there was usually no room for larger instruments like the piano in the flimsy, temporary shacks, built as recreational bars for the off-duty worker. As soon as the area was saturated, the miners would relocate to another area. It was economically unsound for anyone to build a permanent structure.

The boogie-woogie piano style was the predecessor of the Midwestern shuffle style made popular by Count Basie and his band. Although the rolling, repetitious style of boogie-woogie is most often associated with the Kansas City style, the style was also common in other areas such as Oklahoma, Texas, and Arkansas. After World War II, Sugar Child Robinson, one of the last of the young, popular boogie-woogie pianists, became an overnight success with his keen sense of rhythm and flashy right hand. Generally speaking, the boogie-woogie pianists didn't have as much classical technique as the earlier ragtime players, but they did develop a tremendous amount of power and endurance. The constant repetitions in boogie-woogie playing demanded strength and endurance.

Boogie artists were much in demand during the 1920s, in Chicago, as solo artists and as duo acts. In many ways the duo act offered a special musical treat for the jazz fan by featuring a more concise and structured performance. One of the most dynamic of these duos was Albert Ammons and Pete Johnson. Later they teamed up with pianist Meade "Lux" Lewis to form one of the most dynamic jazz boogie-woogie trios in history.

The boogie-woogie pianist traveled throughout the country performing his or her art, even before the introduction of the phonograph recording. Many of the histories and studies done on jazz seem to focus on the recordings of the period. This not only gives an inaccurate view of what was happening musically, but limits our understanding of the music. It is important to remember that recordings give a musical picture only of what the artist was focusing on at the time of the recording. In many cases the only way to know what the artists were trying to do prior to the recording is either by asking them (if they are still alive) or by interviewing someone who was present.

Chicago Jazz

Chicago jazz was the name given to the type of New Orleans music played by predominantly white jazz musicians in Chicago during the 1920s. Most of these musicians credited New Orleans jazz men like Freddie Keppard (cornet), Joe Oliver (comet), Tony Jackson (piano), and Louis Armstrong (trumpet) with introducing them to jazz. Among the many Chicago musicians to gain fame were Benny Goodman (clarinet), Muggsy Spanier (cornet). Mezz Mezzrow and Pee Wee Russell (clarinet), Frank Teschemacher (clarinet, sax), Bud Freeman (sax), Gene Krupa and Dave Tough (drums), Jimmy McPartland (trumpet) and Joe Sullivan (piano).

Chicago Jazz was considered by many to be aggressive, and it usually ended abruptly. These dedicated musicians tried to improve on the music they had heard, taking the best of Joe ("King") Oliver and Freddie Keppard, but introducing a more scholarly approach. This may account for their forceful approach to improvisation. One of the most closely knit groups to emerge from early Chicago Jazz came from Austin High School. This group later became known as the Austin High Gang and developed into one of the most important forces in jazz, during the 1920s.

To understand the importance of Chicago's influence on the history and development of jazz, we must accept that Chicago possessed a certain attraction for jazz artists, during the 1920s, that New York didn't have. Chicago had more nightclubs during this period and was geographically closer to the southern states from which most of the musicians came. In addition, there were more blacks in Chicago and its surrounding area than in New York City. This provided the necessary clientele for club owners and promoters interested in hiring jazz musicians. In fact, it was not until after the economic crash of 1929 that Chicago began to take a back seat to New York City as a jazz capital.

The south side of Chicago was not only a haven for urban blues, but actually became the center of the jazz world. One of the most important pure jazz artists on the Chicago jazz scene was "King" Joe Oliver and his Creole Jazz band. Multi-instrumentalist Erskine Tate, who later operated one of the first African-American jazz schools during the early 1940s, was one of Chicago's top bandleaders. As a performer and teacher, Tate is said to have been proficient on violin, piano, drums, saxophones, guitar, and trumpet. It is important to note that Louis

Armstrong had not received much recognition before coming to Chicago to join King Oliver's group as a "hot jazz" specialist. Since the eyes of the jazz world were now on Chicago, it was natural that Armstrong, too, would benefit from such exposure.

The list of musicians who worked in and around the south side of Chicago is a long one. Musicians like the legendary pianist Teddy Weatherford, whom many claimed was one of the most outstanding pianists in jazz, are at the top of the list. Weatherford later moved to Calcutta, India and died there after contracting cholera. Pianist-arranger Charles "Doc" Cooke, originally from Louisville, Kentucky, had one of the most popular big bands in Chicago, during the 1920s. Cooke was such a good arranger that he was lured to New York, by Radio City Music, to become one of its staff arrangers. Earl "Fatha" Hines, a pianist from Pittsburgh, violinist-saxophonist Charlie Elgar, originally from New Orleans, and Ohio-born pianist Sammy Stewart became three of the city's most prominent bandleaders on the South Side.

If Paul Whiteman was the leader in big band commercial jazz and dance music in New York, Jean Goldkette was his equal in Chicago. Goldkette was a shrewd and skillful businessman who was responsible for hiring some of the top white jazz musicians during the 1920s in Chicago. Soloists like cornetist Bix Beiderbecke, C-melody saxophonist Frank Trumbauer and violinist Joe Venuti all worked at one time for the Goldkette orchestras.

Goldkette preferred not to actively perform with any of his groups, but at one time he controlled over twenty different dance bands. He was also the manager, at one time, of the famed McKinney's Cotton Pickers, an all-black group. Other top white jazz musicians and groups performing around Chicago, during the 1920s, were the New Orleans Rhythm Kings, clarinetist Mezz Mezzrow, saxophonists Frankie Trumbauer and Bud Freeman, trumpeter Jimmy McPartland, the Mound City Blues Blowers, and the Wolverines.

Because of the strong enforcement of segregation laws and codes, there was very little open contact between white and black jazz musicians in and around Chicago, during the 1920s. However, during my brief stay in Chicago during the 1950s, I worked with musicians who often spoke of working in all-white clubs where white musicians occasionally came in for a friendly jam session. Other than learning from recordings or from such established white transplanted groups, like the New Orleans Rhythm Kings, the jam session was probably the most important source Chicago musicians had for learning the "new" music.

Chicago became the center of jazz during the 1920s. During this period in Chicago there was a more relaxed social relationship between whites and blacks than in New York. During my sojourn in Chicago between 1954–56, I heard the older musicians reminisce about how good it used to be in Chicago, during the 1920s and 30s. Black musicians worked all of the best clubs. There was little open prejudice against black musicians. Since blacks were relegated to the role of servants, musicians—especially dance band musicians who performed for high society—were considered servants. A survey I conducted, of older jazz musicians in Pittsburgh, brought out the fact that in Pittsburgh during the 1920s, black musicians and entertainers were able to get a considerable amount of work at all-white functions. It was not until much later, after the triumphs of Whiteman and Goodman in jazz, and an upgrading of the image of musicians, that black musicians and entertainers began to lose their hold on work in previously all-white clubs.

Chicago Dance Bands

During the 1920s in Chicago, many jazz musicians found regular work in one of the many jazz dance bands of Jean Goldkette, a pianist originally from Valenciennes, France. Goldkette was in many ways a midwestern prototype of Paul Whiteman. Goldkette's professional career was mainly spent in Chicago and Detroit. After having lived in Greece and Russia, Goldkette moved to Chicago. Soon he and his musical organization began booking various musical groups under the umbrella name of the Goldkette Dance Orchestra. During this time he was responsible for booking such great artists as trumpeter Bix Beiderbecke, trombonist Tommy Dorsey, violinist Joe Venuti, and later saxophonist Glen Gray.

The Jean Goldkette organization was also responsible for introducing such oustanding dance bands as the Orange Blossoms, which later, after a brief period of reorganizations, became the Casa Loma Orchestra. With Goldkette's business leadership and the superb arrangements of guitarist Harold Eugene (Gene) Gifford, the organization became a hit with the society and college crowd, turning out such popular hits as "It's the Talk of the Town," "Under a Blanket of Blue," and "Black Jazz."

Society Dance Bands

Society dance bands also existed in Chicago, during the 1920s, when, according to some historians, it was the jazz "capital" of the United States. Society bands were, in most instances, big bands with plush arrangements, designed primarily for dancing. Ben Pollack was another important society band leader during this period.

The idea behind the society dance band in Chicago was to develop a sophisticated type of jazz using the ideas of Joe Oliver and other New Orleans musicians. At the same time, the bandleaders didn't want the semi-free improvisational style of the New Orleans musicians to dominate their music. Unfortunately, these bands were so successful that other jazz bands, including the band of King Joe Oliver, tried to copy their style. A careful listen to Joe Oliver during the Chicago years confirms that his music did not possess the same vigor and fire as when he was in New Orleans. Some may dismiss this theory on the grounds that he was older, but even the earlier recordings of Oliver show this "watering down" of his music according to many of the older New Orleans jazz musicians. The New Orleans musician watered his music down once he reached Chicago in an attempt to gain entrance into the society money crowd.

Although not actually from Chicago, Leon "Bix" Beiderbecke is considered by many jazz critics to have been the only white trumpeter/cornetist to have come close to capturing Louis Armstrong's popularity as a jazz musician. Some critics have even gone so far as to say that Beiderbecke was a better jazz trumpeter than Armstrong. Beiderbecke's style was molded more closely after a European concert trumpet style than Armstrong's. According to Marshall Stearns, Beiderbecke's early influence on trumpet was Nick La Rocca of the Original Dixieland Jazz Band. Throughout his career, Beiderbecke was bothered by those fans and critics who insisted that he was a better jazz trumpeter than Armstrong. During his brief life (1903–31), he was often unable to perform because of alcoholism.

For a moment, let's look at the question of whether or not Beiderbecke was as good a jazz trumpeter as Louis Armstrong. Though kept quiet, this kind of question has been one of the forces behind decisions concerning recording, promotion, and so on. In many cases, the music industry has promoted certain artists because they felt they appealed "across the board"—meaning to both blacks

Bix Beiderbecke. Photo courtesy of the Institute of Jazz Studies.

and whites. In recent times, there have been bids for the Native American and Spanish market. The 1970s saw the emergence of groups such as Santana and a number of pop artists who exploited their Native American heritage. In fact, it became accepted to rally behind the cause of the disadvantaged American. But getting back to Beiderbecke versus Armstrong, we must remember that the music we are exposed to at an early age remains with us and shapes our taste for music. Beiderbecke's background (his father was a successful businessman in Davenport, Iowa) was completely different from Armstrong's. Armstrong, for example, spent time in a reformatory. Without a doubt, Armstrong's childhood provided him with the social "tools" necessary to survive in the society in which he lived. This same society gave him his rough, ragtime trumpet sound. Their lives were completely different in every way possible. There is no way that they could have even felt the same about music. Saying one musician is "better" than another is a superficial argument. Of course there are differences in technical proficiency, but after a certain point the only difference is in concept, and that is shaped by one's philosophical, psychological, and sociological views of music and life.

Chicago's Urban Blues

One of the most important periods of my musical career was spent in Chicago performing along lower State Street, better known as the "bucket of blood." The "bucket of blood" referred to the area along State Street between 35th and 18th. Our club was considered the only club in the area that hired modern jazz musicians. The other clubs boasted a lineup that looked like a who's who in blues: Muddy Waters, Bo Diddley, Willie Dixon, Howlin' Wolf, and so on. During intermission, the guitarist and I would go down to the other clubs to say hello to the groups. Much to my amazement, the blues clubs would be twice as full as the club we were playing. As mentioned earlier, Chicago was a mecca for hundreds of migrating blues musicians. As far as I am concerned, it has always been the urban blues center of the North.

Goin Home Blues

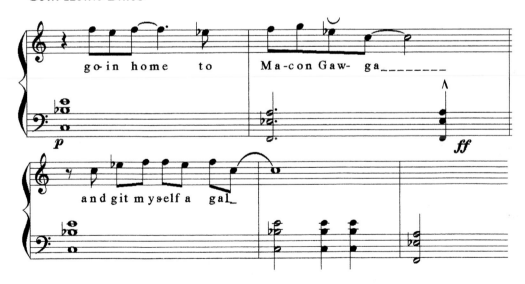

Example 14

New York

Ever since I can remember, New York City has been the home of jazz. New York, during the 1920s, boasted several schools of jazz, among them the Harlem big bands, the Harlem Piano School, society dance bands, urban blues, and a brand of Dixieland that sharply rivaled the famous Chicago Jazz school. In addition, "spasm" bands started to catch on. According to Marshall Stearns in *The Story of Jazz*, "spasm" bands became popular when Jack Bland, Dick Sleven, and Red McKenzie made a recording using homemade instruments such as combs, paper horns, and washboards, much in the tradition of Spike Jones. The idea of "spasm" bands was actually taken from the old minstrel shows when groups of black performers would gather on the corner and advertise the upcoming minstrel event. The idea was to be as funny as possible and to attract attention, so that people would want to come to the actual minstrel performance.

The Harlem Renaissance

Sometime during the mid 1920s, the jazz industry shifted from Chicago to New York. One of the most creative periods in the history of jazz was the Harlem Renaissance. Among the most successful pianists of the Harlem Piano School were Luckey Roberts, Fats Waller, James P. Johnson, Willie "The Lion" Smith, Joe Turner and, later, the incredible Art Tatum. The Harlem piano school was built mainly around small intimate clubs featuring solo piano acts. The piano bar doesn't exist today on the same scale as it did, during the 1920s, in Harlem. During the 1960s, the Mars Club in Paris, and the Living Room, featured two of the best modern barroom pianists in the business: Art Simmons and Aaron Bridges. These two pianists could play any song a customer might want to hear. The same was true of the barroom pianist during the 1920s, in Harlem. The pianist was a jack-of-all-trades. He or she (men for the most part) was expected to serve as entertainer, tourist guide, part-time hustler, psychologist, and just about anything else one might need. In addition to performing at piano bars, the multitalented pianist also played at house rent parties like their boogie-woogie counterparts in Chicago. One difference between the Harlem piano school and the boogie-woogie school of Chicago is that the Harlem pianists were generally better trained than the Chicago players. The Harlem players were careful to master various techniques of playing. Many of them studied with famous teachers and were careful

Art Tatum's incredible, lightning-speed technique, coupled with a musical concept that fused together classical, swing, stride, blues, boogie-woogie, and religious music, raised the level of solo jazz piano to new heights. Tiny Grimes (guitar) and Slam Stewart (bass). Photo courtesy of the Institute of Jazz Studies.

to analyze and study the intricacies of each composition before they perfomed a piece. Both the Harlem piano school and the Chicago boogie-woogie school derived from the ragtime school of piano playing. Many of the "floating" or "stride" effects found in the Harlem school can be traced back to the older ragtime school. The intricate playing of James P. Johnson is a good example of the Harlem school. Johnson was one of those players able to play sophisticated lines with a touch of undiluted "funk." He was at home in both the classical and blues fields. He was also considered one of America's most talented composers. He composed rags, minuets, symphonies, concertos, and operas. Johnson also served as musical Conductor and director for several musicals.

The Harlem Big Bands

The Harlem Renaissance was one of the most fruitful periods in the history of African-American culture. Music, dance, poetry, prose, and art by African-Americans were looked upon with new respect. The country was prosperous and blacks were among those enjoying the "fruit of the land." Harlem was the new playground for rich whites. Jazz clubs in Harlem catered predominantly to whites. There was little or no racial tension in the after-hours spots. Places like the Cotton Club and Lincoln Theatre were havens for black talent. The increasingly lucrative market for African-American music and the move to New York of hundreds of musicians, publishing houses, and recording companies established New York as the new jazz mecca.

Profile

FLETCHER HENDERSON • If there was a dean of the Harlem big bands it was Fletcher Henderson (pianist, composer, arranger). Henderson was typical of the new breed of jazz musician, during the 1920s, who came to New York armed with a college degree. Henderson earned a degree in chemistry at Atlanta College and originally intended to do graduate research while in New York.[1] However, shortly afterward he joined the Pace-Handy Music Company as a song demonstrator. Henderson, more than any other big band leader, was responsible for opening up the improvisational possibilities of the small jazz band for the big ensemble. One of his main contributions was the introduction of the "swing formula" into jazz arranging, though some claim that it was

Fletcher Henderson, Dean of the Harlem Big Bands, together with saxophonist and fellow band member, Don Redman, are responsible for creating the Swing Formula. Photo courtesy of the Institute of Jazz Studies.

Don Redman, Henderson's arranger and alto saxophonist, who was responsible for the swing formula. The swing formula consisted of writing an improvised solo line and composing a countermelody designed to accompany the solo line. The two lines were than harmonized to produce a full big band sound. The idea was to make that arrangement sound as close to the improvised solo as possible. According to Gunther Schuller in *Early Jazz*, Fletcher Henderson was not the kind of leader Duke Ellington or Jelly Roll Morton was, but he did hire the right sidemen. Not that Henderson was untalented or depended entirely on his sidemen, but credit should be given to his often overlooked sidemen, such as Don Redman. As an arranger and composer, Henderson worked for such greats as Benny Goodman, Teddy Hill, and Isham Jones.

Henderson's was one of the most important musical voices of the new "black is beautiful" concept of the Harlem Renaissance. His band not only played regularly at the Roseland Ballroom but was also broadcast live from the club.

Henderson's role as the musical director of Black Swan records, the first major all-black-owned record label, gave him the opportunity to expand his arranging and composition skills. According to John Chilton in *Who's Who in Jazz*, Henderson, after a series of solo and club gigs, joined clarinetist Benny Goodman as arranger and pianist in Goodman's sextet, as early as 1939.

In addition to Henderson and Ellington, a number of other groups were both innovative and creative enough to deserve mention. Pianist Charlie Johnson's ten-piece band began its career in Atlantic City, but caused quite a sensation when they opened for an extended stint at Harlem's Smalls' Paradise. Guitarist/saxophonist Elmer Snowden was another orchestra leader who made important improvisational contributions as well as giving opportunities to other musicians. Snowden, who doubled on guitar and saxophone, met Duke Ellington in Washington, D.C. Later, Snowden formed a group called the Washingtonians, of which Ellington later assumed leadership.

One of the most interesting and innovative of the Harlem big band leaders was pianist/arranger Sam Wooding. In addition to being an exceptional pianist, Wooding toured Europe, as early as 1925, as the leader of the orchestra accompanying the show "Chocolate Kiddies." While in Europe, the group played Berlin, West Germany, the Soviet Union, Hungary, Scandinavia, Turkey, the United Kingdom, Italy and Romania. This made Wooding and his group one of the first, if not the first, American jazz groups to tour the communist countries of the Soviet Union, Hungary, and Romania.

Fletcher Henderson was representative of many of the well-trained eastern bandleaders. As an authentic blues artist, Henderson was not very good. He was constantly under fire from the other musicians to improve his blues playing. His first attempts at accompanying Ethel Waters were futile. Generally speaking, musicians from the East were not as adept at playing the blues, or blueslike material, as musicians from the South and the Midwest. The earlier bands of Duke Ellington and Fletcher Henderson were not as well accepted in the Midwest as the funkier bands of Jap Allen and Benny Moten. Henderson's lack of blues understanding also caused much disagreement in the band. His sidemen often took advantage of his interest in their abilities and would forget to come in at the proper place during the music. Some critics attribute this lack of respect to Henderson's weakness as a businessman-bandleader. Henderson's dependency on Don Redman as both composer and arranger became apparent when Redman left Henderson in 1927 to join McKinney's Cotton Pickers. The Henderson band subsequently suffered while the Cotton Pickers gained in popularity.

Other big bands during the Harlem Renaissance were led by Elmer Snowden (banjo and saxes), Duke Ellington (piano)—Ellington reportedly took over the Elmer Snowden orchestra after Snowden quit the band because of a disagreement[2], Sam Wooding (piano arranger), Chick Webb (drums), William McKinney (drums), and Luis Russell (piano).

"Duke" Ellington was the most celebrated band leader during the Harlem Renaissance. Ellington is one of the most studied composers in American music history. There is hardly an arranger of jazz or pop music who doesn't use some of Ellington's techniques. And for one who had contributed so much, Ellington was one of the humblest persons I have ever met. As mentioned earlier, Ellington's main contribution to the art of arranging was the idea of stylizing each arrangement around the individual players of the orchestra. Ellington's arrangements, when played by a different band, took on an altogether different character. Being an important part of the Harlem Renaissance also shaped the sound of his band. The band was accustomed to playing a lot of shows that called for various sound effects such as street noises and jungle sounds. Musicians like James Wesley "Bubber" Miley (trumpet), and Joseph "Tricky Sam" Nanton (trombone), could reproduce with their instruments just about any type of sound. Ellington was also one of the first African-American musicians to speak out on the subject of equality and racial pride. Many of his early compositions like "Black and Tan Fantasy," "Black, Brown, and Beige," and "Liberian Suite" show his pride in his race. Ellington was also in the forefront in bringing together big band jazz and church music. His composition "In the Beginning God" is an example.[3] Ellington's most precious gift was himself. His easy manner and diplomatic appraisal of seemingly unforgivable social injustices established him as a leader among men and women.

Paul Whiteman

If Fletcher Henderson was the dean of the Harlem big bands, and Duke Ellington the most influential musician of our century, why was Paul Whiteman

Society Band leader Paul Whiteman helped to pave the way for the acceptance of jazz during the 1920s, despite the fact that he was not even a jazz musician in the traditional sense. Photo courtesy of the Institute of Jazz Studies.

known as the King of Jazz during the 1920s? Whiteman's major contribution to jazz was introducing more people to jazz during the 1920s than any other person. He did this by organizing a series of well-planned concerts (one of which was the now famous Aeolian Hall concert in New York, February 24, 1924) and publicity campaigns. Whiteman, who played violin in a number of symphony orchestras, was not an authentic jazz musician. At best, he was a semi-classical or light-pop musician. But he often employed some of the better jazz musicians such as Bix Beiderbecke (trumpet), Joe Venuti (violin) and Bunny Berigan (trumpet). Whiteman also hired Don Redman to write several ararrangments for his orchestra.

Whiteman was a fine businessman. He acted as impresario for a number of groups including his own. He was so successful that when the stock market fell in 1929, a time when most other bandleaders gave up, he was able to continue working with his band until retirement.

Conclusion

Chicago and New York during the 1920s were the two most important cities for jazz. Groups were mainly piano trios and some "small" big bands. The typical instrumentation used by leaders, like Fletcher Henderson, consisted of three trumpets, two trombones, three and sometimes four reeds (saxophones), and four rhythm instruments. The music was mostly a sophisticated kind of New Orleans Dixieland. Although the majority of the music was written out, some of the more established musicians preferred to learn the arrangements by heart. At the end of each night's performance, the musicians remained on the bandstand and learned each part by rote.

The 1920s was known as the Jazz Age. Everything was centered around the big sound of the jazz band. With the war over and the economy on the road to recovery, the country was more than ready to dive into the new "hot music." Speakeasies, gambling, prostitution, and organized crime gave America an atmosphere of delinquency, though without this atmosphere jazz might not have developed so powerfully.

The 1920s also marked the beginning of big business in jazz. Paul Whiteman's success at organizing and producing concerts proved that one could make a sizable amount of money in the music business. Others followed his lead. "Race records" showed that blues as well as society jazz bands could make money. Race records, with their emphasis on black talent, proved to be an important source of income for many major labels.

Suggested Readings and Listening

Books

Ellington, Duke. *Music is My Mistress*. New York: Doubleday & Co., 1973.

Hadlock, Richard. *Jazz Masters of the Twenties*. New York: MacMillan, 1965.

Higgins, Nathan I. *Harlem Renaissance*. New York: Oxford University Press, 1971.

Records

Henderson, Fletcher, "Wrappin in Up," Smithsonian Collection, #7.

Trumbauer, Frankie, and His Orchestra. "Riverboat Shuffle," Smithsonian Collection, #5.

Waller, Fats. "Ain't Got Nobody," Smithsonian Collection, #1.

Lewis, Meade "Lux," "Honky Tonk Train Blues," Smithsonian Collection, #2.

CHAPTER 8

Kansas City: The Focal Point of Jazz in the Late 1920s

Profile

COUNT BASIE • Never in the history of jazz has there been a more prolific leader than William "Count" Basie. Surprisingly, Basie started out as a drummer and later switched to the piano, studying with a local pianist. His early influence on the piano was Fats Waller. Basie, more than any other jazz musician of his generation, introduced the concept of "silence" and made it an integral part of jazz phrasing. By capitalizing on the steady walking rhythms of the midwestern bass players like Walter Page, he was able to strategically place his harmonies and melodic improvisation. Though he was born in Red Bank, New Jersey, throughout his career Basie has been associated with Kansas City jazz, and it was in Kansas City that he first caught the eyes of the jazz world.

After brief stints with Elmer Snowden in New York, Walter Page's Blue Devils, and the Bennie Moten bands, Basie established himself as a leader while broadcasting over station WXBY, during an engagement at the Reno Club. The famous impressario John Hammond heard the band and arranged for them to go on tour. Possessing one of the most distinctive sounds in jazz, the Basie

William "Count" Basie, pianist and big band leader, helped to establish the Kansas City sound as the standard for big band swing.

group became a success playing such clubs as The Famous Door. Other great innovators in Basie's early group include Lester Young on tenor sax, Freddie Green on guitar, Joe Jones on drums, Jimmy Rushing, and Joe Williams.

The sound of the band always centered around the pulse of the walking bass. The free flowing, blues shuffle style of the Kansas City blues (boogie-woogie) was the foundation of the band. During the territory band period of the late 1920s, when touring bands often tried to expand their club appearances by winning the battle of the bands, Basie's band was considered the "king of bands." Later, during the 1940, the band was a who's who for tenor saxophonists with such personnel as Don Byas, Buddy Tate, Illinois Jacquet, and Paul Gonsalves. Other top brass men who have worked with Basie are Thad Jones (who also served as an arranger for the band), Vic Dickenson, J.J. Johnson, and Clark Terry.

During the 1950s, Basie was forced to abandon the big band for a smaller group that included trumpeter Clark Terry, saxophonist Wardell Gray, and clarinetist Buddy DeFranco. The small group was an all-star group of some of the most important soloists in jazz. But thoughout this period it was the sound of the big band that Basie's followers wanted to hear. Eventually he reassembled the larger unit. In addition to serving as a launching pad for some of the most important soloists in jazz, the Basie band has provided an opportunity for a number of jazz composers and arrangers like Thad Jones, Frank Foster, Ernie Wilkins, Johnny Mandel, Manny Albam, Neal Hefti, and more recently Sammy Nestico, Frank West and Frank Foster. One of the most successful commercial and musical associations for Basie was with Frank Sinatra.

Basie's style of utilizing space and silence in playing the piano did not develop overnight. During his earlier ragtime period, Basie showed as much technique as any of the ragtime pianists. His association with various groups shaped his sparse style of composing and soloing. For it was the group's ability to perform certain rhythmical figures that prompted each member to alter his style to fit the concept of the group.

Profile

LESTER YOUNG • Tenor saxophonist Lester (Prez) Young was considered, by most musicians, one of the most important voices in jazz since Louis Armstrong. His laid-back sense of time, coupled with one of the most lyrical melodic concepts ever, made him one of jazz's greatest exponents. ("Laid-back" because his playing suggested a kind of behind-the-beat shuffle feeling.) Young, who was born in Woodville, Mississippi, was taught to play by his father, who was a carnival musician. Because of the traveling schedule of the elder Young, the family was constantly on the move, though they did settle for brief periods of time in New Orleans and Minneapolis. As a youngster, Young took lessons from his father on trumpet, violin, drums, and finally alto sax. According to Young he gave up playing drums because it took so long to pack up the drums after each gig. And by that time, all of the "chicks were gone." Young often paid tribute to his father when speaking about the major influences on his playing.

According to most critics, the other major influence on Young's playing was C-melody saxophonist Frankie Trumbauer. Young, who was playing the larger B♭ tenor sax, was intrigued by Trumbauer's smooth, light sound on the smaller C-melody and tried to duplicate this sound. Young's musical ideas came from various artists, including his father.

It was in the band of Art Bronson and the Bostonians that Young made the "official" switch from alto to tenor saxophone. As a young tenor saxophonist, Young worked with the bands of King Joe Oliver, Walter Page and the Blue Devils (during the beginning of his Kansas City period), Benny Moten, George Lee, and Andy Kirk.

Lester's next big break came when he joined Count Basie's band in the 1930s. It was in the Basie band that he left his mark on the jazz world. His cool "unorthodox" approach to playing the tenor sax brought mixed reactions from musicians and critics. Some felt that his light, airy sound was not the way the saxophone was supposed to sound. Before this, saxophonists, to be heard over the sound of the soaring brass sections of a big band, developed a hard, cutting sound. With the aid of the microphone, which was now being used to greater advantage, Young was able to play with a softer, lighter, cleaner sound and still be heard over the soaring brass sections. It was also during the Basie Kansas City days that Young made a reputation for himself as a tough "session" tenor who was hard to beat. During these jam sessions, Young created such a sensation that he became a sort of folk hero among the younger Kansas City musicians.

Together with Coleman Hawkins, Young helped bring the saxophone out of obscurity. Before this, the saxophone had been thought of as a sort of "clown's" instrument, used mainly as a joke in the earlier minstrel shows.

Contrary to the cliche of the unreliable jazz musician, Young was very conscientious and often on the job before starting time. The one habit that did plague him was excessive drinking. According to close friends and fellow musicians, Young drank because he felt that he was not getting the recognition he deserved. He was aware of his position as one of the liberators of the saxophone and of his influence on contemporaries, like alto saxophonist Charlie Parker and trumpeter Miles Davis. His musical marriage to the style of vocalist Billie Holiday, whom he called "Lady Day" because of her elegant, sophisticated approach to singing, helped set the trend for the future of jazz.

Lester "Prez" Young with his cool laid back, soft airy sound was responsible for introducing a new concept of saxophone style that influenced Charlie "Bird" Parker, Paul Quinichette, Stan Getz, and Sonny Stitt. Photo courtesy of the Institute of Jazz Studies.

His fear of doctors prevented him from seeking much needed medical treatment. By the time that Young had gone to Europe, on what was to be his last trip abroad, he was in poor health. In Paris, he worked with Kenny Clarke's group, which included Clarke on drums, Jimmy Gourley on guitar, and the incomparable bassist Pierre Michelot. According to Gourley, Young was, despite his drinking, a friendly person and easy to get along with. He often told jokes and tried to keep things loose. Needless to say, his playing was superb. Although he didn't practice much during his later years, his experience gave him the tools to play whatever he wanted. After it had become apparent that Young was in desperate need of medical attention, he was persuaded to return to the States by his long-time associate and promoter Norman Granz. He died in New York City of heart failure.

Lester Young's style and approach to improvisation can be seen in the work of almost every saxophonist of the 1950s. Even the modern, singing style of tenor saxophonists Sonny Rollins, Dexter Gordon, and John Coltrane owe much of their rhythmic concept to Prez.

Kansas City during the late 1920s was one of the most important cities for jazz. It was not only a focal point in the twenties but probably one of the most innovative cities in the history of jazz. It was the Kansas City style of jazz that first introduced the concept of playing four beats to the measure.

Before the introduction of what was called the "southwestern" style or "shuffle," eastern bands were still playing two beats to the measure. The main reason for introducing four beats to the measure was that southwestern musicians found it impossible to play the "rolling" bass lines, common in ragtime music, in the two-beat style typically found in the East. Many bands touring the Midwest found they could no longer play their familiar brand of two-beat music.

Example 15

The "unsophisticated" dance audiences of the Midwest did not readily accept the eastern brand of jazz because they could not dance their "native" dances to it. Another factor was that the midwestern bands were predominantly blues-oriented. The typical midwestern big band sound was a duplication of the blues "shout." In fact, most instrumental music is usually so closely related to vocal music that it is almost possible to identify the vocalist being imitated. No one doubts that Billie Holiday and saxophonist Lester Young influenced each other's style.

How and why did Kansas City become such an important city in the development of jazz? Kansas City and the midwestern and southwestern states like Oklahoma, Missouri, and Texas have always produced outstanding jazz musicians, but it was not until the stock market crash in the late 1920s that the world began to realize the southwestern contribution. This, along with the second largest migration of blacks from the rural areas of the South and Midwest and the migration of unemployed musicians from eastern cities drew attention to Kansas City.

The "opening up" of Kansas City by its controversial Mayor Tom Pendergast and Tom's brother, Jim Pendergast, laid the groundwork for jazz in that city. Together they developed one of the most sophisticated political machines in the United States during the late 1920s.[1] Under Mayor Tom Pendergast's leadership, Kansas City became another "Storyville." Prostitution, gambling, and other illegal activities were a way of life. For the unemployed musician, this meant work. Musicians from all over the country began to pour into Kansas City. Local musicians were able to find work as well as introduce visiting musicians to their style of jazz. Jam sessions went on well into the early hours of the morning. Big band leaders such as Benny Moten (piano), Jap Allen (bass), Alphonse Trent (piano), Walter Page (bass), Harlan Leonard (sax), and Andy Kirk (bass, sax, and tuba) set the standard for big band jazz in the Midwest. Musicians like Artie Shaw (clarinet), Benny Goodman (clarinet), and Lionel Hampton (vibes) engaged in jam sessions with local artists. Many of the artists thought to be natives of Kansas City were, in most instances, just passing through and found themselves stranded there. Such was the case with William "Count" Basie, who originally came from Red Bank, New Jersey; tenor saxophonist Lester "Prez" Young, from Woodville, Mississippi; pianist Mary Lou Williams, who came from Atlanta, Georgia, but grew up in Pittsburgh; saxophonist Andy Kirk, who came from Kentucky but grew up in Denver; and saxophonist James "Jimmie" Lunceford, who was from Missouri but was raised in Denver.

Kansas City, like Texas, was known for its saxophonists. Ben Webster (tenor sax), Lester Young (tenor sax), Coleman Hawkins (tenor sax), "Chu" Berry (tenor sax), Jack Washington (alto sax), Herman Walder (alto sax), Buster "Prof" Smith (alto sax), Hershel Evans (tenor sax) and later "Jumping" Joe Thomas (tenor sax) were saxophonists to be reckoned with in Kansas City. During my early childhood in Kansas City, my parents often told me stories about the early "carving" sessions held by the musicians. One of the stories had Lester Young returning to an all-night jam session several times in one evening in an effort to regain his "title" from the newly-arrived Coleman Hawkins. The day I received my first saxophone, my next door neighbor, Reverend Paul Kidd, invited me into his home and played several recordings of Coleman Hawkins. After an hour or so of listening, he said, "Don't even think about playing unless you're going to try to get a big sound like that."

As mentioned earlier, the sound of Kansas City was robust. One reason for this hard, big saxophone sound was that microphones were seldom used during the earlier years. Later, using a microphone, it was possible for an instrumentalist to concentrate on a soft but purer sound and not worry about being heard. Lester Young did just that. His sound was revolutionary during the late 1920s. It was full, round, pure, and soft, as opposed to the sound of Coleman Hawkins or "Chu" Berry. Many critics have claimed that Lester fashioned his sound after saxophonist Frankie Trumbauer, who played the C-melody saxophone with orchestras such as Jean Goldkette's and Paul Whiteman's. I feel that critics have overplayed the Trumbauer influence. Having studied the style of Lester Young for a number of years, I have concluded that Young played with such a light, airy, pure sound mainly because of his earlier experience as a clarinet player. Listening to Young on clarinet shows his sound on clarinet and saxophone to be the same. Even if Young patterned his style after Trumbauer, he would have been imitating the sound of the C-melody, which is a lighter sounding instrument than the larger B♭ tenor saxophone that Young played.

The "big" sound of Kansas City applied not only to saxophonists and other instrumentalists but also to vocalists. The "shouting" blues singers like Jimmy Rushing, Joe Turner (not to be confused with pianist Joe Turner mentioned earlier), and later Jimmy Witherspoon turned out some of the most inspiring blues ever. The blues shouters had to sing over a big band without the aid of a microphone. Most bars didn't even hire a vocalist independent of the band. The vocals were often rendered by the bartender or waiter who, on demand, belted out the blues.

Med. Swing

Example 16

The riff was a short melodic motif repeated at regular intervals. The musicians used the riff as a unifying point behind a soloist or as a melodic line instead of the usual written arrangement. Using the simple riff gave the musicians enough freedom to let the melody swing freely and at the same time helped to hold the band together. The riff became so much a part of the big band musicians' style that many bands created simple riffs instead of playing precomposed arrangements. Many musicians felt that the precomposed arrangement took all the "soul" out of the music. As mentioned earlier, bands often remained two or three hours after a performance to learn new riffs for the next night.

The Count Basie band became the most innovative big band of the late 1930s. Basie himself was declared a genius not for virtuoso technique at the keyboard, but for his unequalled use of silence. He knew when and when not to play. Freddie Green, the band's rhythm guitarist, was responsible for laying down a solid foundation without interrupting the steady four-four time of bassist Walter Page. Drummer Jo Jones' even steady pulse on the "hi-hat" cymbal took drumming away from the older two-beat "trap" concept to a more modern four-beat style. Lester Young, with his revolutionary light and airy, but firm, tenor sax sound, became a leader in three different schools of jazz: swing, cool, and bebop. Count Basie's band has been one of the most innovative in jazz. Regardless of the style or period, the Basie band's four-four midwestern shuffle beat remains one of its identifying features.

Some critics of Basie's band have stated that Basie received credit for the earlier efforts of bandleader Bennie Moten. Basie did play in the Moten band and later formed a group that included some of Moten's top players. It is to Basie's credit that he was respected enough by those musicians for them to join him as sidemen. Basie was not the usual kind of bandleader. According to reports he was an easy-going, likeable person, which helped him cope with some of the more outspoken jazz giants who worked with him through the years.

Conclusion

Kansas City during the later 1920s was a hotbed of jazz. The style of jazz played in Kansas City, during this period, was more blueslike and employed what was commonly known as the midwestern shuffle beat. The midwestern shuffle was a take-off of the earlier piano and guitar boogie-woogie style that developed in the mining camps of the Midwest. This style differed so much from the smoother dance band style of the eastern bands that many of the more sophisticated bands from the East found it difficult to please midwestern audiences. Another name for the Kansas City type blues bands was *territory bands*. In fact, this period is often called The Territory Band Period.

Battles of the bands took place in the territories during the late 1920s. The territories included Kansas, Missouri, Oklahoma, Texas, and Arkansas. Each band usually covered a particular territory. Most of the jobs were in hotels and dance halls. The main feature often centered around the battle of the bands. Each band would take its turn in trying to outblow the other. Clever arrangements and outstanding soloists were the major attraction of the bands. Major bands of the Kansas City Territory Band Period were those of Alphonse Trent, Andy Kirk, Harlan Leonard, Jap Allen, Walter Page and the Blue Devils, and Bennie Moten.

"Andy" Andrew Dewey Kirk, was one of the most prolific bandleaders during the 1920s Jazz age. Born Andrew "Andy" Dewey Kirk in Newport, Kentucky, May 28, 1898 he gained his early music musical training as a tuba player in the Denver-based orchestra of violinist George Morrison. Kirk died in New York City on December 11, 1992.

According to Leonard Feather and Ira Gittler in *The Biographical Encyclopedia of Jazz*, Andy Kirk was a well-schooled musician who studied singing, alto and tenor saxophone and theory with Wiberforce Whiteman—Paul Whitman's father. He later switched to bass saxophone and soon emigrated to Kansas City where he teamed up with jazz pianist Mary Lou Williams to form the famous "Andy Kirk and His 12 Clouds of Joy" orchestra. In this orchestra Kirk served as bandleader and conductor. Mary Lou Williams was featured soloist and composer/arranger. A "dapper" dresser, Andy Kirk was a striking diplomatic, charismatic figure and in many ways was a mirror of Duke Ellington in his approach to running the band.

Walter Page, born Walter Sylvester Page, was perhaps the most authentic of the Midwest bands representing the Kansas City territory bands. While Andy Kirk's band was more of a sophisticated "Duke Ellington" type orchestra, Page's group was more blues oriented. Born in Gallatin, Missouri on February 9, 1900, Page died in New York City on December 20, 1957.

Walter Page began playing a number of different instruments including drums, eventually switching to bass. It is on the bass that Page makes his most important contribution to the development of jazz as a member of the Bennie Moten and Count Basie orchestras. It was Page's collaboration with pianist-bandleader Count Basie that initialized the concept of playing four beats to the measure instead of the customary two beats that was an integral part of the Midwestern dance music of that period.

Pianist/bandleader Bennie Moten was one of the most authentic big band leaders ("the big 3") of the Kansas City Territory band period. Born Benjamin "Bennie" Moten in Kansas City, Missouri, November 13, 1894 and died April 2, 1935 in Kansas City, Moten was primarily a bandleader who led one of the most respected territory dance bands of the 1920s. It was in his band that the idea of the Kansas City Shuffle began to take shape with the teaming up of bassist Walter Page and pianist Count Basie. According to Feather-Gittler in *The Biographical Encyclopedia of Jazz,* his sidemen consisted of some of the most famous names in jazz: Count Basie (piano), Jimmy Rushing (vocal), Hot Lips Page (trumpet), Ben Webster (tenor saxophone), Harlan Leonard (saxophone), Buster Smith (alto saxophone), etc.

If there was a representative style or sound of the Territory Band Period, it was that of Count Basie and his band. The laid-back shuffle beat combined with the big blues shout made the Basie band one of the major big bands in the history of jazz. Basie's reserved use of space and Lester Young's elegant and gentle tenor saxophone sound, combined with the walking four-four beat of Walter Page's bass and Jo Jones' drums, and later Freddie Green's guitar, to give the Basie band one of the most innovative sounds in jazz.

Suggested Readings and Listening

Books

Russell, Ross. *Jazz Styles in Kansas City and the Southwest*. Berkeley: University of California Press, 1971.

——. *Bird Lives: The High Life and Hard Times of Charlie (Yardbird) Parker*. New York: Charter Books, 1973.

Records

Williams, Martin, and Moten, Bennie, Kansas City Orchestra, eds. The Smithsonian Collection of Classic Jazz, #8 (Moten Swing).

Boogie Woogie, Folkways Jazz Anthology, vol. 10.

CHAPTER 9

Swing

Profile

BENJAMIN (BENNY) DAVID GOODMAN • Benjamin (Benny) David Goodman (clarinet and alto sax) was born in Chicago, Illinois on May 30, 1909 and died in New York on June 13, 1986. He began his early music studies at the local synagogue and later at Chicago's Hull House. In Chicago, he performed with fellow Chicagoans, drummer Dave Tough, alto saxophonist Frank Teschemacher, trumpeter Jimmy McPartland, and Russian-born pianist Art Hodges. He later joined Ben Pollock's Orchestra, where he recorded with the orchestra.

According to Leonard Feather in *The New Edition of the Encyclopedia of Jazz*, Goodman made his first recorded solo with Pollack's orchestra in Chicago, as well as his only recordings on alto and baritone saxophones.[1]

Goodman was quite active as a studio recording musician who got into jazz at the suggestion of fellow musicians and later John Hammond. He formed his first big band in 1934 and immediately began to have success as one of the premiere dance bands in the country. During this time Goodman continued to work as a studio musician for radio and recording companies. His

Benny Goodman, clarinetist and big band leader, was dubbed the "King of Swing" by critics and fans. Goodman was a master clarinetist who played classical music as well as jazz. Photo courtesy of Rutgers, the Institute of Jazz Studies.

reputation as an excellent sight reader and flawless technician won him the praise of his fellow musicians.

One of the most important moves that Goodman made as a new band leader was to hire Fletcher Henderson to write arrangements for the newly formed group. Fletcher, who had previously enjoyed minimal success as one of the major big band leaders of the Harlem big bands during the Harlem Renaissance period, brought a totally different concept to Goodman's band. Benny Goodman was also known as a perfectionist. Perhaps because of his early training with Franz Schoepp, a clarinetist with the Chicago Symphony Orchestra, Goodman was more inclined to strive for technical proficiency and exactness of pitch than did his colleagues who lacked such training. His drilling of the band, by having them repeat a musical phrase over and over until it was the way he wanted it, was legendary.

After his appearances on the popular coast to coast "Let's Dance" radio show, Goodman was propelled into the national spotlight as a big band leader and became a household name as the "King of Swing." His concert at Carnegie Hall helped establish jazz as a respectable art form in the public mind.

In 1935, Goodman formed the Benny Goodman Trio, with Goodman on clarinet, Gene Krupa on drums, and Teddy Wilson on piano. Later in 1936, Lionel Hampton joined Goodman, thus forming Goodman's highly-publicized racially integrated quartet.

Benny Goodman was the first active Jazz big band leader and soloist to gain wide recognition as a classical performer. Perhaps his most celebrated collaboration in this area was his work with the European composer Bela Bartok. Goodman recorded "Contrast," which he had commissioned Bartok to compose for him, with violinist Joseph Szigeti. (*Jazz* by Frank Tiro, W.W. Norton)

The Swing Era started in the middle of the 1930s and continued into the early 1940s. Swing was one of the most popular types of jazz. It was, if nothing else, "danceable." The periods in jazz that produced the most danceable music were also the most popular and profitable. The 1920s also produced a tremendous amount of dance music. But it was the 1930s that created the publicity to sell the idea to the general public. Radio programming and high-powered sales tactics made the music industry one of the prime sources of revenue in this country.

A number of big bands achieved national recognition during the Swing Era, like those of Benny Goodman (clarinet), Artie Shaw (clarinet), Glen Gray (sax), the Casa Loma Orchestra, Glenn Miller (trombone), Earl "Fatha" Hines (piano), Tommy and Jimmy Dorsey (trombone, sax), Les Brown (sax-arranger), Teddy Hill (sax), Duke Ellington (piano), Erskine Hawkins (trumpet), and later the big band of Lionel Hampton (vibes). The Swing Era was predominantly a big band era, but a number of small groups also played a significant role. The most popular figure during the Swing Era was Benny Goodman. Goodman's band was, in its earlier stages, primarily a dance band. With the help of a number of arrangers, including Fletcher Henderson, Goodman's band began to take on the characteristics of a true jazz orchestra.

What is the difference between a "true" jazz band and a dance band? The main difference is in the concept and the type of music performed. Dance bands played music designed mainly for dancing. Hot, improvised solos were minimized.

The idea was to tailor the band's sound and rhythm around the current popular dance. On the other hand, the true jazz band's aim was to play in an improvised style. Improvisation was the main objective. Jazz orchestras like the orchestra of Fletcher Henderson were criticized because they often played music that sounded uneven, out of tune, or just plain sloppy. They also aimed at getting the audience to dance, but their main objective was to play as much jazz as they could. One of the achievements of Goodman was to bring together the loose, "funkier" approach of Henderson's band and the more European dance band approach of Paul Whiteman.

Goodman was one of the first white bandleaders to integrate bands in the United States. He hired pianist Teddy Wilson in 1936 and later also hired vibraphonist Lionel Hampton. This was an unusual move for a successful bandleader. Touring through the South and some parts of the North with a mixed group was practically unheard of. Whether Goodman hired Wilson and Hampton because of their unique musicianship or because it was a good publicity move is not certain. I have asked several musicians this question and received both answers. One thing is certain: Goodman tried to build the best jazz group possible. He must have realized that adding two extraordinary musicians like Wilson and Hampton could only improve his band.

Applying the title "King of Swing" to Benny Goodman must have seemed an injustice to the other big bandleaders of the 1930s. Many of these band leaders were equally as talented and in some instances had as many good sidemen as Goodman. Why didn't one of these musicians receive the distinction? We must keep in mind that many of the older New Orleans bandleaders like King Joe Oliver, King Freddie Keppard, and King Buddy Bolden also used the title "King" as a promotional gimmick. Goodman did the same, only twenty to thirty years later. Nobody doubted Goodman's ability as a clarinetist or bandleader. He was a perfectionist and demanded the same from his men. He began his career as a successful studio musician and later went on to perform works by von Weber, Aaron Copeland, Stravinsky, and others. He also appeared with a number of symphony orchestras, including the Chicago, Philadelphia, and Cleveland orchestra. The question here, though, does not concern Goodman as a symphony musician, but his role as a jazz musician and one of the most celebrated figures in the Swing Era. Technically, Goodman was an excellent clarinetist. Through his close association with black musicians, he learned the language of their music. His association with agent John Hammond also contributed to his business success. It was Hammond who engineered his recording contract with English Gramophone when the American companies refused to record him in a pure jazz setting. Some critics also give Hammond credit for persuading Goodman to hire Teddy Wilson and Lionel Hampton.

With the business guidance of Hammond and the arranging talents of Fletcher Henderson, along with Goodman's musicianship, success was certain. Ironically, many of the arrangements that helped Goodman achieve stardom had been used some years earlier by Henderson in his unsuccessful career as a big band leader. It is important to point out that it was Henderson's lack of good business practice that was responsible for his decline and not his lack of musical talent.

In 1934, Goodman and his band participated in a nationwide radio broadcast called "Let's Dance." Designed by an advertising executive of the National Biscuit Company as an advertisement campaign for the newly released Ritz Cracker, the program helped make Goodman's name a household word. The next big boost in Goodman's career came with his production of a Carnegie Hall concert. The Carnegie Hall concert was an exact replica of Paul Whiteman's "triomphe" at Aeolian Hall. As a result of this concert, Goodman gained a new audience. People who had never before attended a jazz concert were now convinced that jazz was a valid art form. Goodman's financial success paved the way for other big bands during the Swing Era, among them the innovative band of Count Basie. The Basie band's free, relaxed, midwestern style was responsible for introducing blues into the big bands of the 1930s. Earlier, during the 1920s, jazz had been known as "hot" music. The use of the term "hot" started a wave of criticism from the press and general public. For many the term "hot" had immoral connotations. Story after story told of how "Negro" music destroyed the sexual morals of young people and how jazz was sinful music not fit for people of the "higher class." Whiteman in the 1920s and Goodman in the 1930s helped change public opinion about jazz. They made jazz respectable. As more and more businessmen took an interest in jazz, musicians began to be treated like royalty. Many musically talented performers began to incorporate jazz into their acts. The bands of Basie, Ellington, and Goodman became first-rate industries. One of the best examples was the association between Irving Mills of Mills Publishing Company and the Duke Ellington orchestra. Little by little, Mills took over the affairs of the orchestra, serving in the same capacity John Hammond did for Goodman.

One thing became evident during the Swing Era: money could be made from jazz. Major bands became the target for big-time investors. After a while, many bandleaders did not even own their own bands. Long, weary road trips from one end of the country to the other became a common occurrence for musicians. Bandleaders were forced to keep a strenuous series of engagements. As far as the investors were concerned, business was business.

Another controversy during the Swing Era had to do with the Glenn Miller "sound." Miller, a trombonist turned arranger, studied in New York with Professor Joseph Schillinger at New York University.[2] Miller is credited with popularizing the idea of using a clarinet lead over four saxes. This produced a unique sound.

A careful study of Duke Ellington's scores reveals this and many other similar voicings. Why then was Miller credited with being the first one to use this technique? We must remember that Ellington and Miller performed in completely different circles. Ellington, although a jazz musician, did not receive during his early career the same exposure as Miller. Again, we see just how important the music industry is in shaping jazz history.

Hits like "String of Pearls," "Little Brown Jug," and "Chattanooga Choo-Choo" established Miller's band as one of the country's leading dance bands. Miller's popularity rose to even greater heights after he volunteered for active duty with the U.S. Air Force during World War II. He was eulogized, after his sudden death in a plane crash over the English Channel.

One of the most overlooked big bands of the Swing Era was that of Cab Calloway. Calloway, who was born in Rochester, New York, and raised in Baltimore, was not primarily an instrumentalist like many of his predecessors but a vocalist and entertainer known throughout the world for his famous call, "Hi-di-hi-di-ho." Calloway's band played some of the most invigorating jazz of the period. Dizzy Gillespie, the famous trumpeter, recalls that Cab was not really a fan of

Med. Swing

Example 17

the then new sound of bebop. As the story goes, Dizzy and Cab soon parted company after Dizzy allegedly hit Cab in the back of the neck with a spitball during one of his famous cries.

Swing was America's answer to the 1930s. Life in America was a mixture of excitement and boredom. Teenagers were looking for a new lease on life, something that freed them from the apron strings of their parents, who had tried in vain to hide the "evils of prohibition" from them. Amid this superficial revolt, Swing found its niche. Musicians and the public alike were caught up in the concept of bigness. Everything had to be grandiose. America was big, so everything associated with America had to be big. Sometime during the late 1930s swing began to decline. All publicity was built around the bandleaders, some of whom were the least talented musicians in the band. When musicians who had spent years traveling all over the country decided to quit, they could not find work. It was the name of the bandleader that was on the lips of the public, not the name of the sidemen. Some musicians within the big bands asked themselves why they should continue to work for little money while the bandleaders got rich and famous? Some also felt there was little room for their creative ideas within the complicated arrangements of the 1930s big band. Most of the bandleaders were becoming more and more obsessed with highly-technical arrangements that left little room for the soloist. Many of the musicians left to form their own groups. In 1942, the musicians union ordered an end to all recordings by musicians associated with the union. Gasoline rationing during World War II greatly restricted the movement of all entertainers, but the big bands were especially hard hit because their livelihood depended on traveling. For financial reasons it was almost impossible for a large group to remain in one spot over a long period. These things, along with a tax on entertainment, helped put an end to the big dance bands of the Swing Era.

Profile

SIDNEY BECHET • Sidney Bechet was one of the most important soprano saxophonists in jazz. His clear, highly-developed vibrato caught the ear as he caressed it with his sophisticated but jazzy blueslike melodies. Born in New Orleans in 1887, Bechet grew up hearing the great marching bands of that era. In fact, his first opportunity to play jazz came by "sitting in" with various street bands in New Orleans. In his book *Treat It Gentle*, Bechet credits his talent to

Sidney Bechet, often referred to as the Father of the Ex-patriot Movement of Jazz musicians living in Europe, together with jazz drummer Kenny Clarke is responsible for establishing jazz as a major art form in France. Photo courtesy of the Institute of Jazz Studies.

his grandfather, Omar, who according to Bechet could do anything in the way of entertainment. During his early years, Bechet played clarinet in the bands of cornetists Freddie Keppard and Manuel Perez. In addition to marching bands, Bechet also worked with carnivals and traveling road shows. In 1917, around the time New Orleans jazz was in demand in other parts of the country, Bechet joined the Bruce & Bruce Touring Company, touring Georgia, Alabama, Ohio, and Indiana.[3]

It was not until Bechet's visit to London in 1919, with Will Marion Cook and the Southern Syncopated Orchestra, that he bought his first straight model soprano saxophone—by accident, he later said. At first, Bechet used the soprano only as a feature in certain numbers. He did not play it on a regular basis until much later.

The first time Bechet played Paris was in 1920, at the Apollo Theater with the Southern Syncopated Orchestra. It was this first trip to Paris that gave Bechet mixed feelings about his adopted homeland of France. Bechet and a fellow musician were arrested and accused of rape. (They had picked up a couple of girls after a gig and had gone back to the friend's apartment.) Finally, the attempted rape charges were dropped, but Bechet was asked to leave France. Bechet's second brush with the law in Paris came as a result of a disagreement with a fellow American musician. According to Bechet, pianist Glover Compton, at the urging of banjoist Mike McKendrick, began to make obscene gestures at Bechet as he walked past a club where the two were sitting. Bechet ended up in a gun battle in which Glover, a young girl, and a French woman were wounded. Although it was clear that Bechet acted in self-defense, he and McKendrick were found guilty and each served eleven months in a French prison. Bechet was clearly the victim of circumstances. Bechet was a strong-willed individualist who stood up for his rights. If pushed, he pushed back harder.

After returning to the States and working with the bands of Duke Ellington and Noble Sissle, and stints with Revue Negre with Josephine Baker, Bechet finally returned to France in 1951. He occasionally returned to the States to tour and record, but for the most part he remained in France.

In France, Bechet was considered somewhat of a national hero. To show their appreciation for his work, the French erected a statue of him in the south of France. His name is synonymous with the word jazz. During the 1960s, veteran French jazz men like Claude Luther and Maxim Saury were constantly paying tribute to Bechet through their music. During my stay in France, I had the pleasure of meeting Bechet's French widow and son through the American drummer Art Taylor. Although the conversation never really got around to Bechet, his presence was strong as we talked about the Paris jazz scene. It was almost impossible for a saxophonist, especially a soprano saxophonist, even to touch the instrument without being compared to Bechet. This was even more true during the time that American clarinetist Mezz Mezzrow was living in Paris. Mezz's admiration for Bechet was tremendous. In a way, Mezz spoke for the French whenever he was asked about Bechet and his work: "Il etait formidable." ("He was great.")

Dixieland Revival

The Dixieland Revival Period (early 1940s) was one of the most financially unsuccessful periods in the history of jazz. Dixieland was old music and therefore not "hip." During the late 1930s and early 1940s, a group of young white musicians got together and tried to revive interest in the New Orleans music of King Joe Oliver, Freddie Keppard, and Sidney Bechet. The revival of New Orleans music appealed mainly to young middle-class whites. There was a certain snobbish intellectualism involved that did not appeal to blacks. The thrust of the movement was on the West Coast, mainly in San Francisco and Los Angeles. Among the leaders of the Dixieland revival period in the United States were instrumentalists like Lu Watters (trumpet), Turk Murphy (trombone), Bob Wilber (sax and clarinet), and Bunk Johnson (cornet).

Outside the United States the revival of Dixieland met with much more success. In the forefront of Europeans playing traditional New Orleans music were Claude Luther (soprano sax) and later Maxim Saury (clarinet) in France and Chris Barber (trombone) in England. Even today, traditional New Orleans music is played more in Europe than in the United States. Albert Nicholas, one of the last original New Orleans Creole musicians, spent his last years living and working in France and Switzerland because, as he put it: "These people over here know how to appreciate good music when they hear it." Nicholas spent most of his time touring with one of Europe's outstanding traditional groups, The Dutch College Swing Band. I had the pleasure of hearing this group perform with Nicholas on several tours, and they were as good as any traditional group I have ever heard.

Still, although the revival of Dixieland was more successful in Europe, several musicians in the United States did profit financially from the movement.

Soprano saxophonist Sidney Bechet was one of the main reasons for the success of Dixieland music in France. According to the musicians who worked with Bechet, he felt more at home in France than in the United States. He considered himself part French. During my stay in France, I heard many stories about Bechet and his influence on the local musicians. In 1967, I did a television special with Mezz Mezzrow (clarinet) who had often worked with Bechet as a second horn. The show was built around black expatriate musicians in France and was entitled "Harlem à Paris." I had just started playing the soprano sax and the producers wanted someone to fill in with a soprano. As we were playing, Mezz leaned over to me and said, "Don't play with such a dry sound. Use more vibrato, you know, the way Sidney used to do." I never got over that because Bechet played the soprano with a special vibrato like no one else. On another occasion, George Selmer of the Selmer Instrument Company handed me a mouthpiece and said: "Here, take this mouthpiece, it's the model we built especially for Sidney." Bechet's influence as a soprano saxophonist was so powerful that for years it was almost impossible for any soprano player to set a different style.

One of the most important controversies that existed in jazz during the late 1920s and 1930s was that of changing the name "hot jazz" to that of swing. Many felt that the term "swing" was actually a way of commercializing the real jazz—hot jazz. The fact that the term "swing" was not really used by the musicians themselves to describe the music added to the confusion. Fletcher Henderson stated that there was a definite difference in the interpretation of the music. Swing, he felt, was predetermined or less spontaneous than jazz.[4]

One of the most important boosts for the usage of the term "swing" came when the music began to take on a more commercial style and appealed to a less jazz oriented dance band clientele. Jazz bands, including those of Fletcher Henderson, Duke Ellington, Chick Webb, changed to a more commercial dance band approach—thus giving way to the concept of swing. (It is important here to note that throughout the history of jazz, jazz artists have embraced the more commercial forms of jazz in order to increase their earnings.) Some of those bands were among the most successful big bands during the Swing Era and included Lionel Hampton, Erskine Hawkins, Jimmy and Tommy Dorsey, Earl "Fatha" Hines, Glenn Miller, Artie Shaw, and Benny Goodman.

One of the most changed roles in the history of jazz is that of the jazz vocalist. During the 1920s and 1930s, jazz vocalists were used primarily as an added attraction. In recent years (1950–80), the vocalist took on a more "star"-like role. In fact, today (1990) a commercially successful jazz vocalist usually commands triple the amount of money that an instrumental earns. One of the reasons for the success of this role reversal is that the audience can relate to the lyrics of the song. If one looks at the commercial success of such jazz innovators as Louis Armstrong, Sarah Vaughan, and others, it is obvious that their ability to sing greatly enhanced their careers. In the case of Sarah Vaughan, it gave her a new career.

The fact that the swing bands of the 1930s were primarily employed to play dances meant that the bands who played the best dance music were the most successful. The "ballroom" orchestras of the 1920 and 1930s were often responsible for stimulating new dances.

One of the important questions concerning the popularity of the Swing Era centers around the acceptance of Benny Goodman as the King of Swing. While most Black Americans consider artists like Duke Ellington, Jimmy Lunceford, Count Basie, and of course Fletcher Henderson to be the leaders of jazz, white Americans had embraced the music of Goodman, Glenn Miller, and The Dorsey Brothers, etc. Due to a lack of good business practice and declining bookings, Fletcher Henderson was not able to keep his band fully booked. After disbanding his band in 1934, Goodman manager John Hammond proposed to Goodman that he hire Fletcher as his arranger (*The Swing Era*, Schuller, p. 7). According to Kenny Clarke on a television show sponsored by the French National TV show, several critics agreed that Goodman really owed much of his success to the newly-acquired arrangements of Fletcher Henderson.

Duke Ellington's idea of constructing an arrangement or composition tailored to fit the individual talents of his orchestra is further proof that the jazz composer-arranger leaned heavily on the individual jazz soloist for ideas. Yet other composers, like Ferde Grofe and William Grant, still tended to be more traditional in form. One of the most important arrangers of the Swing Era was Melvin James (Sy) Oliver. Oliver, who was from Zanesville, Ohio, contributed some of the most innovative arrangements during his tenure with the Jimmie Lunceford Orchestra and the orchestra of Tommy Dorsey.

The Swing period produced many fine orchestras, among them Jimmie Lunceford, Tommy and Jimmy Dorsey, Andy Kirk, Cab Calloway, The Casa Loma Orchestra, Edgar Hayes, Erskine Hawkins, and Bob Crosby. To imply that the most important contribution during the Swing era was the big band is to ignore the enormous contribution of some of the greatest soloists in the history of jazz.

Tommy Dorsey on the trombone. His clear, smooth distinct trombone sound played a vital role in establishing the trombone as a solo instrument during the swing era. Photo courtesy of the Institute of Jazz Studies.

Soloists like tenor saxophonist Ben Webster, pianist Teddy Wilson, trumpeter Louis Armstrong, and Bix Beiderbecke, although now well-established in the name orchestras of the period, were responsible for some of the most important innovations in jazz. It is often the individual soloist who is responsible for influencing the arrangers-composers who transfer these new ideas to paper. Many well-known composer-arrangers seek out particular soloists and study their styles, in an attempt to get new ideas for their own works.

Most historians will agree that it was the innovative trumpet stylings of Louis Armstrong that took America by storm. Furthermore, Armstrong was responsible for changing the concept of arranging during the 1920s.

The impact of Swing was unpredictable. The nation embraced the new music with an enthusiasm that resembled the excitement of the acceptance of New Orleans Jazz in Chicago and New York during the 1920s. The key element in the new music was dancing. The new dances provided the big bands the opportunity to perform at ballrooms throughout the country. Although at that time dances tended to be regional, the Jitterbug and other similar dances received national exposure. Thus, jazz bands found themselves in the position of bringing the nation together by influencing the style of dancing through music.

Conclusion

The Swing Era produced some of the most danceable music ever, which was one reason for its success. Another reason was that the music business had grown so much that agents and promoters were able to launch publicity campaigns that ensured large audiences. Radio, recordings, and the rapidly maturing motion picture industry's use of jazz and jazz musicians also helped popularize Swing. The financial success of Paul Whiteman and his numerous orchestras helped establish a profitable business.

The most popular big bands of the Swing Era were those of Duke Ellington; Benny Goodman, and Count Basie. Others were led by James Reese Europe, Noble Sissle, Erskine Hawkins, Vincent Lopez, Chick Webb, Glenn Miller, Hal Kemp, Cab Calloway, Jimmie Lunceford, The Dorsey Brothers (Jimmy and Tommy), Artie Shaw, Harry James, Earl "Fatha" Hines, Les Brown, and Glen Gray. One of the most fruitful musical collaborations during the Swing Era was that of arranger/composer Fletcher Henderson and clarinetist/leader Benny Goodman. Goodman was one of the first, major big bandleaders to take an integrated band

Belgium-born Django Reinhart was the first European jazz musician considered by most American jazz musicians to be a major innovator. However, because of his heavy reliance on his native Gypsy musical background when improvising, some U.S. critics were reluctant to consider him a pure Jazz player. © William Gottlieb. All rights reserved.

of black and white musicians on the road. Duke Ellington, though he entered the jazz scene in the 1920s, was probably the one person responsible for bringing together big band blues and an elegant touch of sophistication. His ability to tailor his compositions and arrangements to the musicians in his band set a standard for bandleaders.

The Dixieland Revival followed the Swing Era. In fact, the Dixieland Revival occurred simultaneously with the inception of Bebop—during the late 1930s and early 1940s. The movement was most successful outside the United States, particularly in France and England. Claude Luther and Maxim Saury were two of its most important figures in France, while trombonist Chris Barber contributed in England. One reason for the acceptance of Dixieland music in Europe was the presence of American jazz musicians like Sidney Bechet. Bechet was revered by the French. Many young musicians and fans were first exposed to jazz through Bechet's soprano saxophone. In the States, Bob Wilber, Lu Watters, Turk Murphy, The Crosby Brothers (Bing and Bob), and Eddie Condon had the top bands during the Dixieland Revival. If any musician typified the sound and image of the Dixieland Revival, it was trumpeter/cornetist Bunk Johnson. The restoration of the unique Bunk Johnson sound made the Dixieland Revival a true revival.

Suggested Readings and Listening

Books

Berendt, Joachim. *The Jazz Book*. New York: Lawrence Hill, 1975.

Esquire's World of Jazz. New York: Thomas Y. Crowell, 1975.

Fernett, Gene. *Swing Out: Great Negro Dance Bands*. Midland, Mich.: Pendell Publishing Co., 1970.

———. *Thousand Golden Horns*. Midland, Mich.: Pendell Publishing Co., 1966.

Records

Count Basie and his Orchestra. "Doggin' Around." Smithsonian Collection, record #5, side #7.

Benny Goodman Sextet with Charlie Christian. Smithsonian Collection, Blues Sequence, record #6, side #3.

Jimmie Lunceford and his Orchestra. "Lunceford Special." Smithsonian Collection, record #8, side #5.

Profile

EARL KENNETH ("FATHA") HINES • Earl Kenneth (Fatha) Hines, piano composer and big band leader, was born on December 28, 1905. Earl Fatha Hines' contributions to jazz are numerous, but perhaps his most important contribution was his introduction of the single solo, trumpet style, approach to improvising on the piano. In addition, he led one of the most important big bands and was responsible for helping to launch the 1940s bebop era.

Hines studied piano as a young student and originally planned to become a concert pianist. Because of his serious study of the classics, he developed a formidable technique on the piano that served him well when he began duplicating trumpeter Louis Armstrong's solos. Hines' single-line solo technique revolutionized jazz piano, thus giving birth to later styles such as Bud Powell and Oscar Peterson.

In 1928 Hines formed his first big band for an engagement at Chicago's famed Grand Terrace. Hines' flare for entertaining, as well as taking a serious approach to playing, gave him an advantage over many of his peers. He was successful as a solo pianist and much in demand as a trio performer. His work with the legendary Louis Armstrong's Hot Five propelled Hines to the top of the jazz world. But it was his role as the leader of one of the most innovative big bands in the history of jazz, especially bebop, that helped to launch the careers of some of the most important musicians of that era.

According to jazz critic and historian Leonard Feather in *The Encyclopedia of Jazz*, Hines' band included at various periods Dizzy Gillespie (trumpet), Charlie Parker (alto sax), Wardell Gray (tenor sax), Bennie Green (trombone), Benny "Little Benny" Harris (trumpet), Rossier "Shadow" Wilson (drums), Billy Eckstine (vocals), and Sarah Vaughan (piano). Other members of the 1943 band included A. Crump, Andrew Gardner, Scoops Carry, John Williams, Jesse Simkins, Jimmy Mundy, Albert "Budd" Johnson, Walter Fuller, Omer Simeon, Darnell Howard, Herb Jeffries, Arthur Lee Simpkins, and Ida James. What was so impressive about this particular roster was that many of the same musicians served as the basis for the Billy Eckstine big band that was to follow. Budd Johnson, who wrote arrangements for both the Hines and Eckstine bands and also recommended various musicians for them, was probably more influential than any other musician during the transitional period between bebop and Swing.

Earl "Fatha" Hines created a style of improvising on the piano using single note lines that was derived from his idol and mentor Louis "Pops" Armstrong. Photo courtesy of the Rutgers Institute of Jazz.

Profile

LIONEL HAMPTON • Lionel Hampton, vibraphonist and drummer, was born in Louisville, Kentucky on April 20, 1908. It is impossible to talk about the history of jazz without discussing the contributions of vibraphonist, drummer, and big band leader Lionel Hampton. Over the years Hamp's bands have given musical birth to the careers of such major innovators as Milt Buckner (organ/piano), Cat Anderson (trumpet), Illinois Jacquet (saxophone), Monk Montgomery (bass), Johnny Griffin (saxophone), Arnett Cobb (saxophone), Clifford Brown (trumpet), Art Farmer (trumpet), Quincy Jones (trumpet/composer/arranger), Dexter Gordon (saxophone), Milt Buckner (piano), and Betty Carter (vocals).

Hampton's contribution to Benny Goodman's small ensembles has tended to overshadow the fact that he produced some of the best big band jazz of the 20th century. For years Hampton led the way in establishing the vibraphone as a major solo instrument in jazz. He possesses one of the fastest techniques I have ever seen on the vibes. During a 1987 appearance in Antibes, France, the members of the Paris Reunion Band and I (Johnny Griffin, tenor sax; Nathan Davis, tenor sax; Woody Shaw, trumpet; Dizzy Reece, trumpet; Slide Hampton, trombone; Kenny Drew, piano; Jimmy Woode, bass; and Billy Brooks, drums) were approached and asked if we would accompany Lionel Hampton for his set at the festival. We agreed and immediately set up a rehearsal so that we could learn his tunes. To our amazement, in addition to playing his old classics like "Flying Home" and "Air Mail Special", Hamp wanted to play John Coltrane's "Giant Steps" and "Moments Notice"—and he played them as if they were his own compositions.

As a master of his instrument, the vibraphone, Lionel Hampton is very underrated. In addition to an incredible technique, he is abundant in ideas. Perhaps his ability to entertain an audience with such flair and showmanship, as demonstrated on such tunes as "Hey-ba-ba-re-bop" and "Flying Home", has overshadowed his real talent in the eyes of the more serious critics. Throughout the years Lionel Hampton has remained a positive force in Jazz and has served as a role model for community socially-minded people all over the world.

CHAPTER 10

Bebop

Profile

CHARLIE "BIRD" PARKER • If there is one genius in the history of jazz, it is Charlie Parker (1921–55) (Parker's date of birth has been listed as August 29, 1920. However, in an interview with Parker's brother, John A. Parker, I learned that Parker was actually born on August 29, 1921.) "Bird," as he was known to his fellow musicians, had both a positive and negative influence on young musicians during the Bebop Period. Bird was a positive influence because he set musical examples that were almost impossible to attain. On the other hand, his habitual use of narcotics was one of the most detrimental influences on young musicians in the history of jazz. Bird was introduced to narcotics by a friend when he was fifteen, and he continued using drugs off and on until his death on March 12, 1955. The question of whether Parker was a genius has been the subject of many discussions at seminars and jazz clinics throughout the world. The answer lies in one's definitions of a genius. If a genius is, as Howard H. Kendler states, a "gifted person," then Charlie Parker was a genius.[1]

Charlie "Bird" Parker, alto saxophonist and composer, set a standard during the bebop era that musicians are still trying to reach. Photo courtesy of Rutgers, the Institute of Jazz Studies.

Kendler also states that:

> *"Geniuses are not only characterized by exceptional intelligence, but by persistence of motive and effort, confidence in their abilities and great strength or force of character. We would expect this because, by definition, a genius is a person who creates something new. As an innovator he would have to be a radical nonconformist in his own field to persist in his unusual way of doing things. Otherwise he would not be a genius."*

Parker qualifies on the grounds that he not only possessed an unusually high IQ,[2] but he was persistent in motive and effort; he created something new.

Parker was not born a genius. While a student at Lincoln High School, he often suffered insults from his fellow musicians because of his inability to "keep up." Finally, Parker joined the band of George Lee for a stint at an Ozark vacation resort. Here, Parker is said to have learned the tools of the trade by "woodshedding" (practicing) eight to ten hours a day. Here, Parker also spent much time memorizing the solos of tenor saxophonist Lester Young. (Young was one of the most influential musicians in the history of jazz. Saxophonists, trumpet players, piano players, and vocalists all tried to imitate his style.)[3] After having mastered the saxophone and music theory, Parker went on to play in the big bands of Jay McShann, Noble Sissle, Earl "Fatha" Hines, Andy Kirk, Billy Eckstine, and others. His photographic memory, tonal memory, and keen sense of rhythm made Parker one of the most exceptional musicians the world has ever known. Musically, he was comfortable in any setting. He recorded with strings, large ensembles, and small combos. His many compositions often showed rare insight.

As a businessman Parker was equally sharp. However, because of his involvement with drugs and inconsistent appearances during his later years, he didn't benefit from this keen sense of business. He composed many of his pieces using the harmonic structure of standard songs. In this way, he proved his musicianship by improvising on the jazz classics, while at the same time collecting royalties on his original melodies. (The copyright law at that time protected the original composer of the melody, not the harmonic scheme.) Thus Parker showed musicians how to be "hip" (to be "hip," a musician had to be able to improvise from the "chosen standards") and how to collect composer's royalties at the same time.

Profile

DIZZY GILLESPIE • One of the most representative musicians of the Bebop Era is John Birks "Dizzy" Gillespie, though of course his talents are not confined to this era. But it was during the Bebop Era of the 1940s that Dizzy developed his musical talents. According to Gillespie, he inherited his talent for music from his father, who was a part-time musician. Dizzy's first instrument was the trombone. He also studied theory and "fooled around" with a few other instruments at an early age.

His first jazz influence was jazz trumpeter Roy Eldridge. Like other musicians of his day, Gillespie began imitating the style of his musical idol. His early career included stints with the bands of Frank Fairfax, Cab Calloway, Earl "Fatha" Hines, and Billy Eckstine's big band. According to the musicians who worked with the Eckstine big band, Gillespie was the actual musical director and shaped the band's concept. As a major innovator, Gillespie is often viewed as having contributed to the development of Bebop as a partner of alto saxophonist Charlie Parker. While Parker was indeed a genius, and rightfully considered the most important influence at that time, many critics and historians have underplayed Gillespie's contributions. Because of his showmanship on and off stage, some jazz purists failed to recognize his talent. But carefully listening to Gillespie will confirm his greatness. Both he and Parker were original and explorative in their approach to harmony and rhythm. Both were masters of their instruments. A thorough listen to Gillespie's "Woody 'n' You" (RCA-Victor LPV530) shows he was and still is a master trumpeter and improviser. Numerous other recordings not only highlight his trumpet playing but confirm his brilliance as a composer/arranger. One attribute that places Dizzy ahead of many of his contemporaries is his thorough knowledge of chords and various exotic scales. Musicians like Dizzy, who travel to various foreign countries and incorporate the music they encounter, are our "first-line" ethnomusicologists and musicologists. Their contributions and insights into the music of other cultures enable us to explore new horizons of sound.

Another contribution of Gillespie's that is often overlooked is his style of singing. Gillespie was one of the most original scat singers in jazz. He sang the way he played, using both long and short interweaving, chromatic phrases. One of the best forms of training for a musician is to sing the phrases he or she is attempting to play. Gillespie's style of scat singing has influenced a host

Dizzy Gillespie performs with his curved trumpet. The 'High Priest of Bop' was so popular that he was actually drafted to run for President of the United States. Dizzy for President signs were seen all across the country.

of other Bebop or scat singers such as Eddie Jefferson, Joe Carroll, and King Pleasure (Clarence Beeks). Over the years, a number of groups have borrowed from Gillespie's trumpet playing and singing, such as The Double Six of Paris, Lambert, Hendricks and Ross, and The Manhattan Transfer. When all is said and done, history will record Dizzy Gillespie as one of the most important musicians not only in jazz, but of the twentieth century.

Bebop was the name given to the music played in and around New York during the early 1940s. As mentioned earlier, bebop started as a quiet revolution in the big bands of the late 1930s. One of the most important of these bands was that of Earl "Fatha" Hines (piano).

The name *Bebop*, according to drummer Max Roach, came from the sound musicians heard in the music as they played. As an example of this, take Kenny Clarke's nickname, "Klook-a-mop." Most of the time I spent in Paris was as a member of Kenny Clarke's quintet. Each night, I found myself listening to the various sounds "within" the music. If you listen to the sound between Kenny's sock cymbal and ride cymbal, the "klook-a-mop" becomes loud and clear. The "sound" theory seems the most readily accepted by jazz musicians, but some jazz historians have claimed that the term *Bebop* derives from the word "arriba," which is Spanish for "up."[4] While it is true that during the 1940s there was a considerable amount of Spanish influence in jazz, the theory that the term *Bebop* was taken from the sound heard within the music seems more likely.

Now that we've established the origins of the name Bebop, let's examine the many theories of this music's origins. First of all, Bebop did not develop only in New York. In an interview with Dizzy Gillespie, I learned that long before they began to perform and record together in New York, he and Charlie Parker had freely improvised and experimented with various chords in Kansas City—though no one was present to declare them the innovators of the new jazz. According to drummer Kenny Clarke, after a year-long tour with Teddy Hill's band, Hill decided to stop touring, taking advantage of an offer to manage a club, Minton's Playhouse, recently acquired by ex-bandleader Henry Minton. Clarke was Hill's first choice as house band. The idea appealed to Clarke because it meant less traveling and a chance to work in New York. As Clarke stated, "Everything was cool because Teddy didn't interfere with my choice of musicians or the type of music

Vocalist Ella Fitzgerald is considered by most critics and historians to be the greatest jazz vocalist of all time. Her fluid, innovative, and improvisational style of scatting is both unique and original.

we played." According to Ira Gitler in his book *Jazz Masters of the Forties*, Clarke's lineup was as follows: Joe Guy (trumpet), Thelonious Monk (piano), Nick Fenton (bass), and Clarke (drums). The impact of these four musicians cannot be overestimated. Nor can we simplify the origins of Bebop by saying that the entire movement started at Minton's Playhouse. The fact is that Teddy Hill, a former bandleader, hired one of his former sidemen, Kenny Clarke, as the house band at Minton's. Both Henry Minton and Teddy Hill were musicians and ex-bandleaders, and because of this they didn't interfere with the experimentation of these musicians.

In New York, Minton's became the place to hear good jazz. Jazz musicians like Dizzy Gillespie (trumpet), Charlie Christian (guitar), and Milton Hinton (bass) would join forces with already established names like Roy Eldridge (trumpet), Mary Lou Williams (piano), Lester Young (tenor sax), Jimmy Blanton (bass), Don Byas (tenor sax) and many others. As a result of the sessions becoming overcroweded and boring because of "unqualified musicians" taking long, uninteresting solos, Clarke, Monk, Gillespie, and others would work out intricate chord substitutions designed to discourage the "beginners." The music was often so foreign that the potential improviser got into trouble. (I was fortunate enough to have grown up in an environment where this kind of "musical chess game" was still being played. There is nothing quite as embarrassing as finding yourself "out there" in the middle of a familiar song and suddenly feeling the bottom fall out of your musical story.) The musicians were constantly testing each other's abilities. Tempos were increased to unbelievable speeds. Original keys were replaced by a modulation of a half step or more. Substitute harmonies were used to give the song "character." After having read about these tricks, one might accuse the young boppers of being malicious.

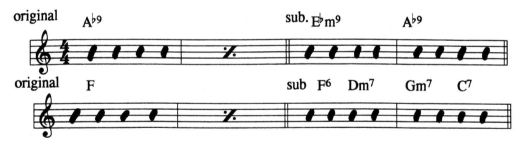

Example 18

Experimentation in jazz raises the question of criticism. Critics and the media were quick to put down the new music of the 1940s. Many of the jazz critics who had previously chastised Bebop found themselves in an uncomfortable position after bop had proven itself as a major force in music. We must consider that Bebop was a concept so completely foreign, compared to the music of the past, that not even all the professionals supported it, and critics often are guided by the opinion of current professionals. Both Roy Eldridge and Louis Armstrong, two of the top jazz musicians of the period, stated in public their disapproval of Bebop. The critics naturally felt safe in following their lead.

When I made my first recordings in Europe for Saba Records (German label), I was bombarded by a number of critics who had come to the Blue Note Club in

Paris where I was working to get my opinion about the music of the 1960s. Most of them wanted to know what I thought of Albert Ayler (tenor sax), Archie Shepp (tenor sax), and other avant-garde saxophonists. My fellow musicians advised me not to answer these questions but to let the critics figure it out for themselves "since they were being paid for it." The critics were looking for some kind of support before committing themselves to the new music. The same was true during the beginning of Bebop. Many critics looked for approval from musicians before supporting a new music. The critic indeed has a tremendous responsibility. Now that I find myself in the role of both professional jazz musician and music scholar, I wonder just how I might have re-

Master drummer, historian, and composer Max Roach is one of the most important innovators in the history of jazz.

acted to Bebop. Musicians were searching for new methods. There were no ground rules. The best thing the critics could have done was to wait before making a final evaluation of the music. And they should have supported the experimentation.

The Philosophical and Sociological Implications of Bebop

That Bebop was a revolutionary music is an accepted fact by most historians and critics, but the extent to which if affected society and the musicians who played it has not been fully explored.

First of all, most of the musicians who performed Bebop were out to prove a point. They wanted respect as artists, not as entertainers. Artists were thought to be more sincere about their art. Artists studied, practiced, planned, and cultivated their art form until they had reached a high degree of proficiency. On the other hand, the entertainer's goal was merely to entertain. To refute the minstrel image of 1940, many of the bebop musicians refused to acknowledge applause, refused to announce the name of compositions, refused to acknowledge requests, and so on. Intellectualism was the fashion. Many musicians wore "Bebop glasses" (sometimes only frames without lenses) because they thought eyeglasses made them look more intelligent. The Bebop tam (the brimless French beret) was adopted by musicians who had traveled to France and other European countries. The tam was a symbol of freedom, the freedom many of the musicians had experienced in Europe. Some of the musicians adopted the Moslem religion (not to be confused with the Nation of Islam, otherwise known as the Black Muslims). This was a symbol of religious freedom. Intellectualism and artistic freedom were the immediate aims of the new artist. As the period progressed and the musicians perfected their new art form, the public began to accept the music. Anybody who wanted to be "cool" dressed, talked, and acted like the jazz musicians. They were the new leaders of the "hip," the new intellectual gurus of the cultural revolution of the 1940s. Bebop is considered by most critics, historians, and practitioners one of the most complicated and artistically stimulating periods in the history of jazz.

To understand the period, we must closely examine the various musical components that make up the music. First, the melody in bebop was constructed of short rhythmical phrases with lots of syncopation.

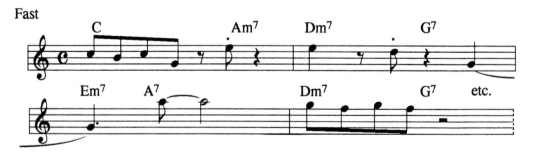

Example 19

Many of the phrases were built around chromatic runs—the actual notes appearing to be unrelated to the tonality implied by the harmonic symbols. Long melodic phrases with difficult sequences made it more difficult for the untrained musician even to play the melody. Musicians often found themselves "going to the woodshed" (that is "practicing") to be able to play the melody. If a musician could remember the sometimes long, complicated melodic lines and then improvise on the difficult harmonic sequences, he was ready.

Example 20

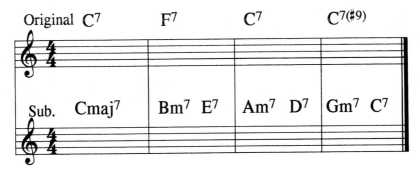

Example 21

Profile

KENNY CLARKE • Born in Pittsburgh, Pennsylvania January 2, 1914, died in Paris (Montreuil-sous-Bois) January 25, 1985.

According to Ursula Davis in her book *Paris without Regret*, the actual date of birth for Kenny Clarke was January 2, 1914 and not January 9th as some biographers have recorded. "Kenny Spearman Clarke, alias Liaquat Ali Salaam, better known as 'Kenny' or 'Klook', was born in Pittsburgh. Since his birth was never officially recorded, most sources quote his date of birth as January 9,

Jazz legend drummer Kenny Clarke returned home to Pittsburgh to participate in the University of Pittsburgh Jazz Seminar and to receive the key to the city from Mayor Richard Caliguiri. Photo by R. Szoszorek.

1914. His actual birthdate, however, was January 2 of that year." (*Paris without Regret*, University of Iowa Press and Tomorrow International Press, 2nd edition.)

Kenny Clarke's contribution to Jazz, and especially to Jazz drummings, is undeniable. One of the advantages that I have in writing about Kenny Clarke is the fact that I actually played with "Klook" night after night, primarily in Paris but also all over Europe and Africa. During the eight years we played together in the 1960s, we discussed everything from religion to politics to music. Kenny personally told me that he was born on the 2nd of January and not the 9th. He also took great pleasure in showing me his passport where his race was listed as "White". He seemed to derive pleasure from pointing out how stupid it was to list the race of a person on the official document from one's government.

Ironically, Kenny first started his career as a musician on the trombone. According to Kenny, he and his brother Chuck were always competing with each other. "Chuck started playing music first, so naturally I wanted to do the same." Kenny only began playing drums when a friend who was the drummer in a local Pittsburgh club told him, "If you want to play these drums, you can have them." The drummer's wife, who was extremely jealous of his staying out late at night playing gigs, gave him the ultimatum of quitting the gig or moving out. Kenny, who had been filling in on the drums occasionally to cover for the adventurous drummer, gladly accepted—thus beginning his career as one of the most important drummers in the history of jazz.

Kenny is credited with changing the concept of the way drums were played in jazz. He introduced the technique of "dropping bombs"—the playing of heavy accents on the bass drum at various places within the measure. According to Kenny, "I would hit the bass drums harder at certain places in the measure so that it would be easier for the musicians to hear the beat and know where they were whenever we would play those fast flag wavers." ("Flag wavers" refers to fast show tunes designed to showcase the band or a feature act.) Kenny is also credited with changing the keeping of time—keeping the main beat by playing a steady rhythm—from the sock cymbal to the large "crash" cymbal. The crash cymbal had previously been used as a way of focusing attention on a particular movement such as a dance step or to announce an act.

Kenny was one of the founding members of the ever-popular M.J.Q., Modern Jazz Quartet. Kenny states, "I went to Dizzy (Gillespie) after one of our concerts and told him that I thought it might be a good idea if we would let the rhythm section play as a small group in-between shows or acts. My thinking was that this would add some variety to our show and would also give us a chance to play some different kinds of tunes." Dizzy agreed. With Kenny in charge, the group began to rehearse special numbers and eventually developed into the original M.J.Q. After leaving Dizzy's big band, "Klook" began working with numerous musicians and developed a reputation as one of the most reliable and "swingingest" drummers in Jazz.

Another milestone in Kenny's career was his collaboration with Belgian arranger-composer Francy Boland. Kenny Clarke's swinging drum rhythms, combined with Boland's innovative arrangements and Italian-born entrepreneur Gi Gi Campi, produced some of the most inspirational big band music of the decade.

Tenor saxophonist James Moody, originator and creator of the now famous composition of "Moody's Mood for Love," is one of the most lyrical and dynamic soloists in jazz. Many critics and historians also consider him to be the best flutist in jazz. Photo by Curt Gustafsson.

During the 1940s, the Bebop Era, Bud Powell established himself as one of the most influential voices on the piano since Art Tatum. Photo courtesy of the Institute of Jazz Studies.

Harmony

The harmonic sequences of many of the so-called standard songs of the day were often changed to make them more interesting.

Thelonious Monk was known for his intricate harmonic progressions. Dizzy Gillespie is one of the most thorough musicians I have ever known, when it comes to analyzing the harmonic structure of a song. Every sequence, cadence and modulation is carefully thought out and mastered before he even attempts to perform the piece. Vibraphonist Milt Jackson once astonished me by sitting down at the piano and explaining the "inside" chords as they related to the Thelonious Monk composition "Around the Midnight." In fact, many of the bebop musicians whom I have worked with seemed almost fanatic about the harmonic make-up of the compositions they played. A good example of the various ways a particular harmonic sequence can be altered is shown in the following interpretation of the blues.

Rhythm

As mentioned earlier, the rhythms in Bebop were unusually difficult because they were extremely syncopated and polyrhythmical.

Example 22

As you can see, the rhythms alone would be enough to discourage the average musician. At this point, I would like to clarify Kenny Clarke's concept of modern drumming. Clarke is said to have revolutionized modern drumming by changing the main emphasis of keeping time from the hi-hat drum to the large, round cymbal. While doing this, he also further developed the concept of dropping "bombs." He would play strong accents on the bass drum with his foot pedals that were designed to emphasize the beat. During my tenure with the Kenny Clarke quintet—Jimmy Gourley (guitar), Michel Gaudry or Gilbert "Bibi" Rovere (bass), Rene Urtreger, Raymond Fol, or Marc Himmler (piano), Kenny Clarke (drums)—I asked Clarke about his use of the ride cymbal and "dropping bombs." He said that he did play strong accents on certain beats to give the other musicians an idea of where the tempo was. Contrary to many reports, he didn't stop using the foot pedal altogether. Clarke was quite concerned that younger musicians had taken his gesture of emphasizing the beat with the foot pedal as a sign that they only had to use the foot pedal when emphasizing the beat. Many drummers think that this kind of drumming without a consistent use of the foot gives a bottomless sound to the rhythm section. According to Clarke, the best method is to use the foot pedal all the time while being conscientious not to cover up the bass line.

Profile

J.J. JOHNSON • J.J. (James Louis) Johnson was born on January 22, 1924 in Indianapolis, Indiana. In the eyes of most jazz musicians, J.J. Johnson dominated the jazz trombone. Regardless of the number of trombonists, whether modern or traditionalist, J.J. always seems to reign as the favorite. His early training as a pianist prepared him for his later love of composition, orchestration, and arranging, and he developed into one of the best. In fact, his writing was revered almost as much as his trombone playing. I remember the first time I met J.J. at a concert in Berlin—Kenny Clarke introduced me to him as one of the greatest trombonists and composers in jazz. In Kenny's own words, "If you think he can play, then you'll love his writing." Benny Carter, with whom J.J. began working in 1942, served as a role model for his writing.

One of the reasons that J.J. single-handedly dominated the trombone from the 1940s until his retirement was that at first many people felt the trombone was not suited for the quick, often difficult, intricate phrasing found in bebop. They were wrong. Just as Dizzy Gillespie would prove that the intricate phrasing of bebop could be played with a big band, J.J. proved that the same thing could be accomplished on the trombone. In the hands of a master like J.J., the

Dr. J.J. Johnson (left) with David Baker, Distinguished Professor of Music and Chairman of the Jazz Department at Indiana University School of Music (right). J.J. received an honorary Doctor of Music degree from Indiana University. Photo courtesy of Lida Baker.

trombone became as sensitive, and capable of playing the same intriguing melodies, as Charlie Parker or Dizzy Gillespie achieved on their instruments. In fact, it was J.J.'s work with Miles Davis, Bud Powell, Dizzy Gillespie, Max Roach, and Kenny Clarke that helped accelerate him to the top of the jazz world. In 1954 J.J. joined forces with Danish trombonist Kai Winding to form one of the most successful duos in jazz. J.J.'s sojourn in Los Angeles as a television and film composer was just as successful as his playing career. He was in demand to write scores for everything from action movies to TV thrillers.

A number of other jazz musicians made their mark during the Bebop Era— among them the famous trumpet saxophone duo of Charlie Parker (alto sax) and Dizzy Gillespie (trumpet). More than any other combo, this duo established the sound of Bebop. The trumpet-saxophone combination was an ideal front line for the small quintet that was so common during the 1940s. There were also a number of big bands involved in the deveopment of Bebop: Earl "Fatha" Hines (piano), Billy Eckstine (vocals), and the incredible big band of Dizzy Gillespie (trumpet) and Woody Herman (clarinet). It was the Hines band, and other similar big bands, that gave birth to the bebop revolution. The Eckstine band provided the momentum, and the Gillespie orchestra proved that the intricate bebop phrases so commonly associated with the small combo could be played with a big band. The members of the Eckstine band made up a who's who in jazz during the Bebop Era. The orchestra included at one time or another Dizzy Gillespie, Fats Navarro, Miles Davis, and Kenny Dorham on trum-

Anita O'Day was one of the most impressive jazz vocalists during the 1950s and had an original style of "scat" singing. Photo courtesy of Hozumi Nakadaira.

Billie "Lady Day" Holiday has the voice that changed the sound of jazz. She influenced vocalists as well as instrumentalists, such as trumpeter Miles Davis and tenor saxophonist Lester Young. Original painting by Carol Genova.

pets; Gene Ammons, Dexter Gordon, and Lucky Thompson on tenor saxes; Charlie Parker on alto sax; Leo Parker on baritone sax; John Malachi on piano; Art Blakey on drums; Tommy Potter on bass; arrangements by Budd Johnson, Tadd Dameron, and Jerry Valentine; vocals by Sarah Vaughn; while Eckstine himself sang and played valve trombone.[5] Although it is impossible to mention all of the musicians who contributed to the bebop movement, a few deserve to be added to the list—among them J.J. Johnson (trombone), Freddy Webster (trumpet), Al Haig (piano), Bud Powell (piano), Oscar Pettiford (bass), James Moody (sax), Dodo Marmarosa (piano), and Hank Jones (piano).

The Bebop movement, in addition to producing the genius of Charlie Parker, Dizzy Gillespie, Kenny Clarke, and Thelonious Monk, produced more innovators than any other period in the history of jazz. The very nature of the music required the ultimate in skill and creativity.

If Charlie Parker was the king of the alto saxophonists, then John Jackson, alto saxophonist, was considered his immediate successor, if not his equal. I have heard solos of Parker and Jackson together on a recording made by the Jay McShann Band on which Jackson proved himself Parker's equal. Both men were also members of the Billy Eckstine Band. In later years, Jackson switched to the tenor sax but did not really find his own on the instrument. Jackson's sweet, almost piercing sound made him a natural lead player. The influence of pianist Bud Powell is still being felt today. Powell was one of those rare pianists who could utilize the left hand when needed, while playing with incredible accuracy and speed with the right hand. His ideas, though classified today as typical bebop, are as modern as ever. His numerous compositions were among the most frequently played during the Bebop Period. Younger pianists like Herbie Hancock, Cedar Walton, Chick Corea, and McCoy Tyner, owe much to Powell's innovative piano stylings of the 1940s.

Often the transitional periods between the various movements are overlooked. One such period is the transition between swing and bebop. Musicians like Oscar Pettiford, Kenny Clarke, Jimmy Blanton, Charlie Christian (one of the first musicians to play the electric guitar), and Don Byas were more than just innovative musicians: they were pioneers. Perhaps the lack of writing on the work of Christian is the result of his having died at an early age. But as a major pioneer of the electric guitar, one of the most used instruments in modern music, he deserves more attention. According to Leonard Feather in *The Book of Jazz*, Eddie Durham is thought to have been the first to introduce the electrically amplified guitar. But regardless of who actually played the instrument first, Christian's style

Jazz legend and tenor saxophonist Dexter Gordon performs at the University of Pittsburgh Annual Jazz Seminar with fellow musicians Woody Shaw and Mike Longo. Gordon was one of the most powerful tenor saxophones in jazz and paved the way for a new generation of young giants, including John Coltrane.

of performing on the instrument is what established the instrument in jazz and pop music. His phrasing and rhythmic concept were far ahead of his time.

Don Byas was one of the greatest tenor saxophonists. His big, powerful sound often intimidated other saxophonists. His melodic ideas were often long and covered the entire range of his instrument. While tenor saxophonist Coleman Hawkins received much credit for his saxophone innovations, Byas seems to have been overlooked. One reason may be that he spent a considerable amount of time traveling and living in Europe. Almost every jazz saxophonist I know will confirm that Byas was one of the first "swing" tenor saxophonists to make the big jump into the then not-so-popular area of bebop. Although most of his time was spent in Europe, Byas did do a number of European recordings that showed his talent as a masterful soloist.

Betty "Bebop" Carter is considered by most critics to be one of the most original vocalists performing in jazz today. Photo by Werner Stiefele.

In speaking about the transitional period between Bebop and swing, any professional jazz musician will attest that Lester (Prez) Young was one of the most influential figures. Not only was Young's style of playing the saxophone important to musicians during the Bebop Period, but many of them copied his style of living. Prez, as he was called, was the most important influence on Charlie Parker. He bridged the gap between swing and bebop and is responsible for what later became known as the "cool sound" in jazz so popular during the 1950s. I once saw Young at a concert in Kansas City with the Count Basie Orchestra. The band was playing a very fast, up-tempo number, and everybody was deeply involved in trying to make the piece happen. As the band played hard and fast, out strolled Young. As he approached the microphone, he eased out one light and almost inaudible sound, in the midst of what seemed like a thousand notes played by the Basie band. Needless to say, the audience went wild. This was typical Lester Young. He was composed and relaxed, but at the same time there was a certain tension that let you know his music was full of energy. His personality was reflected in everything he did both on and off the bandstand.

The incredible, 'divine', Sarah Vaughan was one of the major jazz vocalists of all time, together with Ella Fitzgerald and Carmen McRae. Photo courtesy of Hozumi Nakadaira.

Narcotics and Jazz

Whereas the 1930s was the "age of alcohol," the Bebop Period was the "dope age." (Later during the 1960s, John Coltrane was referred to as the "messiah" when he "cleaned up" the scene. Coltrane's life style as a health fanatic sent, at that time, many of his disciples to the health-food store.) Ever since jazz's early association with New Orleans, jazz musicians have been linked with immorality. If it wasn't alcohol, gambling, or prostitution, it was narcotics. In my opinion, musicians have been victimized by society. With the help of law enforcement officers and the media, jazz musicians have often been singled out as the number one users of hard drugs in the United States. The problem reached such proportions in the early 1950s that a survey was conducted on the use of hard drugs in the United States. Much to everyone's surprise, jazz musicians placed extremely low on the list. Suburban housewives, medical doctors, lawyers, and other professional people ranked fairly high. However, the number of drug arrests among young professionals was considerably less than among musicians. Even in recent years, the number of arrests involving entertainers accused of using drugs has increased.

One reason for the arrests of jazz musicians during the 1940s was that many law enforcement officers, in response to political pressure, sought to arrest those whose arrests would generate publicity. Jazz musicians were famous enough to ensure front-page headlines. Take, for example, Charlie Parker and his many drug-related arrests. Parker was a known addict. At any time an arresting officer could be sure that Parker was in possession of drugs. The agent only had to be at the right place at the right time. In the United States, as in some other countries, crimes are punished not according to the injustice done to society, but according to the social or economic status of the criminal. This has been the hidden factor in the unjustified incarceration of many jazz musicians. The drug user who has enough money to support his or her habit is more likely to escape a drug-related arrest than someone who is poor—such as a jobless jazz musician.

"It might come as a surprise to some that during the Bebop Period a number of symphony conductors and classical musicians were users of 'hard' drugs, especially cocaine. They, however, were not in society's eyes 'musical outlaws.' They maintained the society's values. Their reward from society was immunity for their transgressions. One conductor, who shall remain anonymous, could not, for reasons that later became clear, begin his Sunday afternoon concert at Tanglewood. Just before the concert, he dropped into the greenroom, head bowed, a look of agony on his face. The general manager seemed furious at the delay and intent on hiding the spectacle from general view. A few minutes later an expensive car sped from the main entrance to the stage door. Out came a dignified looking man carrying a little black bag, the type doctors use. He immediately went to the greenroom. In a few seconds out came the maestro, this time smiling and full of zest. The concert went splendidly, the conductor's arms thrashing wildly as he beat the tempo up to a frenzy. We in the orchestra knew that he had gotten his 'fix.'"[6]

This and other similar incidents are, for obvious reasons, kept from the general public. I am not advocating that society also cover up the illegal actions of jazz artists, but society should treat its artists and citizens equally. Jazz musicians or any other artists should not be prejudged because they perform a different kind of music than those who control society.

Can drugs help the artist reach higher spiritual levels? Many young artists seem to think that older musicians and artists used drugs to expand their art. Nothing could be further from the truth. I grew up in an era when taking drugs was the thing to do if you wanted to be accepted by your fellow musicians. I have seen many exceptionally talented musicians fall from stardom to obscurity because of their involvement with drugs. The only sure way to greatness is through practice and hard work. If an artist is creative, he or she will be twice as creative without drugs.

Progressive Jazz: The Industry's Answer to the Decline of Bebop

Progressive jazz was the music industry's answer to a decline in record sales during the Bebop Period. Many of the leading jazz musicians were drafted into the military. Sales declined partly because most people felt Bebop was too difficult. Shabby treatment of jazz fans by the musicians caused bebop to lose its popularity. The United States government also attempted to stop the production of recordings so that the materials from which records were made could be rechanneled into war-related products. I have personally seen photographs of U.S. servicemen destroying records that were a part of the A.F.N.'s (Armed Forces Network) daily programming.

The larger record companies concentrated on the music of Stan Kenton (piano-composer), Boyd Raeburn (saxophonist-composer) and Claude Thornhill (piano-composer). These bands combined the big band instrumentation of the 1940s with a highly theoretical compositional technique to create a new style during the mid 1940s. Kenton's was by far the most successful of the big bands representing the progressive period. Some of his most impressive work during this period concentrated on sound featuring a large, polished brass section. Kenton also introduced a number of outstanding soloists to the jazz scene.

Profile

STAN KENTON • Stan Kenton was born Stanley Newcomb in Wichita, Kansas on December 15, 1911 and died in Los Angeles on August 25, 1979. Kenton started his career as a dance band leader and pianist in Southern California. According to Jazz historian Leonard Feather in *The Encyclopedia of Jazz*, Kenton's first band included Chico Alvarez, trumpet; Red Dorris, tenor sax and vocals; Bob Gioga, baritone sax; and Howard Rumsey, bass. Their recording, "Artistry in Rhythm" in 1943 for Capitol records, was the beginning of the band's success. But it was Kenton's eventual shift to an all-jazz format and the addition of trumpeter and arranger Pete Rugolo to the band that placed it in the middle of the jazz popularity scene. Rugolo, who was classically trained as a composer, combined his earlier experience as a dance band-jazz pianist and his more academic training as a classical composer to help Kenton in shaping the band's stule. During this time the Kenton style focused mainly on a strong brass sound with occasional emphasis on the reed.

Many of the band's early recordings centered around vocalists (Anita O'Day, Gene Howard, June Christy, and Ann Richards). Kenton's various big bands were instrumental as a launching point for many historical figures in jazz. In this regard, Kenton established himself in the same elite group of band leaders as Duke Ellington, Count Basie, and Woody Herman. Among the great artists who passed through the Kenton band were Art Pepper (alto sax), Lee Konitz (alto sax), Stan Getz (tenor sax), John Haley "Zoot" Sims (tenor sax),

Park "Pepper" Adams (baritone sax), Vido Musso (tenor sax), Maynard Ferguson (trumpet), Kai Winding (trombone), Frank Rosolino (trombone), Shelly Manne (drums), Edward "Eddie" Safranski (bass), David Baker (trombone), Candido Camero (latin percussion), and Laurido Almeida (guitar). In past years, Stan Kenton has suffered from a reputation for being against the inclusion of African American musicians in his bands, but history proves this to be incorrect. Kenton did in fact include African Americans in his bands at various periods. Among this group were Willie Smith (alto sax), Curtis Counce (bass), Lucky Thompson (tenor/baritone sax), and David Baker (trombone).

During the late 1950s Kenton shifted his attention towards launching a number of summer jazz camps, in cooperation with the National Stage Band Camps. He was one of the first active big band leaders to do so.

Eventually Kenton focused his attention on the Los Angeles Neophonic Orchestra. This group served as a platform for the introduction of more adventurous works. He often experimented with the marriage of classical sounds and jazz.

Generally speaking, the Progressive Jazz Period concentrated on big band sound, but there were also some small combo efforts by Billy Bauer (guitar), Pete Rugolo (trumpet-arranger), Jimmy Raney (guitar), and Johnny Smith (guitar). This period also produced a number of instructional materials explaining the nature of the music. The word "progressive" suggested a search for intellectualism in jazz. Unfortunately, the jazz public did not respond to the idea, so the recording companies began to search for a new, more appealing package.

Without doubt, Kenton was the leader of the Progressive Jazz Period. Kenton's concentration of sound clusters (especially in the brass) distinguished his music. As a leader Kenton attracted some of the most gifted artists of that period, including arranger Pete Rugolo, drummer Shelly Manne, tenor saxophonists Vido Musso, Zoot Sims, and Richie Kumuca, alto saxophonist Lee Konitz, trombonists Frank Rosolino and Kai Winding, and vocalist June Christy.

Later Kenton became one of the first successful jazz musicians to devote a considerable amount of time to jazz education at United States colleges and universities when he launched the Stan Kenton clinics.

Clarke Terry at the University of Pittsburgh Jazz Seminar playing both the trumpet and flugelhorn simultaneously. He has proven to be one of the most influential and innovative forces in jazz, having impacted numerous jazz giants such as Miles Davis, Wynton Marsalis, and Wallace Roney. Clarke has recently joined the ranks of jazz artists who combine a career as performer and scholar and has a university music institute established in his name with him as its director.

Conclusion

Bebop was perhaps the most innovative form of jazz ever. Many of its practitioners not only developed into top-rate artists during the Bebop Period but contributed to the music of later periods. Musicians like Kenny Clarke, J.J. Johnson, Al Haig, Billy Taylor, Phil Woods, Charlie Parker, Ray Brown, Dizzy Gillespie, Tadd Dameron, and Max Roach were at home not only in bebop, but in cool, third steam, and even European classical music. Parker did a number of recordings featuring strings and rhythm sections. During his later years, Parker was said to have favored the use of a classical string ensemble and jazz rhythm section as his permanent group.

Although Bebop started as a revolutionary music during the 1940s, it continued well into the 1950s. Its influence was so powerful that even today elements of bebop phrases are heard in the recordings of many younger players like Joe Henderson, Herbie Hancock, Freddie Hubbard, Chick Corea, and others. Without a doubt, bebop is still alive and going strong.

Minton's Playhouse was the meeting place for the younger, experimental musicians of the 1940s. Jam sessions went on well into the early hours of the morning. The more established musicians employed various tricks like changing the rhythm of a tune, or altering the harmonic structure of a composition to test the abilities of the unproven younger musicians.

Unfortunately, many more musicians began using drugs during the Bebop Period, and it became the jazz period most associated with drugs. Drug use during the Bebop Period, however, was overemphasized because jazz musicians were easy prey for overzealous drug agents seeking headlines and promotions.

As a sociological phenomenon, Bebop reflected the discontentment of young musicians who could no longer accept the social and musical values of the previous generation. They revolted in every way possible. Established artists were pitted against younger colleagues. The younger musicians fought back and eventually won the right to present their music to a musically-conscious audience. As a result, the new jazz musicians were no longer regarded as entertainers but as artists. In many ways, bebop gave dignity to all musicians. One might even say that the young Bebop rebels trained the audiences of their day. Progressive jazz centered around the sound of big band brass and western European compositional techniques. Large ensembles like those of Stan Kenton, Boyd Raeburn, Eddie Sauter,

Tenor saxophonist, arranger, and composer Jimmy Heath, "Lil' Bird," is one of the most respected and innovative forces in jazz. A professor at Queens College, NY, he joins the ever-growing number of performers who teach at major universities. Photo by Saul Mephisto, Paris.

Bill Finegan, and others, launched what was later labeled a forerunner of third stream jazz. Although the music was not as intellectual as third stream, it did concentrate more on compositional styles than had previous periods such as Bebop and Swing. The Progressive Jazz Period was short, dying mainly because it did not provide enough challenge to the individual soloists and did not appeal to the general audience.

Suggested Readings and Listening

Books

Berendt, Joachim. *The Jazz Book.* New York: Lawrence Hill, 1975.

Esquire's World of Jazz. New York: Thomas Y. Crowell, 1975.

Feather, Leonard. *The Book of Jazz.* New York: World Publishing Co., Meridian Books, 1959.

Gitler, Ira. *Jazz Masters of the Forties.* New York: McMillan, Co., 1966.

Records

Gillespie, Dizzy. *Groovin High* (Savoy MG 12020)

Parker, Charlie. *Bird* (Savoy SJL2201, 1107)

Powell, Bud. *Bud Powell Trio* (Roost LP2224)

Johnson, J.J. *The Eminent* (Blue Note BST.81505.6)

CHAPTER 11

Cool and Third Stream

Profile

MILES DAVIS • Alto saxophonist Charlie Parker may have been the most influential jazz musician of all time, but trumpeter Miles "Dewey" Davis is one of the most popular trumpet players in jazz.

Miles Davis was born May 25, 1926, in Alton, Illinois. His first professional job was with Eddie Randall's Blue Devils Band.[1] But he came to national attention in the 1940s as a sideman in the band of alto saxophonist Charlie Parker. It was Davis' period as a sideman with the legendary Parker that gave him the opportunity to develop both musically and socially. Socially, Davis was an inexperienced "kid" when he first joined Parker in the 1940s. His playing, though melodic, showed him to be a young, inexperienced improviser. However, one must consider that playing in the shadow of a musical giant like Charlie Parker would intimidate anyone.

The true test of any art form is the test of time. If it is valid, it will survive. Davis' music has. He developed into a first-class soloist during the mid-forties, and later became the major musician of the 1950s Cool Period. I once talked

Trumpeter Miles Davis with his penetrating, haunting, mellow trumpet sound is credited with launching the cool jazz era of the 1950s. Photo courtesy of Hozumi Nakadaira.

to tenor saxophonist Joe Henderson about his brief stay with Miles Davis' band. Henderson told me that Davis always wanted to be a big band leader. It was the lure of "fronting" a big band that Capitol Records used in getting Davis to lead the studio recording of *Birth of the Cool*. These series of recordings established Davis as a first-rate leader and soloist. His all-star sidemen, including such major talents as saxophonist Gerry Mulligan and Lee Konitz, captured what was known as the "cool sound."

During the early 1950s, Davis was often criticized for his light, vibrato-less sound. His answer was that his sound was what he heard in his "inner ear" and as long as it fit with what he was playing that was all that was necessary. As the leader of various size groups, octets, nonets, and so on, during the 1950s Cool Period, Davis experimented with sounds rarely heard in the new jazz of the 1940s and 1950s. The French horn and tuba gave an added dimension to Davis' sound. During the mid 1950s, Davis' playing moved in yet another direction. His group, which consisted of Philly Joe Jones (drums), Red Garland (piano), Paul Chambers (bass), and John Coltrane, forced Davis to play in a more hard-driving blues style, leaving the cooler, brooding approach for the slower ballads. It was also during this period that Davis took the leadership in establishing what he called the "modal" school of jazz.

One of Davis' most important attributes is his ability to survive change. There are but a handful of musicians who not only participate in various periods of jazz (bebop, cool, hard bop, avant-garde of the 1960s, fusion, etc.) but emerge as trend setters. Davis is one of these musicians. During the Bebop Period, Davis, the small town "kid," was completely dominated by the powerful Charlie Parker. In the 1950s, Davis was a more sophisticated, self-assured leader who was laid back, but at the same time let everyone know that he was in charge. As a more dominant figure during the late fifties, Davis and his group laid out the musical "ground rules" and introduced what was to follow in the 1960s—modal jazz.

During the 1960s free jazz period, Davis waited patiently while many of his colleagues cursed the efforts of younger, free players. After careful observation, Davis, with a group of young, energetic, well-schooled musicians, produced an LP entitled *ESP* which somehow gave notice that it was all right to play free. This group included Wayne Shorter (tenor sax), Herbie Hancock (piano), Ron Carter (bass), and Tony Williams (drums). This recording, along with earlier collaborations with composer-arranger Gil Evans, produced some of the best music Davis ever recorded.

Davis' popularity grew even more when he recorded *Bitches Brew*. The recording sessions for *Bitches Brew* included some of the most promising young musicians in jazz and gave birth to a number of new groups that later became trend setters themselves. The artists on these sessions included Wayne Shorter (tenor and soprano sax), Bennie Maupin (bass clarinet), Chick Corea (piano), Larry Young and Joe Zawinul (keyboards), John McLaughlin (electric guitar), Dave Holland (bass), Harvey Brooks (fender bass), Lenny White, Jack DeJohnette and Charles Alias (drums), and Jim Riley (percussion).[2] Out of this recording group, assembled by Davis, were born such groups as Weather Report, Herbie Hancock's Head Hunters, John McLaughlin's Mahavishnu Orchestra, and Chick Corea's Return to Forever. After *Bitches Brew*, Davis appeared to take things at a slower pace, recording and playing sporadically. Davis' self-imposed exile from music and society during the late 1970s left a void in the music community. There were rumors of death and bar fights.

Any mention of Davis led to hopes and expectations that Miles Davis, the "guru" of the jazz world, would once again return to the music scene. Davis's return to live performance accompanied by the release of a new LP, *Man With a Horn*, and his marriage to actress Cecily Tyson, gave the jazz world renewed hope that Davis had indeed returned to lead the music world to even greater heights.

The cool school was "officially" launched with the 1949 Capitol recording by Miles Davis entitled *Birth of the Cool*. Although the cool school was geographically centered on the West Coast, mainly in Los Angeles, many of its practitioners were actually from the East Coast. Shorty Rogers (trumpet), Gerry Mulligan (baritone sax), Lee Konitz (alto sax), Russ Freeman (piano), and so on. Many of the musicians associated with the cool school came west to do studio work and to work as arrangers in the booming motion picture industry. Bassist Red Mitchell once told me that he averaged somewhere in the six figures annually from his work recording motion picture background sound tracks.

It is easy to understand why the West Coast recording studios became the headquarters for most of the recordings being done on the West Coast. Established jazz musicians with big names had begun to demand enormous sums for their talents, and rightfully so. The record companies were more interested in a good marketable product than in the individual musician's artistic efforts. It was possible to use studio jazz musicians in place of the professional free-lance jazz soloist and more profitable for the recording producer. Increasingly, scientific marketing and the combined efforts of distributing companies made the job of selling an unknown artist an easy task for the professional promoters. Talent and individual creativity were no longer the major concern of the large record conglomerates. Studio jazz had come of age. The old days of bands, like Count Basie's or Woody Herman's, going on the road to learn the new book before going into the recording studio were over. "Instant jazz" was the name of the game.

Some critics of the cool school have described the Cool Period as predominantly white. Many Hollywood studios segregated against black musicians during the early 1950s. Whether or not they segregated against black musicians solely because of race has been debated by musicians, both black and white. Most of the jazz recording during this period was done in the same studios that produced background music for the movie industry. In many cases, the producers of jazz recordings used those same musicians who recorded motion picture sound tracks. Some studios claimed that they used the best musicians and that the segregation was based on whether a musician could read or double on an instrument.

In addition to the segregation by the studios, contractors (the musicians who hire the other musicians for the recording date) also obviously determined who was called for sessions. Here we find a different kind of segregation at work. In many instances, musicians were hired because they were socially acquainted with the contractors or producers. The fact that white and black musicians traveled in different social circles made it difficult for the contractors to meet those black musicians who were qualified to work.

Musical expression and sound often played a role in whether or not a particular musician was hired. In the 1970s, the "soul" sound was very popular and was therefore courted by the record producers. But what about during the 1950s, when the soul sound was not the most sought after? The cool sound was not classified as a soul sound, even though it was tenor saxophonist Lester Young who started this way of playing. This is further proof that the popularization of a particular style of musical concept does not necessarily follow racial lines. In the long run, people tend to buy what they like, regardless of racial associations.

The omission of so many talented black musicians from the recording scene on the West Coast during the 1950s, prompts me to recognize another school of West Coast musicians active during the Cool Period—the "hard school within the cool school." This school consisted of musicians of the bebop and hard bop schools. Among these musicians were Dexter Gordon (tenor saxophone), Wardell Gray (tenor saxophone), Sonny Criss (alto saxophone), Hampton Hawes (piano), Frank Butler (drums), and Joe Gordon (trumpet). These musicians rarely worked in the studios and often found it extremely difficult to earn a living from playing jazz.

It is important to remember that the term "hard school" was not an official label given to those musicians during the Cool Period. I have so named this school because these musicians were actually "hard" players. Most of them in fact were bebop players from the 1940s.

Not all of these hard players were neglected by the industry. Some were drafted into the armed forces; others were not qualified, and some did not confine themselves to studio work.

Flutist Herbie Mann, one of the most creative soloists in jazz, is credited with being the first jazz musician to adopt the flute as his primary instrument. Photo by Clyde Hare.

The cool school has often been described as the least innovative period in the course of jazz. Most critics agree that no earthshaking developments took place during this period. The main objective of the players was to be relaxed, cool, and reserved. Musicians were interested in producing a pure, unemotional, steel-like sonority on their instruments. Lester Young (tenor saxophone), who had produced a pure vibratoless sound during the late 1920s and early 1930s, became the new role model. Regardless of the instruments they played, musicians tried to imitate his sound. This is ironic since Young was greatly influenced by "Lady Day" (Billie Holiday), and everyone knows that she was very emotionally involved in her singing. The almost pure sonority of jazz, especially that of the saxophone during the Cool Period, was very closely linked to the pure sound used by classical musicians. In fact, certain European classical saxophonists thought about adopting the pure sound of the cool saxophone as the "legitimate" sound for saxophone. However, this did not work out, so classical saxophonists continued using the sharp-edged sound of Marcel Mule and Sigurd Rascher as their model.

During the Cool Period, a common size group was the semi-big band, similar to the chamber group. The Cool Period was a composer's period, and composers such as Gerry Mulligan, Shorty Rogers, and John Lewis used the opportunities to expand their writing. Instruments such as the flute, French horn, and tuba were often added to give a special sound to the music. Some groups sounded almost like a light cocktail chamber orchestra.

Many of the composers during this period looked to the European classics for direction. European composers such as Darius Milhaud, Paul Hindemith, Claude Debussy, and later Oliver Messiaen were often quoted by jazz composers of the 1950s.

The cool school was one of the most popular in the history of jazz. It was successful mainly because the musicians took full advantage of the promotional expertise of the already established motion picture industry. Its popularity extended well into the 1950s. Musicians like British-born George Shearing (piano), Dave Brubeck (piano), Herbie Mann (flute), Bud Shank (reeds), Miles Davis (trumpet), Art Farmer (trumpet), Gerry Mulligan (bartitone sax), Chet Baker (trumpet), Stan Getz (tenor sax), Art Pepper (alto sax), Jimmy Giuffre (reeds), Buddy Collette (reeds), Chico Hamilton (drums), and Lars Gullin (baritone sax) became overnight successes.

Dave Brubeck discovered that by carefully presenting his music in semi-academic fashion he could appeal to the college audience. Shortly after his first successful college date at Oberlin College in Oberlin, Ohio, Brubeck recorded a

The Modern Jazz Quartet. First row: Connie Kay (drums), John Lewis (piano). Second row: Milt "Bags" Jackson (vibes), Percy Heath (bass). The Modern Jazz Quartet (M.J.Q.), one of the most innovative groups in jazz, was first formed from within the rhythm section of Dizzy Gillespie's big band and has been together longer than any other group in jazz. Photo courtesy of Rutgers, the Institute of Jazz Studies.

series of records that appealed to the college and university markets. His success was one of the first major breakthroughs for record companies into the college market since the 1920s. A growing snob appeal accompanied the new interest in jazz on the college campus. This proved an obstacle for the musicians. During the 1920s and 30s, jazz was considered a people's music; now it was considered an intellectual music for a smaller, select group. As this group became smaller and as the jazz musicians grew more intellectual, jazz suffered from lack of a sizeable audience.

It is impossible to talk about the cool school without talking about the M.J.Q.—the Modern Jazz Quartet. The M.J.Q. was one of the most consistent groups to gain notoriety during the Cool Period. With John Lewis as its musical director, the group began to explore combining a classical chamber style with true jazz. Although Lewis wrote most of the music, it was the group effort that led the group to its international reputation as one of the most exciting jazz groups of all time. The other members of the group were Percy Heath (bass), Connie Kay (drums), and Milt Jackson (vibes). The contrast between Jackson's "funky" vibes, the "down-home" walking style of bassist Heath, the relaxed brush and cymbal work of Kay, and the compositional piano style of Lewis gave the group its character. (Kenny Clarke was the group's original drummer and co-founder.)

More than any other musician, Miles Davis typified the cool school. The way he walked, his cool, relaxed manner, and self-assurance made him the symbol of what cool was all about. Bebop was "cool" because it projected an intellectualism, but cool gave the impression that nothing mattered. If you didn't like the music, that was okay. Davis became a folk hero. Among jazz musicians and fans he was high priest, with a following equaled only by that of certain spiritual leaders of the 1970s. Every note that he played was revered.

As the cool school became more popular, the music industry began to assume more control over the lives and music of the performers. Advertising firms began influencing the outcome of the major polls. Some of the musicians were even reluctant to talk about their placement in the various critic and popularity polls, for fear of being incorrectly quoted. During an interview with Lee Konitz (alto sax), I sensed his reluctance to talk about winning the polls over saxophonist Charlie Parker. He said that he often wondered just how that could have happened. Obviously he greatly admired Parker. Konitz was, and still is, a great jazz musician, but he must have felt strange being compared to and winning a jazz poll over one of the few undisputed geniuses in jazz history. Alto saxophonist Julian "Cannonball" Adderley was another victim of the same publicity gimmick. During the first year of his recording career, he was constantly being compared to Charlie Parker. Some articles went so far as to hail him as the successor to Parker. Adderley complained about the publicity campaign for his new album, but was told to let the company handle such matters. Cool was an industry controlled period. Those who controlled the business were less concerned with the music than with building the correct image.

Lennie Tristano (piano) has often been identified with both the progressive and cool schools, but actually he was neither. Tristano's highly intellectual approach to playing the piano placed him in the unusual position of being the leader of his own "school." In a way Tristano, and his disciples Lee Konitz (alto sax), Warne Marsh (tenor sax) and Billy Bauer (guitar), set the stage for a more experimental approach.[3]

Third Stream

The term *third stream* was used to describe the combination of West European art music and mainstream jazz that was played during the late 1950s and early 1960s. Composer Gunther Schuller (French horn) is credited with inventing the term. Leonard Feather, in *The Book of Jazz*, states that John Lewis of the Modern Jazz Quartet and Gunther Schuller were "co-founders" of the movement. The music was called "third stream" because there are two mainstreams of music—jazz and classical—and bringing the two together signaled the emergence of a new or third stream. Although earlier attempts (1920s) had been made to bring elements of European classical music together with jazz (by violinists George Morrison, James Reese Europe, and Paul Whiteman), third stream was the first real direct attempt to combine the two musics into a permanent style.

Third stream was a composer's music. The major composers were John Lewis (piano), Bill Smith (clarinet), Gunther Schuller (French horn), Jimmy Giuffre (reeds), George Russell (piano), Gary McFarland (vibes), and Gil Evans (piano). (Evans' work seemed to fit more in the category of cool than third stream.) Their works were performed by such top orchestras as the Stuttgart Symphony Orchestra and Orchestra U.S.A. Many historians outside the area of jazz have confused third stream with other attempts by classical musicians to play jazz. In true third stream, jazz musicians perform within the European art music tradition. In addition, each group usually performs the same precomposed music. A classical

Composer Gunther Schuller examines one of his scores. Schuller first gained international recognition during the late 1950s when he coined the term "Third Stream" to represent the combining of Western European classical music and jazz. © 1994 Jimmy Katz, Giant Steps.

musician simply playing jazz does not produce true third stream. Nor does the jazz musician who attempts to play classical music produce third stream.

Third stream was not very successful financially. The concerts and festivals were usually supported by patrons of the arts. Perhaps the biggest disappointment of the period was that European audiences did not really accept third stream. European jazz fans responded to third stream by saying: 'If it is classical music we would rather hear a good symphony orchestra; and if it is jazz, we would rather hear someone like Louis Armstrong or Duke Ellington.'

Although critics have different opinions of third stream, they do agree that the standard of musicianship during this period was very high. The fact that jazz musicians had to perform with highly-trained symphonic musicians added yet another dimension to jazz. Problems developed because of how each musician interpreted the music. The idea of accenting the off beat of each group

Third Stream Thematic Material

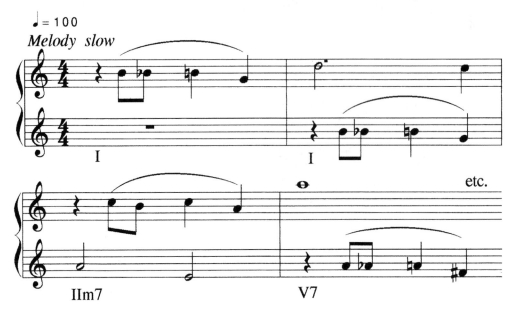

Example 23

of eight notes and the bending of notes presented problems for the symphonic players. On the other hand, intonation and phrasing troubled the jazz musicians.

The third stream period lasted from the late 1950s to the early 1960s. In recent years, there has been renewed interest in this style of music. Young European composers like Krzysztof Kameda and Andre Trazskowski of Poland, Friedrich Gulda of Austria, Elias Gistelinck of Belgium, and the German composer Alexander von Schlippenbach have presented some of the most interesting music along these lines in Europe. In the United States, composers like Don Sebesky, Pat Williams, Bob James, and the German composer Claus Ogerman have all contributed to this field.

Perhaps it could even be said that the laid-back, understated style of Miles Davis and the cool period influenced the highly-intellectualized style of Third Stream. A close examination of the deeply sensitive writing of many of the arranger-composers of the cool era, like John Lewis, Pete Rugolo, Gerry Mulligan,

Trumpeter Chet Baker, considered by most critics, historians, and fans to be one of the most lyrical and creative stylists during the 1950s cool era. Photo by Werner Stiefele.

etc., gives us an indication of what was to come. The same can also be said of the more improvised stylings of pianist Lenny Tristano, and alto saxophonist Lee Konitz. Their highly personalized approach to free improvisation influenced composers as well as instrumentalists.

Because jazz innovations are generally attributed to American artists, European contributors to the field are often neglected. According to Joachim Berendt in *The Jazz Book,* pianist John Lewis was the first person to recognize the importance of European jazz. Berendt attributes Lewis' interest in European jazz to his love for European classical compositional styles. However, it is important to note that in recent years a number of European performers have distinguished themselves on the international scene outside of third stream, notably Jean-Luc Ponty (violin), Gunther Hampel (vibraphone), Fritz Pauer (piano), Dado Maroni (piano), Niels-Henning Orsted Pedersen (bass), Palle Mikkelborg (trumpet), Albert Mangelsdorff (trombone), etc.

Another factor that one must take into consideration when examing the effects and popularity of third stream is that it did not appeal to the tastes of many

Tenor saxophonist Stan Getz, one of the most dynamic tenor saxophone voices during the 1950s cool era, is credited with helping to launch the Bossa Nova wave during the late 1950s–1960s. Photo courtesy of Hozumi Nakadaira.

young jazz fans who related to jazz as an African-American derived dance music. They felt that the "roots" were not there. As I had mentioned earlier, this feeling was in some way similar to that of the Western European jazz purist.

Conclusion

The cool school was basically centered on the West Coast of the United States, mainly in Los Angeles, though many of the musicians involved in this school were actually from the East. Many of them had gone to the West Coast to work in the motion picture industry as studio musicians. Although Lester Young is acknowledged as the "Father of the Cool School," it was the Miles Davis Capitol recording *Birth of the Cool* that announced the beginning of cool.

Discrimination against black American musicians by many studios led to the emergence of a completely different school—the "hard school" within the

Composer Gil Evans, a new voice in jazz orchestration. Photo courtesy of Hozumi Nakadaira.

cool school. These musicians, led by Dexter Gordon, Hampton Hawes, and others, kept the hard sound of the 1940s alive during the Cool Period.

Arrangers-composers like Gerry Mulligan, Shorty Rogers, John Lewis, Dave Brubeck, J.J. Johnson and Gerald Wilson created a new standard for jazz composition during the Cool Period. In addition, the team of Eddie Sauter and Bill Finegan, along with Woody Herman and Stan Kenton, produced one of the most interesting orchestras during the cool movement.

Dave Brubeck made an important move when he began appearing on college campuses throughout the country. Jazz had been popular among college audiences before this, but beginning with Brubeck, colleges and universities grew to be the largest market for jazz in the United States.

The concept of cool featured complete reserve. The hot, straight-ahead playing of the 1940s was replaced by a quieter, softer, relaxed style. Musicians held back the aggressive approach to improvisation that had been so popular during the 1940s. The chamberlike ensembles of the Modern Jazz Quartet, Gerry

Mulligan, Jimmy Guiffre, and George Shearing, were typical of the Cool Period. Another important group sound was Woody Herman's "four brothers" sound. According to Joachim Berendt in *The Jazz Book*, the four brothers sound was actually created by arrangers Gene Roland and Jimmy Giuffre. The sound consisted of four tenor saxophones playing together instead of the usual five saxophones (two alto, two tenor, and one baritone) found in the big bands of the 1950s. According to Berendt, Herman was so impressed that he hired three of the tenors and added one of the greatest baritone saxophonists of all time—Serge Chaloff.

The four brothers sound typified the light, fast-moving phrasing of reed sections during the Cool Period. Many of the big bands of the 1950s began to imitate the sound of Stan Getz, Herbie Steward, Zoot Sims, and Serge Chaloff. Thus, the Herman band became one of the most important big bands of the Cool Period.

Suggested Reading and Listening

Books
Hodeir, Andre. *Jazz: Its Evolution and Essence*. New York: Grove Press, 1956.
Stearns, Marshall. *The Story of Jazz*. New York: Oxford University Press. 1956.

Records
Miles Davis and his Orchestra. *Boplicity*. Smithsonian Collection, #1.
Dexter Gordon Quartet. *Bikini*. Smithsonian Collection, #3.

CHAPTER 12

Hard Bop (Late 1950s)

Profile

ART BLAKEY • Art Blakey was one of the most explosive drummers in the history of Jazz. His driving rhythms and sensitive use of dynamics placed him in a category by himself.

Born in Pittsburgh, PA on October 11, 1919, he grew up performing with local bands and even developed into a fairly accomplished tap dancer. Although he was basically self-taught, he eventually developed into one of the most visible drummers of his era, performing with such artists as Billy Eckstine, Fletcher Henderson, and Mary Lou Williams.

His quest to lead a big band influenced Art's decision to organize a 17-piece big band under the name of the Jazz Messengers. A list of his sidemen reads like a Who's Who in Jazz, and included such luminaries as Clifford Brown, Hank Mobley, Horace Silver, Donald Byrd, Jack McLean, Johnny Griffin, Benny Golson, Wayne Shorter, Bobby Timmons, Curtis Fulton, Nathan Davis, Freddie Hubbard, etc.

Art Blakey died on October 10, 1990 in New York City.

Pittsburgh drummer Art Blakey and his Jazz Messengers became one of the major training grounds for future jazz musicians. Photo by Werner Schifele.

Hard Bop was the East Coast answer to the cool school. The sound was hard, swinging, and very much alive. There was an emphasis on returning to the roots of jazz, the blues. African-American artists like gospel singer Mahalia Jackson and blues singer Ray Charles were the guiding light for the movement. The "over-polished" jazz musician began searching for the roots that during all jazz's transformations, seemed to have disappeared from jazz. Music from the following people signaled a return to the blues: Max Roach (drums), Clifford Brown (trumpet), Clark Terry (trumpet), Sonny Rollins (tenor sax), Horace Silver (piano), Art Blakey (drums), Lee Morgan (trumpet), Oscar Peterson (piano), Carmell Jones (trumpet), Kenny Dorham and Donald Byrd (trumpet), Hank Mobley (tenor sax), Phil Woods (alto sax), Lou Donaldson (alto sax), Pepper Adams (baritone sax), Yusef Lateef (tenor sax), Slide Hampton (trombone), Julian "Cannonball" Adderley (alto sax), Stanley Turrentine (tenor sax), Leo Wright (alto sax), Clifford Jordan (tenor sax), Tommy Flanagan (piano), Johnny Griffin (tenor sax), John Gilmore (tenor sax), George Coleman and Ira Sullivan (tenor sax), James Moody (tenor sax and flute), Jimmy Woode (bass), Kenny Drew (piano), Benny Bailey (trumpet), and Harold Land (tenor sax). Actually the blues had never left jazz; it had only been camouflaged. The small combo was the standard for the hard bop musicians. Even the small piano and organ trios of artists like The Three Sounds and organist Jimmy Smith, played hard and funky. Hard bop was extremely popular and financially rewarding for many musicians. One reason for its success was that people could dance to it. The simple melodies and strong back-beat rhythms provided an excellent rhythm for young dancers. The marriage of Bebop with Rhythm and Blues was a successful one. Everyone prospered—even the musician. One of the most successful small combos during the Hard Bop Period was Art Blakey and the Jazz Messengers. Blakey's Jazz Messengers was a training ground for many of the giants of the 1960s, among them Donald Byrd, Kenny Dorham, Hank Mobley, Horace Silver, Doug Watkins (bass), Lee Morgan, Bill Hardman (trumpet), Johnny Griffin, Benny Golson (tenor sax), Bobby Timmons (piano), Freddie Hubbard (trumpet), and Wayne Shorter (tenor sax).

Hard Bop, like every other period in jazz, produced a cultural language all its own. Terms like "put the pots on," "funky," "cookin'," and "burnin'," showed a return to the emotion of early blues. Funk pianist and composer Bobby Timmons joined the ranks of other "soul" composers with such compositions as "Dis Here" and "Dat Dere." Timmons' "Moanin" and Horace Silver's "Sister Sadie" and "Filthy McNasty" emphasized the return of African-Americanism in jazz.

(To be "nasty" was to be hip.) It was during the late 1950s that the term became synonymous with African-American music. The spirituality of oppression became the main theme of musical expression.

Profile

CLIFFORD (BROWNIE) BROWN • Clifford Brown, trumpeter, was born in Wilmington, Delaware on October 30, 1930 and died in an automobile accident on the Pennsylvania Turnpike on June 26, 1956.

During the 1950s hard bop Clifford Brown was one of the most exciting musicians on the jazz scene. His brisk, crisp, brilliant execution of post-bop musical ideas ignited the musical fire of both the jazz fans and jazz musicians. Not since the advent of Charlie Parker and Dizzy Gillespie had the jazz world been so completely swept off its feet. Musicians and critics alike agreed that "Brownie," as he was affectionately called, was the new prince of jazz. Jazz fans lined up to purchase his records. Musicians waited for his new release, just as they had eagerly awaited Parker's, so that they could know the latest "hip" new jazz "licks."

Clifford's early training as a pianist provided him with a thorough grounding in music theory, and assured him a solid understanding of the proper interrelationships between melody, rhythm, harmony, and structure. A careful examination of Clifford Brown's recorded works reveals a clever musical melange of the styles of Dizzy Gillespie, Fats Navarro, Miles Davis, and Charlie Parker. According to Leonard Feather in the *Encyclopedia of Jazz*, Clifford studied harmony theory, trumpet, piano, vibes, and bass with Robert Lowery in Wilmington. Trumpeter Donald Byrd often referred to the time when he first heard Clifford during a club engagement. Byrd had just completed playing a solo when he heard a "heavenly" burst of "slick" soulful lines. As Brownie continued his exciting flurry of hip new, well-executed ideas, Donald said to himself, "This is the new star." Within the jazz community all over the country, jazz fans and musicians overwhelmingly embraced Clifford as the new Messiah. His undeniable influence can be heard in the later work of trumpeters like Donald Byrd, Lee Morgan, Freddie Hubbard, Randy Brecker, and Woody Shaw. Brown gained early experience in the bands of Art Blakey, Lionel Hampton, and Tadd Dameron.

Trumpeter Clifford Brown was considered by musicians and critics to be the most innovative trumpet soloist since Dizzy Gillespie and Miles Davis. His explosion on the jazz scene during the 1950s created an excitement and renewed interest in jazz. Photo courtesy of the Rutgers Institute of Jazz.

Unfortunately Clifford Brown's career was cut short when he and pianist Richie Powell, the younger brother of jazz pianist Bud Powell, were killed in an automobile accident on the Pennsylvania turnpike. Their group, which was co-led by jazz innovator drummer Max Roach, was on its way to play an engagement at a popular Chicago Jazz club.

According to Chicago trumpeter and local jazz historian Melvin Williams, Donald Byrd has established a Brown/Byrd museum at Delaware State University in honor of Clifford Brown. The museum houses Clifford's original trumpet, mouthpieces, mutes, and music. Melvin Williams' own experience upon being first exposed to the music of Clifford Brown is typical of the feeling of many musicians. "I was visiting some friends and listening to our favorite jazz artists when one friend put on Clifford Brown's 'Clifford Brown with Strings' (Emarcy record label). My first reaction was it's not possible to play like that on a trumpet—that recording changed my whole life."

Hard Bop produced a kind of "rigid" musical freedom that led to the free style of the 1960s. In comparing the style of tenor saxophonist Wayne Shorter during the later 1960s to that of John Coltrane in the early 1960s, I found them quite similar. As a member of the Jazz Messengers during the late 1950s, Shorter reiterated the simple, churchlike riffs of his contemporaries, such as Hank Mobley, Booker Ervin (tenor sax), Junior Cook (tenor sax), Jackie McLean (alto sax), Johnny Griffin (tenor sax), Kenny Dorham, and Clark Terry (trumpet). (Terry is a musician who can adapt to any style and is therefore impossible to label. He has influenced Donald Byrd, Miles Davis, Freddie Hubbard, etc.) The hard bop style of Shorter and others was, in a way, free. The style centered around a blues-like cliche repeated over a blues background. During the 1960s, John Coltrane did the same by improvising freely over a modal-like harmonic figure that was, in many ways, similar to the blues. Both artists played without strict harmonies. Freedom was a part of the blues.

The partial restriction of the rhythm section did not prevent the soloist from creating freely. To a certain degree, rhythm sections have always been more restricted than the other instruments. This has led many rhythm section players to stick together both on and off the bandstand. One of the worst things a horn man or woman can do is aggravate a rhythm section player. I learned this lesson the hard way during a series of concerts featuring trombonist Slide Hampton and

Donald Byrd is a complete musician in every way. The Detroit-born trumpeter performs, composes, conducts, and produces. He is a scholar and university professor who has taught at several major universities. Photo by Alan Bergman, courtesy of Elektra.

myself. I remarked to the drummer that I thought the tempo was dragging. This so infuriated him that he signaled the rhythm section to purposely drag on each section of the composition featuring me as a soloist. Regardless of what I did, each time we came to my solo the entire band began to drag. Afterwards, Slide informed me that I had just been taught a lesson in "rhythm section protocol."

One of the most important stylistic changes during the Hard Bop Period was the combination of gospel, bebop, and rhythm and blues. It is annoying to hear critics referring to the marriage of rock and jazz as if it were the first time such a union had taken place. The term *rock* was invented by a midwest disc jockey who was referring to what was actually rhythm and blues. Present day rock musicians are credited for bringing blues and mainstream jazz together when actually the credit should go to the early rhythm and blues players like tenor saxophonist Jimmy "Night Train" Forrest, Louis Jordan (alto sax), bandleader Buddy Johnson, saxophonists King Curtis and Junior Walker, Illinois Jacquet (tenor sax), and Earl Bostic (alto sax). These musicians were a few of the major innovators responsible for bringing together bebop, gospel, and blues.

One of the most important big bands to emerge during the 1940s and 1950s was that of vibraphonist Lionel Hampton. Hampton is directly responsible for launching the careers of hundreds of musicians, including Clifford Brown, Dexter Gordon, Illinois Jacquet, Johnny Griffin, and Art Farmer. According to the musicians who worked with him, Hampton was a strict and demanding leader. His bands were always well-rehearsed and performed a variety of music. Because the band was known the world over for the exciting show they put on, some critics overlooked the band's musical contributions.

Another important development of the Hard Bop Period was the introduction of the organ trio. One of the leading soloists of this period was organist Jimmy Smith. Smith, along with Larry Young, Jack McDuff, Jimmy McGriff, and Shirley Scott, brought the organ to the forefront of modern jazz. In recent years, organists Lonnie Liston Smith and Charles Earland have been successful in combining the elements of gospel, blues, and mainstream jazz.

One of the most exciting groups to come out of the Hard Bop Era was the quintet led by drummer Max Roach and trumpeter Clifford Brown. Brown's debut signaled a return to the hard and driving straight-forward style of improvising that was common during bebop. "Brownie," as he was known, was a combination of Dizzy Gillespie, Fats Navarro, and Miles Davis. His big, full, round sound, fluid ideas and incredible technique influenced young trumpeters the world over. Unfortunately, in 1956, Brown's life was abruptly ended in an automobile accident

Freddie Hubbard has established himself as one of the most influential trumpeters on the scene since Clifford Brown. Photo courtesy of Blue Note.

Trumpeter Art Farmer and saxophonist Benny Golson were the catalyst that propelled the jazztet to the top of the jazz world. Golson is a prolific composer who has contributed several innovative standards to the standard classical jazz repertoire. He is currently working on a scholarly treatise on the saxophone.

Bassist Charlie Mingus, one of the leaders of the new avant-garde. His hard, direct, no-nonsense style helped to pave the way for the new era of the 70s.

along with Richie Powell, the younger brother of pianist Bud Powell. Virtuoso drummer Max Roach, the co-leader of the group, was and still is a musical giant. His impeccable sense of time, along with his intelligent interpretation of the intricacies of modern music, has kept him in the forefront of jazz.

Modality: "The New Thing" (1959–60)

During the transitional period between the late 1950s and the early 1960s, a type of music called *modality* emerged. Instead of using scales, musicians like Miles Davis, John Coltrane, and Eric Dolphy returned to the earlier church modes (Dorian, Lydian, Aeolian, etc.) in an effort to discover newer and richer melodic materials. Modality did not enrich the natural musical elements of jazz as musicians had hoped it would. Instead, it restricted the harmonic possibilities of the improvisers, particularly the keyboard players.

Instrumentalists found that the modal concept offered a challenge in permitting the soloists to play "inside and outside" the harmonic scheme. But

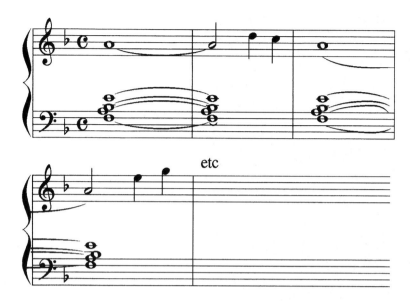

Example 24

during this melodic and harmonic freedom, the rhythm section found itself restricted to a straight four-four to the beat. The keyboard player was even more restricted because he or she had to follow the soloist. The role of the bass in Hard Bop was to keep time as well as to stimulate the soloist by creating a mood out of the monotonic sound implied by the modes. The drummer was expected to keep time and to create the rhythmic stimulus for the group. Modality was difficult because unlike Bebop there were no harmonic guidelines for the musicians to follow. This meant that the musicians had to create a feeling out of the "oneness" so often implied by the restrictions of the mode. Many of the less harmonic players welcomed modality because it appeared to offer them the opportunity to improvise without learning hundreds of chord sequences usually associated with a bebop tune. In a way, modality resembled swing because neither style required the soloist to concentrate as strongly on the harmonic structure of a given composition.

The one record that more than any other typifies the sound of modality was Miles Davis's *Kind of Blue*. On this LP, Miles introduced what was to become one of the most popular compositions in jazz—"So What." "So What" uses a regular

Bill Evans, during his tenure with Miles Davis, emerged as one of the most influential pianists in jazz. Photo courtesy of Hozumi Nakadaira.

ABA format but replaces standard harmonies with two modes. Another outstanding feature of the composition is that the bassist introduces the theme while the horns provide a subtle but effective background. The unusual, highly spirited alto saxophone work of Cannonball Adderley, and the extremely disciplined tenor saxophone solo of John Coltrane, help make this one of the most important works in the history of jazz.

One of the most effective though subtle musical marriages in jazz was the addition of Cannonball Adderley's alto saxophone to Miles Davis's cool trumpet sound and John Coltrane's piercing, penetrating tenor saxophone. Adderley's southern-bluesy, guttural alto was the perfect contrast and balance to the more subtle, controlled sound of both Davis and Coltrane. Unfortunately, many critics at that time could not relate to this particular blend. They had not quite forgotten the smooth alto sax sounds of the earlier Cool Period. However, such a contrast in sound and concept was needed to offset the almost hypnotic flow of modal sounds.

In France, a number of young jazz musicians experimented with the concept of modality. These musicians, mostly inspired by the recordings they had heard of Davis and Coltrane, seemed more comfortable with the concept of

Tenor saxophonist Sonny Stitt, a proponent of the hard bop era, proved to be one of the giants of jazz during the late 1950s through 1970s.

Guitarist Kenny Burrell has proven to be one of the most reliable and innovative stylists in jazz. Here he is seen together with bassist Richard Davis.

modality than with other styles of jazz. When Miles Davis went to France during the late 1950s, he surrounded himself with a group of young musicians, many of them already attuned to his music. Rene Urtreger (piano), Pierre Michelot (bass), and Barney Wilen (tenor sax) were among these. The presence of American jazz musicians in Europe was responsible for the acceptance of many local jazz musicians. In France there was no exception. Recording companies responded to the local demand for jazz by recording local artists accompanied by their American guests. Sweden, the European country most active in jazz during the 1950s Cool Period, was replaced by the Hard Bop school of France as the leading European country for jazz.

To say that Hard Bop was just another attempt at playing music that would appeal to the masses is to dismiss the fact that hard bop produced some of the most innovative music ever. It would be totally irresponsible to dismiss the

Sonny Rollins, the living legend of the tenor saxophone, is considered to be the greatest tenor saxophonist playing today. Photo courtesy of Hozumi Nakadaira.

The Oscar Peterson Trio, one of the most dynamic forces in jazz. Photo courtesy of Hozumi Nakadaira.

intricate phrasing of trumpeter Clifford Brown or the highly-personalized and intellectual lines of tenor saxophonist Sonny Rollins. Upon close examination of the work of these and other artists from this period (the work of drummer Max Roach, tenor saxophonist Hank Mobley, trombonist J.J. Johnson or Europeans such as German bassist Peter Trunk), one cannot help but marvel at the level of authenticity and commitment.

The fact that many of the Hard Bop musicians were also active in previous periods such as Swing, Bebop, Progressive, and Cool provided them with a variety of experiences, which was reflected in their music. Again, this is evidence that the true artist is one who is able to go smoothly from one period to another. However, one cannot overlook the fact that many artists are prevented from making this transition simply because they can no longer find an outlet through recording or performing opportunities. Perhaps two of the most influential musicians of this period were Chicagoans Nicky Hill (tenor sax) and Ike Day

Tenor saxophonist Johnny Griffin, the "Little Giant," is one of the most important original jazz saxophonists in history. Photo by P. Brunner.

(drums). Unfortunately for the jazz world, both artists died early in their careers and did not have an opportunity to be properly recorded and exposed to a world-wide audience. But their individual influence could be felt and heard through the work of such artists as Johnny Griffin (tenor sax), Max Roach (drums), and Clifford Jordan (tenor sax).

Conclusion

The Hard Bop Period was, in many ways, one of the most important developments in jazz. The return to the blues and to the natural swing in earlier jazz restored some of the original colloquialism to the music. Without such a move-

Dizzy Gillespie, Donald Byrd, Nathan Davis, and members of Dizzy's Quartet in concert at Pittsburgh's Three Rivers Arts Festival.

Kenny Clarke (drums), Woody Shaw (trumpet), Terry Pollard (vibraphone). Vibraphonist Terry Pollard was one of the most creative voices on vibes since Milt "Bags" Jackson.

ment, jazz might have become so deeply entrenched in the West European classical tradition that it would have lost much of its original drive. Musicians like Clifford Brown, Max Roach, James Moody, Art Blakey, Phil Woods, Lee Morgan, Horace Silver, Donald Byrd, and others returned to the musical concepts of the African-American church. The relaxed, low-key sounds of the cool school soon gave way to the fiery riffs of harder players. The emphasis on "hot" playing was reflected in the language of the new boppers. Terms like "put the pots on," "cookin'," "soul," and "burnin'" described the feelings evoked by this music. Small combos were the favored format for musical expression. The most popular instrumentation of Hard Bop groups was tenor or alto sax, trumpet, trombone, piano, bass and drums. The organ trio (organ, tenor sax or guitar and drums) was also a popular combination.

One of the most important big bands to emerge during the Hard Bop Period was that of Lionel Hampton. Hampton launched the careers of hundreds of musicians—Dexter Gordon, Art Farmer, Johnny Griffin, Clifford Brown, and so on. Although the band was known more by the general public for its ownership, Hampton's band produced some of the most important music in jazz.

During the late 1950s and early 1960s, Miles Davis, John Coltrane, Eric Dolphy, Gil Evans (and earlier Lennie Tristano) introduced the concept of modality to jazz. Modes replaced the intricate harmonic sequence used during the Bebop period. Musicians began experimenting with collective improvisation built around a single sonority, which led to the free jazz, avant-garde era of the 1960s.

Suggested Readings and Listening

Books
Cole, Bill. *Miles Davis*. New York: William Morrow, 1974.
Tanner, Paul, and Gerow, Maurice. A *Study of Jazz*. 5th ed. Dubuque, Iowa: William C. Brown, 1984.

Records
Sonny Rollins—Plus Four. "Pent-Up House." Smithsonian Collection
Max Roach—Clifford Brown Quintet in Concert (GNPS 18).

Mellon Jazz Festival Spectacular. L–R: Vince Genova, piano; Donald Byrd, trumpet; Dwayne Dolphin, bass; Harold Betters, trombone; Jimmy Heath, tenor saxophone; Nathan Davis, soprano saxophone; and Roger Humphries, drums. Photo courtesy of Robert Bowman and Associates, Inc.

CHAPTER 13

Free Jazz and the Avant-Garde (1960s)

Profile

ORNETTE COLEMAN • Multi-instrumentalist (alto saxophone, trumpet, violin) Ornette Coleman was born in Fort Worth, Texas, on March 19, 1930. When Ornette first emerged on the jazz scene during the late 1950s he was immediately hailed by a multitude of critics and musicians as the jazz "voice" of the future. His haunting alto saxophone sound seemed to suggest some kind of futuristic direction in Jazz. In part, the type of sound he produced on the alto saxophone was due to the white plastic saxophone that he preferred to use.

In 1965, during the time that I lived in Paris, Ornette used to come by the Blue Note Jazz Club where I was playing with the Kenny Clarke group and sit in. In most instances we would play standards and a few blues. Ornette's ability to play fast was limited at that time so he approached me about coming over to my apartment so that we could practice together.

But even more than the sound, it was his highly personalized concept that separated Ornette from his peers. His previous experience as a rhythm and blues saxophonist in southwest Texas during his teens, coupled with a general

curiousity for beauty and naturalism, produced an unusual marriage of freedom and funk that appealed to the more adventurous jazz fan. In addition, his
ability to create interesting melodic lines that complimented his sound and
concept produced a kind of elevated simplicity that was easy for the listener
to follow.

Soon after moving to Los Angeles, Ornette began attracting the attention
of local musicians who were curious about what he was trying to accomplish.
Perhaps the group of musicians who admired Coleman's work the most were
the composers—who, by the very nature of the process of composing, were
always searching for new and different ways of making music. As a composer,
Ornette was one of the most creative among his peers. His works "Lonely
Woman" and "Skies of America" are considered classics and rank among the
major works of the period. His collaboration with trumpeter Don Cherry suggested memories of Charlie Parker and Dizzy Gillespie. Ornette's later collaboration with his group "Prime Time," which often included his son Leonardo
on drums, saw Coleman turn to more folk-traditional ethnic music (Morocco,
Spain, Turkey for instance).

As a multi-instrumentalist, Ornette's work invited even more controversy.
His left-handed playing of the violin, coupled with his unusual approach to
playing the trumpet, enraged musicians who considered his technique on both
instruments unorthodox and counterproductive. But what these critics forgot
was that Ornette's concept of technique and music was different from theirs.
Needing to say what he wanted to say musically was most important to him,
and he continued to experiment with various techniques to produce his own
special brand of music. As far as he was concerned, he was accomplishing his
goal of playing the best music he knew. The proof was in the music. Regardless
of all the negative criticism Ornette Coleman received, he remains one of the
truly innovative figures in jazz.

Profile

Eric Allan Dolphy • Eric Dolphy, according to many musicians, was
the "unofficial" father of the new avant-garde movement in jazz during the

1960s. This recognition has often been challenged by those who did not accept Dolphy's unconventional approach to improvising. However Dolphy's association with John Coltrane and his superb technique gave him an edge over other musicians.

Dolphy was born in Los Angeles, California, on June 20, 1928. There he later became an active member of the young jazz community which featured such jazz greats as reedman Buddy Collette, alto saxophonist Sonny Criss, and composer/bandleader Gerald Wilson. Despite New York City's status as the mecca of jazz, the avant-garde movement got its impetus in California (where the cool movement of the 1950s also got started). Although Dolphy was a part of the Los Angeles jazz scene, it was not until he joined drummer Chico Hamilton in the late 1950s that he received national attention. During this time Dolphy was more of a straight-ahead player. But in the 1960s, when he joined the band of bassist Charlie Mingus, he began to show promise as an avant-gardist.

Mingus gave Dolphy the opportunity to explore the elements of musical freedom. Although the music of Mingus appeared to be completely free of form, there was at all times a kind of implied structure that required the utmost in musical discipline to perform. To perform the music of composers like Mingus, a musician must possess a thorough knowledge of harmony and a keen sense of time (rhythm). Dolphy had both. His work with Charlie Mingus was one of the avant-garde's most creative unions. Perhaps it was the magnitude of this combined musical tour-de-force that contributed to its demise. Both Mingus and Dolphy were strong-minded, independent thinkers who were determined to maintain their own way of doing things.

I first met Dolphy at a party in West Berlin, Germany at the apartment of trumpeter Benny Bailey. During this time, Dolphy was recording with Bailey and also worked with him at one of the Jugendheims in West Berlin. The next time I saw Dolphy was shortly after he left bassist Charlie Mingus for Paris. But before that, Dolphy had teamed up with trumpeter Booker Little for a recording club-date at the famous New York club—The Five Spot. This union produced some of Eric's most brilliant work. The combination of complicated twelve-tone inspired melodies superimposed upon multi-phonic harmonies set the standard for new directions in jazz during the early sixties. In 1962, Dolphy teamed up with trumpeter Freddie Hubbard for an association that saw the younger Hubbard blossom musically. Dolphy's influence on Hubbard was tremendous and can be heard in Hubbard's recordings of that period.

Eric Dolphy, considered by many musicians to be the true father of the 1960s Avant Garde movement, was a brilliant instrumentalist who helped change the sound of jazz. Photo courtesy of Rutgers Institute of Jazz.

One of the most successful musical unions in the history of jazz was that of Dolphy and saxophonist John Coltrane. Unfortunately, there were those who criticized this union. Some critics felt that Dolphy was the lesser of the two musicians and had merely taken advantage of the sympathy of Coltrane. Nothing could be further from the truth. His collaboration with Coltrane produced some of the most inspirational music of the period and showcased Dolphy as a prolific arranger-orchestrator as well as a soloist. Once, during our gig at the now defunct Chat Qui Peche, Dolphy and Trane met to discuss going to India to confer with Indian sitarist Ravi Shankar about music and life. During this time both Dolphy and Coltrane were beginning to experiment with improvising to Indian music. It is a fact that Coltrane not only accepted Dolphy as a musical equal but respected him enough to give him the opportunity to write the arrangements for his LP *African Brass*.

As an arranger/orchestrator, Dolphy was one of the most interesting, if not the premiere, experimentalist of the 1960s. His work on *African Brass* showed him to be preoccupied with the then popular concept of writing and playing in fourths. However, some of Dolphy's most interesting writings were the compositions he wrote for Sonny Gray's big band in Paris. This was a big band created by Jamaican trumpeter Sonny Gray and American Donald Byrd. The band was made up of mostly French musicians and some Americans: Lou Bennett (organ), Art Simmons (piano and arranger), and myself (reeds). Dolphy's writing for this group was representative of his playing—very polyphonic. The combination of sound together with his intricate use of polyrhthmic patterns gave to his compositions an excitement rarely heard.

Dolphy was a well-schooled musician who, in addition to self-study, was constantly seeking out European classical teachers to study with. During the period that I worked with Dolphy in 1964, he was almost obsessed with musical perfection. He wrote down everything: tunes, arrangements, short phrases, motifs, and rhythms. Whenever we rehearsed Eric would record everything, then we would all listen to the tapes to figure out better ways of doing things. Eric's knowledge of western European classical composers was astonishing. Not only did he know their histories but he also knew their music because he had already meticulously analyzed it. Dolphy's dazzling technique on all three of his instruments—the alto saxophone, bass clarinet, and flute—is legendary. His frequent visits to the Selmer Music Instrument Factory during his brief sojourn in Paris during the 1960s often found him dazzling the Selmer staff and clinicians with his brilliant technique. On one occasion, when

Dolphy visited Denmark for a performance and recording with the renowned Danish Radio Orchestra, the bass clarinetist, who also played with the classical orchestra, stated, "Now that's the way the bass clarinet is supposed to be played."

Often the question of just who was considered the father of the avantgarde arises. The simple answer is that, according to the critics and a select group of musicians, Ornette was considered the first to have made an impression in that area. However most musicians agree that Eric Dolphy appeared to play with more acceptable technical mastery of his instruments and appeared to be more of a schooled musician. In many ways Dolphy was similar to Ornette Coleman in that Eric also sought to explore new and different ways of expressing himself in jazz. Both men were primarily alto saxophonists who also doubled on other instruments. Eric preferred the bass clarinet and flute while Ornette's doubles were primarily violin and trumpet.

One factor in this argument that appears to be overlooked is the status of jazz outside the United States. During the late 1950s, about the same time that Ornette and trumpeter Don Cherry began experimenting, in England two Afro-Caribbeans—saxophonist Joe Harriet and trumpeter Shake Keane— began experimenting with a way of improvising that borrowed heavily from Caribbean music. What is so coincidental about this fact is that both Harriet and Ornette were of Caribbean descent. In fact, some of the Caribbean musicians that I interviewed assured me that Harriet and Keane began playing that particular music long before Coleman and Cherry did in the U.S. Regardless of who was first, the fact is that both groups had a Caribbean feel to their music. This therefore suggests a closer relationship between free jazz and Caribbean music than had been previously thought.

Much has been written about the sudden death of Dolphy in Berlin, Germany on June 29, 1964. A common misconception is that he died of a drug overdose. This was not the case. The facts are as follows: I had introduced Eric to pianist and vibraphonist Karl Hans Berger and vocalist Ingrid Berger, Karl's wife. They had come to Paris to invite Eric to perform in Berlin. Dolphy agreed to make the date and asked me to form a group to keep the Chat Qui Peche open until he returned from the Berlin job a week later. The night before he left for Berlin, he came by the club to hear the group I had put together and to talk to me about his plans for the future. He spoke about forming a new group and sending for trumpeter Woody Shaw, drummer Billy Higgins, and vibraphonist Bobby Hutcherson.

The next day, Dolphy left to begin his week-long engagement in Berlin. In Berlin, he became ill and started acting strangely. He was rushed to the hospital by some people who assumed that the cause was drugs. Dolphy actually was in insulin shock and soon fell into a diabetic coma. The medical staff had no way of knowing that Dolphy was diabetic—he carried no papers or medical records indicating the disease—so the true nature of Dolphy's condition was not correctly diagnosed in time. He never recovered. The news of his death reached Paris in a matter of hours and shocked the entire jazz community.

Shortly before his departure for Berlin, Eric, Donald Byrd and I began a series of recordings for Jacques Deival for a radio-TV Jazz show entitled "Jazz Au Champs (Elysée)." Every day en route to the studio Eric would insist that we stop by a café juice stand and drink the freshly squeezed fruit and vegetable juices. He was obsessed with these fruit drinks—which were the wrong thing for a diabetic to drink. Later a doctor explained that this habit no doubt contributed to Eric's falling into the diabetic coma.

---

*F**reedom* or *Free Jazz* were the terms used for the music played during the 1960s by artists like Eric Dolphy (alto sax, bass clarinet, flute), Sonny Rollins (tenor sax), John Coltrane (tenor sax, soprano sax), Ornette Coleman (alto sax, trumpet, violin), Archie Shepp (tenor sax), Gary Burton (vibes), Albert Ayler (tenor sax), Don Cherry (trumpet), Booker Little (trumpet), Frank Wright (tenor sax), Jimmy Owens (trumpet), Clifford Thornton (trumpet), Kenny Fisher (tenor sax), Cecil Taylor (piano), J. C. Moses (drums), Roy Haynes (drums), Herbie Hancock (piano), Freddie Hubbard (trumpet), Pharoah Sanders (tenor sax), Sun Ra (keyboards), Billy Harper (tenor sax), Vince Genova (piano), and Don Pullen (piano). A few years later, a number of young players imitated the free style in a more structured way. Among them were Joe Henderson (tenor sax), Clifford Jordan (tenor sax), Wayne Shorter (tenor sax), Andrew White (tenor sax), Arthur Blythe (alto sax), Chico Freeman (tenor sax), Sam Rivers (tenor sax), Miroslav Vitous (bass), Leo Wright (alto sax), Eric Kloss (alto sax), Roswell Rudd (trombone), Jean Luc Ponty (violin), Michel Portal (tenor sax and clarinet), Jan Arnet (bass), Dave Liebman (tenor sax), Charles Lloyd (tenor sax), and Nelson Harrison (trombone). Some dissenting musicians and fans called the new music "space music" or "moon music," meaning that it sounded like something from outer space. "Black music" was the name preferred by the more "militant" musicians.

The 1960s saw the beginning of a cultural revolution in the United States that has had lasting effects. The black American demonstrations that started in the South when Rosa Parks refused to move to the back of the bus in Montgomery, Alabama, changed the entire social structure of the country. Sit-ins and protest marches, led by Dr. Martin Luther King Jr. and his colleagues, set a revolutionary tone that was soon reflected in the music called Jazz. In many ways, the cultural revolution of the 1960s resembled the earlier Harlem Renaissance period. African-American culture once again revealed to the rest of the world the plight of black men and women in the United States. As the movement grew, young whites joined their black brothers and sisters in fighting the injustices of American society.

The music of Eric Dolphy, more than that of any other person, signaled the kind of music that was to emerge from the chaos of the 1960s. It was Dolphy who influenced the playing of John Coltrane during Trane's earlier association with the avant-garde. Many critics have stated that Ornette Coleman was the major influence on Coltrane and other avant-gardists, but Dolphy and Coltrane had begun experimenting and practicing together as early as 1960. Ornette Coleman's main appeal was his uninhibiited melodic and rhythmic simplicity. His free improvisations with their songlike melodic approach were simple compared to the more adventurous jumps and skips of musicians like Coltrane, Rollins, and Dolphy.

Dolphy, although not as popular as Coleman or Coltrane, was hailed as the Father of the new avant-garde. Musicians looked to him not only for musical advice, but for direction in life. I was fortunate enough to have worked in the last group Dolphy and Donald Byrd put together in 1964 for a club date at the now defunct Chat Qui Peche in Paris. Perhaps I should clarify the origins of the Chat Qui Peche date since I have read so many different versions of what took place. Donald Byrd was originally scheduled to open at the club with a quintet, but when Dolphy came to town, Madame Ricard, the owner of the club, asked Byrd if he would consider forming a group with Dolphy. Byrd agreed and the group opened for a month-long engagement. During that time, Dolphy had to fulfill a week's commitment in Holland, and I was asked to fill in for him at the Chat Qui Peche. When Dolphy returned, he asked me to stay with the group. The rhythm section consisted of Luigi Tristardo (bass) and Jacques Tolo (drums). Many of the compositions we played during the Chat Qui Peche engagement were composed by Dolphy and centered around Indian music.

Dolphy was a virtuoso instrumentalist. He could play almost anything on the saxophone. He also had an exceptional knowledge of music theory. During our sojourn in Paris, Dolphy, Byrd, and I played with the Sonny Gray (trumpet) big band. During this period, Dolphy wrote some of the most advanced music for a big band that I have ever heard. If a student of composition wanted to research the various compositional possibilities for big band, these arrangements and compositions would prove invaluable. The Chat Qui Peche group, consisting of Dolphy, Byrd, Tolo, Tristardo, and myself, recorded a number of sides for the O.R.T.F. (French radio and TV station) under the direction of Jacques Dieval, the French producer and pianist. These sides are Dolphy's very last recorded music and some of his best work. Recently, these recordings have been released on various European labels.

Ornette Coleman's influence in jazz cannot be overestimated because he, more than anyone, typified the sound that became synonymous with the 1960s. The sound Coleman got from his plastic saxophone was, in part, a result of the instrument itself. Once in San Remo, Italy, I tried Coleman's saxophone and noticed that my sound seemed to change as a result of playing on the instrument. This particular instrument and Coleman's original concept of music, which was quite experimental at that time, both were responsible for his "outside" sound. Coleman, like many of the new musicians of the 1960s, possessed a certain mysticism, or aura, which was, at least partly, created by the amount of publicity generated by the media to influence record buyers.

The 1960s free jazz movement produced a number of experimental groups. Many of these were actively involved in the cultural-political revolution that lasted until the beginning of the 1970s. Musicians became spokespersons for a number of organizations and causes. One of the most articulate musical spokespersons during this period was tenor saxophonist Archie Shepp. Shepp, along with Marion Brown (alto sax), Ted Curson (trumpet), Clifford Thornton (trumpet), Andrew Hill (piano), Cecil Taylor (piano), Sun Ra (piano), Charles Tolliver (trumpet), composer Michael Mantler, and others, spoke out on issues ranging from politics to racial injustice. Among books, Frank Kofsky's work on black music and its revolutionary role during the 1960s, *Black Nationalism and the Revolution in Music*, is an outstanding contribution to jazz literature.

Profile

JOHN COLTRANE • One of the most gifted soloists of all time was tenor saxophonist John Coltrane. Coltrane, born in Hamlet, North Carolina, on September 23, 1926, was so influential as a soloist that he became something of a guru, much like his former bandleader Miles Davis. When Coltrane embraced the concept of spirituality in jazz, younger jazz musicians immediately became concerned about God, religion, and the relationship between the two. Jazz musicians all over the world began to pray and meditate in order to better their music through a mystical reunion with God.* When Coltrane further changed his lifestyle by eating health food and exercising, his faithful disciples followed suit. During this dramatic change in attitudes among jazz musicians, I was very active in the Parisian and European jazz scene (1960–69) and personally witnessed Coltrane's effect on jazz musicians all over Europe. Influenced by the American jazz musicians who annually toured Europe, the young European musicians also began to eat health food, pray, meditate, physically exercise, and attempt to play hour-long solos just as their mentor did.

What kind of a man was John Coltrane and what was it about his music that gave him such power over his musical disciples? Shortly before he died, I had the pleasure of meeting "Trane," as he was known among musicians, at the Blue Note Jazz Club in Paris. Coltrane was in town to perform a concert with his group, which was composed of McCoy Tyner (piano), Jimmy Garrison (bass), and Elvin Jones (drums). After the concert, he and the group had stopped by the Blue Note to hear Kenny Clarke's group. My recollection of Coltrane, though slightly colored by my reverence for his contributions to music and his influence on my own development as a saxophonist, was of a quiet, sincere, and gentle man who loved to smoke cigars. I had just finished playing a set with Clarke's group when Ben Benjamin, the American owner of the Blue Note, introduced me to Coltrane. In an almost inaudible tone, Trane expressed an interest in my playing and complimented us on our performance. Needless to say, we were elated. Whether out of kindness or sincerity, Coltrane always seemed to have an interesting and kind word for the work of younger musicians.

---

*On his recordings "A Love Supreme" and the controversial "Om," Coltrane clearly emphasizes the spiritual qualities of his music, leaving the technical and theoretical aspects of the music to develop along a less structured format.

Tenor saxophonist John Coltrane, together with Miles Davis, emerged as the leader of the 1960s jazz scene. Photo courtesy of Hozumi Nakadaira.

Not long afterwards, Coltrane gathered a number of younger players to-gether for his controversial recording of *Ascension*. This experimental record-ing, which demonstrates Coltrane's inquisitiveness concerning the theoretical limitations on the jazz soloist, focuses on his flirtation with free group im-provisation—a concept much like that of early traditional New Orleans jazz. Much has been made of Dexter Gordon's influence on Coltrane's style. The very first time I heard Coltrane perform on tenor saxophone was at a dance-concert, in Kansas City's Municipal Auditorium, with another great jazz saxo-phonist, Earl Bostic. During that time (early 1950s), Coltrane's playing, both in ideas and sound, closely resembled that of saxophonist Sonny Stitt. Rhyth-mically, he had a more laid back concept that resembled the shuffle concept of tenor saxophonist Lester Young. This is where the idea of Gordon's influence probably developed. Gordon's time concept, which he admits he developed from listening to Young, influenced Coltrane's rhythmic concept. Harmonical-ly, Coltrane was greatly influenced by pianist Thelonious Monk. During his as-sociation with Monk (1957), Monk showed him how to use polychords.*

From playing extended chords or polychords, Coltrane developed the con-cept of playing the notes so rapidly that he created what one critic called "sheets of sound." This idea, along with practicing music written for the harp, helped Coltrane develop a new concept in jazz. These techniques gave him an unbelievably flawless technique. Another method he used to develop his melod-ic concept was practicing material found in the *Thesaurus of Scales and Melod-ic Patterns* by Nicolas Slonimsky.

That Coltrane developed into one of the most influential saxophonists of all time can be attributed more to his diligent practice than to genius. Obvi-ously, without talent Coltrane could not have achieved such greatness, but he did in fact practice eight to ten hours daily. Both Coltrane and Eric Dolphy constantly practiced during intermission at clubs, concerts, and just about any other place and time.

During the latter part of his life, Coltrane's music became even more ex-perimental. Alice Coltrane replaced Tyner on piano and Rashied Ali replaced drummer Elvin Jones. First introduced to free form improvisation by saxophonist and multi-instrumentalist Eric Dolphy, and later influenced by saxophonists Ornette Coleman and Albert Ayler, Coltrane had become obsessed with this concept shortly before his death on July 17, 1967. Contrary to reports that

---

*Polychords are two or more chords that occur simultaneously.

Coltrane died from a drug usage, his death was attributed to a liver ailment. Coltrane had so great an influence on his contemporaries that when he adopted the soprano saxophone for his recording of "My Favorite Things," sales of soprano saxophones increased tremendously. George Selmer—of the Selmer Brothers of the Parisian saxophone family—once asked me the reason for the sudden increase in the soprano saxophone. At that time, 1960, the soprano saxophone had not enjoyed much popularity since Johnny Hodges played it with Duke Ellington during the big band swing period of the 1930s. Of course there were the rare recordings of Lucky Thompson on soprano and some of Steve Lacy, but that was all. My answer, of course, was John Coltrane.

After his first meeting with multi-instrumentalist Eric Dolphy, Coltrane showed more interest in the flute and bass clarinet as possible extensions of his musical voice. The flute, once established as a solo jazz instrument in the 1950s, was already riding a crest of popularity. But I am sure that had Coltrane lived to record more on flute and bass clarinet, sales of bass instruments and flutes would also have suddenly increased.

The 1960s was a very productive period in jazz. More young musicians were given a chance to express their musical ideas and to establish themselves as artists in residence at many of our leading colleges and universities. Many of them formed their own companies in order to control their careers. One such musician was Charles Tolliver (trumpet), who later became one of the founders of Strata-East Records, Inc. Strata-East was formed with the idea of allowing the participating members to produce and control their own records. The Jazz Composers Orchestra, under the leadership of Michael Mantler, is another organization that was developed during the 1960s to provide a musical platform for the new avant-garde musicians.

What criteria can be used to determine if you are buying the best possible work of an artist? It depends on what you are looking for. If you are concerned about both the artist and his or her music, you will listen for such things as musical competency, tonal quality, technical facility, general musicality (the overall musical sound of the performance), recording technique, engineering quality, compositional structure, improvisational ideas, and musical compatibility between the musicians involved. These are just some of the guidelines to use in determining the validity and sincerity of a recorded or live performance.

Trumpeter Woody Shaw emerged as one of the most gifted and innovative trumpeters of the 1970s and 80s.

Time will prove the quality of the music of the 1960s avant-garde period. The major problem with any experimental period in art is that the critics often rush in and endorse every new artist and style without first objectively analyzing the art form. After time and money are invested in promoting the music, it is almost impossible to discontinue the project. One main reason so much "unproven music" came out of the 1960s was that many jazz writers were afraid to openly disapprove of the music.

The response of the musicians should also be considered. At the very beginning of the 1960s, many established musicians were openly hostile to the new music. Trade magazines newspapers, and other publications revealed that many musicians opposed the music played by Eric Dolphy, Gary Bartz, Don Cherry, Gato Barbieri, Ornette Coleman, Albert Ayler, Sun Ra, Giuseppi Logan, Pharoah Sanders, Cecil Taylor, Sam Rivers, and Archie Shepp. Leonard Feather's *Encyclopedia of Jazz in the Sixties* has documented many of the criticisms made by musicians who opposed the new music of the 1960s. Why then did Dolphy, Coleman,

A young Woody Shaw and Nathan Davis pose in Paris for publicity photos for their engagement at Paris' famed "Chat Qui Peche" Club in 1964. Photo courtesy of Studio Ethel.

Ayler, and Shepp go on to become the new leaders of the period? The answer lies in the power of the music industry to influence buyers. The music industry succeeded in selling the new music to a large enough group, which led to the acceptance of the music by those who normally would have rejected it.

Another point is that many established artists are often threatened by the success of younger and "cheaper" artists. The established musician knows that the younger artist has to work for a lower price while building a name. That the new performer is less expensive seems a threat to the older, more established performer, which leads many established musicians to speak unfavorably of the new, young artist. This is not true in every case, but it certainly does occur. The older, established musicians reacted to the new music of the 1960s in the same way Louis Armstrong and Roy Eldridge reacted to the introduction of bebop.

As I mentioned earlier, one of the more controversial recordings to come out of the 1960s was *Ascension* by John Coltrane, featuring a group of young avant-gardists. The recording was Coltrane's attempt at "big band" playing without preconceived arrangements. Some critics of the LP thought the effort might have been more successful if the abilities of the musicians had been more evenly matched.

The idea of free collective improvisation did not begin with Coltrane's *Ascension*. Free collective improvisation started with the beginning of jazz and was the basis of the traditional music played in New Orleans during the 1800s. In *Ascension*, Coltrane was trying to go back to the roots of jazz—to the idea of musical freedom. Each of the musicians involved was there for a purpose—to contribute to a communal-spiritual element in the music that can also be heard in Coltrane's recording of "A Love Supreme," featuring McCoy Tyner, Jimmy Garrison, and Elvin Jones. The spiritual quality of this recording, even if you do not read Coltrane's prayer, makes it one of the most stimulating performances ever recorded. Here Coltrane, through his music, converses with the Supreme Being by emphasizing the spiritual aspect of musical simplicity.

Few will not agree that John Coltrane was one of the most influential tenor saxophonists in the history of jazz. Trane's "sheets of sound" were perhaps responsible for his immediate acceptance by the jazz elite. His clear, pure tonality seemed to reach out and touch the heart. His LP of ballads appealed as much to the nonjazz fan as to the jazz connoisseur. Some critics have stated that his sound showed influences of Dexter Gordon, Stan Getz, and Sonny Stitt. According to many of Coltrane's close friends and colleagues, he also felt very close to the sound of tenor saxophonist Stanley Turrentine. Trane was impressed with Turrentine's clear, sharp-edged bluesy sound. During the 1960s, Wilton Gaynard, one of the lead soloists with the Kurth Edelhagen big band in West Germany, was another tenor saxophonist who Trane admired. Many saxophonists are supposed to have influenced both Sonny Rollins and Coltrane, but few made lasting impressions on them.

Sonny Rollins and John Coltrane were the two most important established tenor saxophonists during the 1960s. Each represented the sound and concept of the 1960s. During the 1920s, the trumpet or cornet was the most influential. During the 1930s, it was the clarinet. During the late 1930s and early 1940s it was the tenor saxophone (Don Byas, Coleman Hawkins, and Lester "Prez" Young). During the middle 1940s, it was the alto saxophone of Charlie Parker. (Many players of the Bebop Period refused to even consider playing the alto saxophone after hearing Parker perform.) During the Cool Period, Lester Young and Stan Getz were the leaders. (Rollins's earlier sound was greatly influenced by Charlie Parker on tenor; Ornette Coleman's sound on tenor resembled that of

Drummer Elvin Jones, the rhythmic foundation of the John Coltrane Quartet during the 1960s, remains an influential and formidable force in jazz today. Photo by Werner Stiefele.

Jazz drummer J.C. Moses was one of the most explosive and cohesive drummers during his brief life.

Sonny Rollins. I personally had the rare opportunity to hear Ornette play tenor when he sat in with our group at the Blue Note in Paris and borrowed Sony Stitt's tenor.)

Sonny Rollins is considered one of the major jazz tenor saxophonists living today. During the 1960s, Rollins was overlooked by many jazz critics who favored the then popular John Coltrane. This was most unfortunate for an established musician such as Rollins. Not only was Rollins an established musical personality, but he also had developed a large following. During the two years (1954–56) that I spent in Chicago as a free-lance jazz musician, Rollins and Sonny Stitt were the two most copied saxophonists in the jazz world. Every tenor saxophonist in the country sounded either like Rollins or Stitt. Rollins, at that time, often played with a stiff reed. Because the reed was so stiff, he occasionally produced a squeak or pinched sound. I, along with hundreds of other young saxophonists, found a way to squeak in exactly the same way as Rollins.

Perhaps one of the reasons for the semi-neglect of Rollins during the Coltrane years was that, on more than one occasion, he temporarily retired from the jazz scene. During one such period, Rollins was found practicing his saxophone under a New York bridge. When asked why he was there, he replied that it was a nice, quiet place to practice without being interrupted. (The history of jazz is full of interesting stories about musicians. One of the most difficult jobs is to filter out the inaccurate information and place the facts in their proper perspective.) During these exiles, Rollins studied various philosophies, practiced under a New York bridge, and reassessed his role as a performing artist. But the industry and fans of course turned to someone who was currently available.

Sonny Rollins is the kind of musician who continues to grow and develop regardless of what else is happening in the music world. There was a period when he preferred to work with a trio consisting of guitar, bass, and drums. Later, he became totally committed to the new music of the 1960s. His ideas, imagination, and command of the instrument makes him one of the most influential tenor saxophonists in the history of jazz.

Although he entered jazz much earlier than the 1960s avant-garde period, Rollins was a major contributor to the period. His association with trumpeter Don Cherry and other avant-gardists produced an unparalleled body of music.

Conclusion

The avant-garde period in jazz was, more than anything, an experimental period. Because the music was different and not readily understood by many established musicians and writers, the serious younger avant-garde musicians often suffered a great deal of unnecessary criticism.

Aside from igniting a musical revolution during the 1960s, jazz also played an important role in the social revolution of that period. Musicians became leaders in many social causes such as the fight against racial discrimination, equal rights for minorities, political freedom, educational opportunities, and so on. The music became a mirror of society. Freedom in music became synonymous with freedom in life.

Like any other period, the avant-garde period produced its leaders. Eric Dolphy, Ornette Coleman, Don Cherry, Archie Shepp, and Pharoah Sanders were some of the major figures who contributed not only to the musical revolution, but to the social revolution.

Grover Washington, Jr. emerged as the leader of a new school of young contemporary jazz artists. Photo by Gary Guydosh.

Many critics during the avant-garde period were uneasy with the musical development of the new musicians. Some accused the younger musicians of being "musical charlatans." Many critics refused to support or condemn the new music, deciding to "wait and see." Finally, established artists emerged as leaders in the field, while those who were less fortunate disappeared from the jazz scene.

John Coltrane and Sonny Rollins, along with Miles Davis, were respected by the majority of the musicians as leaders of the "new music." Because they had proven themselves during the previous jazz periods, the general public as well as the writers and musicians were not as reluctant to accept them as leaders. After a period of experimentation in jazz, the musicians themselves and the general public demanded a different kind of music. Slowly the avant-garde period in jazz gave way to a blending of musical elements from previous periods.

Suggested Readings and Listening

Books
Cole, Bill. *John Coltrane*. New York: Wm. Morrow, 1974.
Jones, LeRoi. *Black Music*. New York: William Morrow and Co., 1967.

Records
Coleman, Ornette *Shape of Jazz to Come* (Atlantic 1317)
Coltrane, John *A Love Supreme* (Impulse 77)
Corea, Chick *Light as a Feather* (Polydor 5525)
Davis, Miles *Bitches Brew* (Columbia GP-26)
Dolphy, Eric *Out to Lunch* (Blue Note BST. 84163)

CHAPTER 14

Jazz Rock Fusion: "The Big Crossover" (1970–1980)

I n the 1970s, there was a conscious effort on the part of many jazz musicians to reach the general public. The "marriage" of hard bop and blues, together with the enormous growth of the recording industry, led the jazz musician to enter into the area of "pop." It was not that jazz musicians sold out. On the contrary, jazz returned to its origins, the blues.

The blues revival of the 1960s was the basis for the emphasis on rhythm and blues in today's *Fusion*, or *Crossover Jazz*. Because of the many blues recordings sold to young, middle class whites during the cultural revolution of the 1960s, African American blues found its way back into the mainstream of American music. The emergence of a new, "integrated" society, that adopted the cultural patterns and habits of the blues-oriented African American, led to national and worldwide acceptance of blues. Good blues could be heard on top radio stations. It even became fashionable for the President's daughter and the President to listen and dance to the "funkiest music in town." Everybody proclaimed the blues the "in" sound. It was only natural that those jazz musicians who fanatically clung to the "pure jazz" of the 1960s would make the blues a part of their musical performance.

Some of the musicians involved in the exotic, experimental excursions of the 1960s were not preaching the sermon of funk. Musicians like Herbie Hancock, Chick Corea, Don Ellis, Freddie Hubbard, Miles Davis, Donald Byrd, Quincy Jones, Tom Scott, and Hubert Laws, not only found it financially rewarding to play the new "Fusion" music, but many of them found musically acceptable ways to present it. Herbie Hancock's Headhunters group recorded a number of interesting dates. Especially impressive is his LP *Chameleon*. Donald Byrd and his group the Black Byrds broke all sales records at Blue Note Records. Chick Corea, Chuck Mangione, Stanley Clarke, Blood, Sweat, and Tears, Chicago, Billy Cobham, Mahavishnu Orchestra, Buddy Rich, Eddie Harris, Larry Coryell, and George Benson were among the most financially successful artists.

The blues revival of the 1960s and the emphasis on Crossover in the 1970s originated with the industry's interest in hard bop during the late 1950s. The financial success of hard bop influenced the industry's interest in hard bop during the late 1950s. The financial success of hard bop influenced the industry's decisions for the future. The majority of musicians who played hard bop were well grounded in both bebop and blues. Introducing more blues into their performances was simply a matter of playing what was already a natural part of their musical heritage.

Again it was Miles Davis, with his recording of *Bitches Brew*, who paved the way for the music we now call *Jazz-Rock Fusion* or *Jazz Crossover*. Many of the "superstar" groups representing the merger of jazz and rock came out of the Miles Davis Group of 1969, when *Bitches Brew* was recorded. Weather Report with Wayne Shorter (tenor sax) and Joe Zawinul (piano), and Herbie Hancock's Headhunters are two of these groups.

Groups like Blood, Sweat and Tears; War; Earth, Wind and Fire; Stevie Wonder; and Chicago were instrumental in introducing Jazz-Rock to large groups of non-jazz fans. This is important because Davis and his group and other similar groups, did not have the popular following of these groups. Since that time many "antijazz" people (those who claimed jazz too difficult to listen to and that you couldn't dance to it) have accepted jazz.

The marriage of new Blues-Rock and jazz is a very important sociological phenomenon because it shows the degree to which a multi-ethnic culture was accepted. More and more blacks and whites are enjoying the same kind of cultural offerings, and music has been the medium that made this possible.

The return of blues to jazz has caused many critics and musicians to cry "sell out" to those artists who have achieved success with Fusion. Artists like Donald

Byrd and the Black Byrds, Roy Ayers, Chick Corea and Return to Forever, Grover Washington, Jr., Norman Connors, The Brecker Brothers, and The Crusaders (formerly known as The Jazz Crusaders) have been criticized for playing Blues-Rock oriented jazz. Whether these groups have actually sold out, nobody but the artists will ever know. Many of the writers who criticized musicians for "selling out" are those who have appointed themselves society's musical guardians, without having served the necessary apprenticeship in the blues. Blues is jazz and true jazz is blues. The two cannot be separated.

One of the most haunting questions one can ask a serious jazz musician is: Why are you selling out? According to jazz trumpeter Donald Byrd, "most people who ask such questions have not seriously listened to the music they call Fusion, but tend to prejudge the music on the basis of its commercial packaging." If the rhythm has a strong funk beat but not the customary straight-ahead four-four rhythm, or if the harmonic structure centers around a typical bluesy one-two chord pattern (I7 V7), the music runs the risk of being labeled commercial. Artists like Byrd, Grover Washington, Jr., and guitarist George Benson have all been targets of such criticism. During the latter part of the 1970s and early 1980s, new Fusion artists like Spyro Gyra (Pieces of a Dream), saxophonist David Sanborn, trumpeter Tom Brown, Jaco Pastorius' big band, Steps (Mike Brecker, Eddie Gomez, Elaine Elias, Peter Erskine), and Stuff (Eric Gale, Richard Tee, Steve Gadd) gave a revitalized spirit and meaning to Fusion. Critics and musicians began to take a closer look at the previously berated music. The new Fusion music syntheses of veteran trumpeter Miles Davis' group had such a variety of cultural and ethnic origins that most people did not attempt to classify it. Davis' approach on recent LPs, such as *We Want Miles* (Columbia) and *Star People* (Columbia), and his eclectic performance defied categorization. One simply had to accept or reject the performance on its own merit. According to jazz journalist Doug Drown, the *Star People* LP presented some of the "most important and vitalized Miles Davis music in years."

One of the tragedies of remaining a traditional or purist during a time of musical change is that the media and those who produce recorded live music often overlook talented musicians simply because they were not in the spotlight. The number of young musicians refusing to follow the trend of "hot buttered soul" (fusion music) is impressive: Cecil and Ron Bridgewater, Dewey Redman, Eddie Daniels, George Coleman, Curtis Fuller, Billy Harper, McCoy Tyner, Andrew White III, Keith Jarrett, Bobby Hutcherson, Jon Faddis, Garnett Brown, Slide Hampton and Woody Shaw.

Latin music has become such an integral part of jazz during the 1970s "Crossover" Period that it is often hard to tell whether the multiple polyrhythms are Latin or African American. (Theoretically, it is not possible to completely separate the rhythms because African, African American, and African-Latin rhythms are already interrelated.) The highly-syncopated Latin samba rhythms that originated in the religious Condomble of Northern Brazil and later found their way into the more urbanized popular music known as Bossa Nova are still one of the most popular foreign, ethnic influences in jazz. During the 1940s, the most influential ethnic music in jazz other than African American music was Spanish or Cuban music. During the early 1960s it was Indian music. Hardly a jazz or popular recording made today doesn't use African-Latin percussion instruments. In many ways, this return to the African-Latin influence in jazz was a natural outcome considering the origins of the music. Dizzy Gillespie's early use (1940s) of African-Latin rhythms was prompted by his desire to return to the Africanisms of original jazz forms. Gillespie used Chano Pozo, Joe Harris, and Sabu Martinez on Latin percussion instruments during the Bebop Period.

Drummers Elvin Jones, Max Roach, Joe Harris, Billy Cobham, Idris Muhammad, Airto Moreiro, Roger Humphries, J.C. Moses, Alan Dawson, Roy Haynes, Steve Gadd, Alex Acuna, Billy Brooks, Tony Williams, Joe Nay, Mtume, Harvey Mason, Sunny Murray, Dom Um Romao, Lenny White, Jack DeJohnette, James Black, and Alphonse Mouzon are but a few of the drummers, during the 1970s, who have experimented extensively with using multipolyrhythmns. (Some of these drummers represent earlier periods in jazz, but have continued to use the multipolyrhythmic approach.) Popular groups like Earth, Wind and Fire; Blood, Sweat and Tears; M.F.S.B. (the Gamble-Huff inspired group); The Average White Band; Graham Central Station; and Kool and the Gang, together with the more jazz-oriented, established groups of Herbie Hancock, Herbie Mann, Quincy Jones, Ramsey Lewis, Donald Byrd, Santana, Miles Davis, Mahavishnu, and Weather Report are slowly but surely bridging the gap between Blues-Rock and Jazz.

Some jazz purists feel that the introduction of more rhythm and blues and rock material into jazz destroys the quality of the music. They seem to forget that it was not until the development of bebop (1940s) that jazz ceased to be the pop music of the day. During the early years of Dixieland and traditional New Orleans music and during the Swing Period of the late 1930s, jazz was the music people danced to. Dance halls and clubs filled to capacity whenever the likes of

Guitarist George Benson, in addition to his commercial success, is one of the most innovative guitarists in jazz.

Louis Armstrong, Duke Ellington, or Benny Goodman performed. The only attempt during this period to isolate the jazz bands from the more pop-oriented groups of the day came during the 1920s, with the popularity of such groups as Paul Whiteman, James Reese Europe, and other society favorites like the Mound City Blues Blowers, the latter group performing on makeshift paper and toylike instruments.

Throughout history, the serious jazz artist has faced the dilemma of playing what some called "pure" jazz or a more commercial music. In some instances, musicians were coerced by producers and record companies. In other cases, the jazz musicians decided themselves.

During the 1920s, when King Oliver performed in Chicago, his band was well known for being decidedly commercial. Other musicians performing in Chicago during this time tried to change their style to accommodate the more commercially-oriented dance public. Even the great jazz band of Fletcher Henderson attempted to commercialize its music to reach a broader audience. During the 1920s it was common for a jazz band to play commerically-oriented dance music and then "let loose" the resident hot man for the pleasure of the jazz purist. If this was the case throughout history, then why all the fuss over the Jazz-Rock Fusion of the late 1960s and 1970s? Perhaps one reason is the more highly-sophisticiated record industry. Thousands, even millions of pop-oriented jazz records are released each year and can therefore turn the jazz market toward a more "watered down" version of jazz. This is threatening to a jazz purist who thinks he or she must guard against the decline of jazz. But just because a jazz artist introduces rhythms that are danceable or melodic forms that are more rhythm-and-blues rock-oriented, does not mean the music is bad. This music, like the music of the 1960s, will endure or decline on its own merit. If it is good and available to enough record buyers, it should endure.

One artist closely associated with the advent of Jazz Fusion is Donald Byrd. In addition to being an exceptional musician of great musical integrity, Byrd is truly a Renaissance man whose interests include education, law (he has completed two years of law school), art, piloting his own plane, and communication in the arts. In many ways, Byrd typifies the new musician of the 1970s and 1980s, who shows a diversification in music. By listening carefully to artists like Byrd, Grover Washington Jr., the Brecker Brothers, and George Benson, it becomes obvious that there is more to this music than just a "funk" beat and two chords. Before criticizing this music, we should attempt to understand every aspect of its content. One drummer was having difficulty playing a relatively simple funk rhythmic pattern. Throughout the rehearsal he continually criticized so-called Funk Fusion bands, but when it came time for him to play such a rhythm, he couldn't. Unfortunately, the music we call Fusion, or Jazz Rock, suffers tremendously from this type of thoughtless criticism. There is music from this period that can be classified as bad, but there is much that is every bit as artistically sound as the music of Armstrong, Ellington, or Parker.

During the latter part of the 1970s and the early 1980s, an artist like pianist Herbie Hancock or flutist Hubert Laws might record a funk-oriented LP one day and release a straight-ahead jazz work the next. I once asked bassist Richard Davis (who now teaches at the University of Wisconsin as well as continuing to perform) how he was able to record pop, jazz, and country and western all in the same day. Davis simply stated that you had to have the technique of the instrument under control, be alert, flexible, and ready to do whatever was necessary to enhance the quality of the music being performed. This is the kind of flexibility that has permitted jazz to survive through various trends in music.

Fusion, regardless of what many of its critics say, has brought a large number of previously non-jazz lovers to jazz. The effect of Fusion on present-day jazz is similar to that of semi-classical music in jazz. They both attract a larger audience.

A number of Fusion artists have made significant contributions to jazz during the 1970s and early 1980s, some of them outstanding contributions. One such artist is bassist Stanley Clarke. Clarke, who is from Philadelphia, rose to national prominence in the groups of Horace Silver, Stan Getz, and Chick Corea. But it was his personal approach to playing the bass that won him a place among the all-time jazz greats.

Bassists Abraham Laboriel, Alphonso Johnson, and Jaco Pastorius, keyboardist Patrice Rushen, and saxophonists David Sanborn and Ronnie Laws are among the new Fusion artists who have made a tremendous impact in jazz in the seventies and eighties. Among the established jazz musicians who have continued to make significant musical contributions to jazz during the Fusion Period are percussionist/composer Ralph McDonald; trumpeters Miles Davis, Donald Byrd, Chuck Mangione, Randy Brecker; keyboardists Herbie Hancock, Joe Zawinul, Chick Corea, George Duke; guitarist/vocalists George Benson and Earl Klugh; drummers Steve Gadd, Alphonse Mouzon, and Tony Williams; reed players Grover Washington, Jr., Wayne Shorter, Mike Brecker, and Klaus Doldinger; and bassists Ron Carter and Richard Davis.

Fusion has become one of the most popular forms of jazz. It has influenced jazz more than any other form of music since Swing. Record sales attributed to Fusion artists are greater than at any other point in the history of jazz. In addition, attendance at Fusion concerts has more than doubled that of concerts by "straight-ahead" jazz artists.

Whether this is a positive trend in jazz cannot be determined for many years. But the fact remains that jazz Fusion is producing new jazz fans—people who would not otherwise listen to jazz. Rather than criticize the jazz Fusion artists for their lack of musicianship or creativity, we should challenge them to produce a more artistic and stimulating music. We can do this by being more selective when buying records and attending concerts. Art, regardless of its quality, depends on public support. It is the jazz public who holds the key to the stability and future of jazz.

Conclusion

The Jazz Fusion or Crossover Period occurred during the late 1960s and 1970s. Established musicians like Miles Davis, Herbie Hancock, Donald Byrd, Chick Corea, Grover Washington Jr., and Quincy Jones brought together the elements of Rhythm and Blues and mainstream jazz to create a new sound.

The first sign of the "marriage" of blues and jazz occurred in the 1950s with Horace Silver, Art Blakey, and the earlier Hard Bop players. The record industry saw the possibility of increasing its sales by reaching an already established pop-rock market. The cry of "sell out" was heard throughout the music community instantly. That blues was and still is one of the main ingredients in jazz was overlooked by those critics. The established artists were hardest hit by the Crossover. Club dates became more and more a thing of the past as jazz musicians and their agents began to court the lucrative college market.

The next step in the merger was the integration of jazz by established pop-rock groups such as Blood, Sweat and Tears; Chicago; Earth, Wind and Fire; Stevie Wonder and many others.

Suggested Readings and Listening

Books
Coryell, Julie & Friedman, Laura. *Jazz-Rock Fusion*. New York: Dell Publishing Co., 1978.

Records
Byrd, Donald. *Black Byrd*, and *Places and Spaces*
Hancock, Herbie. *Headhunters*
Ohio Players Mercury SMR 1–1122
Different Strokes Columbia Records AS 12

CHAPTER 15

Women in Jazz

Profile

MARY LOU WILLIAMS • Mary Lou Williams was born Mary Lou Scruggs on May 8, 1910 in Atlanta, Georgia, and died on May 28, 1981 in Durham, North Carolina, where she had been teaching at Duke University. She was one of the most dynamic pianists of any generation. Her brilliant technique and inquisitive mind propelled her into the musical spotlight of the jazz world. Although she was born in Atlanta and first began to receive national and international recognition with the bands of Kansas City-based Andy Kirk, it was her early training in Pittsburgh where she grew up that provided Mary Lou with the necessary musical "tools" to become one of the greates innovators in jazz history.

Mary Lou was perhaps the first "legitimate" female jazz instrumentalist to receive critical acclaim (most female artists during the late 1920s and early 30s were vocalists). In addition she was also the very first female jazz artist to arrange and compose for major big bands of the period. As an arranger-composer, she wrote for such bands as Duke Ellington, Benny Goodman, Andy

Pianist Mary Lou Williams, one of the most dynamic and creative forces in Jazz during the 1940s and 50s.

Kirk (her mentor), Earl "Fatha" Hines, and Tommy Dorsey. She also was one of the first jazz musicians to write and publish a book on how to play jazz.

According to another of her mentors, Dizzy Gillespie, "Mary Lou was just like one of the guys." Although she had risen to the top of the jazz world and was considered a celebrity, Mary Lou never forgot her "roots". Periodically she would return to Pittsburgh to visit her sister Geraldine Garnett, and would always stop by the University of Pittsburgh to say hello to me and some of the local musicians who might at the time be listening to the University of Pittsburgh jazz ensemble rehearse. Inevitably she would ask Father Peter O'Brien to go in to the music building and ask me to come out to her car, which she illegally double parked at the corner of 5th and Bellefield. The first thing she would say is, "Nathan Davis, you really think you're something special because you're originally from Kansas City—but I'll have you know that Charlie Parker was running around in short pants when I was there." She would then give me a big smile and ask if I could arrange for her to practice on one of the grand pianos in the music building. After Mary Lou's death, her sister Geraldine Garnett donated Mary Lou's personal piano to the University of Pittsburgh-Sonny Rollins International Jazz Archives and Hall of Fame.

During the 1960s Mary Lou turned her attention towards religion and composed a series of religious pieces. Among the most prominent was "Mary Lou's Mass," which according to the *New Groves Dictionary of Jazz* was commissioned by the Vatican. In Pittsburgh, I had the distinct honor of directing and performing the mass at St. Paul's Cathedral for the Kool Mellon Jazz Festival (George Wein and John Schreiber, producers). The music was a joy to perform because it was well written in the sense that it accomplished Mary Lou's goal of bringing together the best elements of Jazz and religious music.

Later in life, Mary Lou devoted her time to teaching as well as to religious music. It is important to understand that at no time did she rank one over the other. Instead, she envisioned a kind of musical "utopia" where all of the best elements of jazz, religion, and education would work together for the betterment of mankind.

W hen one thinks of women in jazz, vocalists such as Billie Holiday and Bessie Smith come to mind. But there have been a number of outstanding female instrumentalists in jazz, most of whom have been pianists: Lil Hardin Armstrong, Mary Lou Williams, Dorothy Donegan, Hazel Scott, Marian McPartland, Terry Pollard, Toshiko Akiyoski, Carla Bley, Irene Schwitzer, Barbara Carroll, Patti Bown, Patrice Rushen, Geri Allen, and Shirley Scott (organ). Melba Liston (trombone and arranger) is the equal of any top male instrumentalist/composer/arranger in the world. Recently both Clark Terry's big band and Thad Jones have used the services of Janice Robinson (trombone and arranger/composer). Other female jazz instrumentalists and groups are Dorothy Ashby (harp), Willene Barton (tenor sax), Barbara McDonald (trumpeter), Vi Redd (alto sax), the original "Sweethearts of Rhythm" (a big band during the 1940s), Barbara Thompson (saxophone), Carol Kaye (bass), Ruth Underwood (percussion), Sue Evans (percussion), Blossom Dearie (piano), and the Diva (a new group of female instrumentalists based in New York).

Here I would like to focus on female instrumentalists, who have, for the most part, encountered more resistance in jazz circles than female vocalists. The first case of a traveling African-American professional jazz or blues instrumentalist occurred around 1865 after the Civil War. Ex-slaves found it necessary to earn a living whatever way they could. Those who had some experience enter-

Jazz pianist Geri Allen emerged as a leader among the "new breed" of jazz musicians during the 1980s and 90s.

British vocalist Cleo Laine with her husband, saxophonist, clarinetist, composer, and arranger John Dankworth.

taining on the plantation tried to use their talents and experience to earn their keep. But to be successful, many of them had to travel. Thus, the jazz-blues troubadour was born. Such performers often showed up at minstrel shows during the 1800s seeking employment. Women, because of their traditional subservient role in society, were forbidden from following such a profession. The chance of rape, harassment, and intervention by authorities made it next to impossible for a woman to become a jazz performer. Probably the most famous female instrumentalist during the early 1900s was "Lil" (Lillian Hardin) Armstrong. Even before Lil Hardin married trumpeter Louis Armstrong, she had begun to establish herself as an important voice in the entertainment field. Having studied piano as a child and later at Fisk University, Hardin and her family were among the many black families who migrated from the South to Chicago.

In Chicago, Hardin became a song "plugger," or demonstrator, whose job was to play new songs so that potential customers might like what they heard and buy the sheet music. Eventually she gained a reputation as a professional musician. This led to offers to work with various musicians around Chicago, and eventually an offer to lead her own band at one of Chicago's leading entertainment spots, the Dreamland Cafe. Later Hardin became a regular member of King

Joe Oliver's Orchestra at the Royal Gardens. It was during her tenure with Oliver's orchestra that she met and later married the man who became one of the most important figures in the history of jazz. According to Sally Placksin in her book *American Women in Jazz*, it was Lil Hardin who inspired Armstrong to do "bigger and better things." "I feel that if it wasn't for Lil, Louis would not be where he is today," said trombonist Preston Jackson, who had worked with Armstrong. When Armstrong began to record his Hot Five and Hot Seven sides, Hardin acted as pianist and musical director. Besides being a musical and spiritual inspiration to Armstrong, Lil was also involved in the technical success of Armstrong's career. According to Jackson, during this period it was Lil Hardin who wrote down the melodies that Armstrong composed.

Another important instrumentalist and bandleader in Chicago during the 1920s was pianist Cleo Brown. Primarily a pianist who concentrated on performing as an instrumentalist rather than as a vocalist, Cleo also worked with a

Jazz guitarist Emily Remler on stage at Carnegie Music Hall for the University of Pittsburgh Annual Jazz Seminar.

Jazz drummer Terri Lynn Carrington lectures to students at the University of Pittsburgh Annual Seminar on Jazz.

number of outstanding jazz groups in and around Chicago. Later, around 1932, she began appearing regularly on Chicago radio programs. This eventually led to gigs with her own band and recordings.

Saxophonist Peggy Gilbert, bassist Thelma Terry, trumpeter Ernestine "Tiny" Davis, and trumpeter Valaide Snow were among the outstanding instrumentalists of the 1920s and 30s. During the later 1930s and 1940s, the woman who exerted the most influence in jazz was pianist/arranger Mary Lou Williams. Although she had already made her mark in jazz as a pianist and arranger for such notables as Andy Kirk, Benny Goodman, Duke Ellington, Tommy Dorsey, and Louis Armstrong, Williams never received the credit due her. Few males of this period exerted the influence she had on the jazz scene.

I first met Mary Lou Williams at the University of Pittsburgh during the 1970s. Whenever she was in town she would stop by the University of Pittsburgh

Music Department to talk and find a good piano to practice on. I once asked her about her musical relationship with alto saxophonist Charlie Parker and bebop. She smiled and answered, "I was playing bebop in Kansas City when Charlie Parker was still in short pants." Her impact as a performer, innovator, scholar and composer/arranger was tremendous.

Until her recent illness, pianist/vibraphonist Terry Pollard was one of the most articulate soloists in jazz. Once during a concert at the University of Pittsburgh's annual seminar on jazz, she so stunned the audience during an up-tempo piano solo that she received no fewer than seven standing ovations. The next year she returned as a vibraphonist and performed equally as well.

The list of female vocalists is incredible. Some of the most popular vocalists in the history of jazz include Ma Rainey, Bessie Smith, Mamie Smith, Mildred Bailey, Sophie Tucker, Ivie Anderson, Billie Holiday, Ella Fitzgerald, Sarah Vaughan, Carmen McRae, Della Reese, Anita O'Day, Stella Marrs, Nancy Wilson, Abbey Lincoln, Dinah Washington, Annie Ross, Betty Carter, Yolande Bavan, Dakota Staton, Karin Krog, Rita Reyes, Kitty White, The Pointer Sisters, Ursula Dudziak, The Double Six, Novi Singers, Nina Simone, Aretha Franklin, Claude Lombard, Jeanne Lee, Cleo Laine, Lena Horne, Sheila Jordan, Astrud Gilberto, Flora Purim, Jean Carne, The Swingle Singers, Phyllis Hyman, Dee Dee Bridgewater, Betty Roche and Roberta Flack. Women have proven that one's sex need not determine whether one can adequately perform on an instrument. In the near future, perhaps jazz musicians will be hired as instrumentalists solely on their ability to perform. Recently receiving attention have been Diva "The No Man's Band," soprano saxophonist Jane Ira Bloom, and pianists Geri Allen and Renee Rosnes as well as the veterans, multi-talented Toshiko Akiyoshi and Carla Bley, both of whom lead big bands, compose and arrange.

Profile

BILLIE HOLIDAY • Billie Holiday (Eleanora Gough McKay) was born April 7, 1915 in Baltimore, Maryland, to trumpeter/guitarist Clarence Holiday and Sadie Fagan. Her father nicknamed her Bill (which she later changed to Billie) because of her boyish ways. One of her favorite activities was challenging the boys in boxing and bike-riding contests.

Her early childhood was marred by the divorce of her parents. Her father was a traveling professional musician, and there were constant disagreements

Vocalist Billie Holiday influenced generations of jazz instrumentalists. Photo courtesy of Rutgers, the Institute of Jazz Studies.

over financial matters and the fact that he was rarely home. Billie, on the other hand, loved it when he came home from the Fletcher Henderson and Don Redman orchestras and talked to her about music.

Another traumatic event in her already scarred life was the death of her grandmother. At the age of six, Billie had already assumed the responsibilities of a full-time nurse in caring for her. Because of a terminal illness, the old lady could not lie down. One night, in severe pain, she begged Billie to place her on the floor. Billie, out of love for her grandmother, complied and passed the night sleeping in her grandmother's arms. But in the morning Billie found herself trapped in cold arms. Her grandmother was dead. Billie was hysterical for days.

At the age of ten, she was attacked and nearly raped by a boarder who had been taken in by her mother. For this the attacker was institutionalized for five years and Billie was placed in a Catholic institution for what the judge called "enticement." During this same period (she was now 13), Billie earned most of her money scrubbing floors. She soon learned that if the carried her own equipment (brushes, soap, etc.) she could earn more. She was already acquiring the business skills that would later serve her in her music career.

At the age of 14, Billie was already a heavy user of marijuana. When she was 16 (by then the family had moved to New York) she was jailed for prostitution for refusing the favors of a Harlem political leader. In her words, "I felt like a social misfit or a social cripple." The only sanctuary she found was in singing. With her mother acting as a chaperone, Billie started working in various clubs in Harlem. First she tried working as a dancer and waitress and finally out of desperation persuaded one club owner to let her sing, and sing she did! During her career she turned out such masterpieces as "The Man I Love," "God Bless the Child," "She's Funny that Way," "Body and Soul," and "Strange Fruit."

It has often been said that Billie Holiday was not a singer but a song stylist. One must remember that music is an expression of the inner self, a mirror of the soul, a reflection of life. The voice is an instrument, like the trumpet or saxophone, a vehicle through which the artist communicates his or her feelings. In jazz as in other forms of music, it is the message that counts most. Thus, Billie Holiday was more than a singer; she was a complete musician, a "spiritual communicator." She often said that she patterned her singing style after the exciting trumpet of Louis Armstrong and later the mellow, brooding tenor saxophone of Lester "Prez" Young. Although her vocal range was rather limited, no one could phrase with more meaning and soul.

It was her sophisticated approach to life and music that prompted her colleagues to call her "Lady." According to one story, she refused to perform an indecent act, collecting tips between her thighs, and she was fired from the job. But she gained the respect of her fellow workers and the nickname Lady. Another theory is that she was named Lady by Lester "Prez" Young because she refused to sing unless she had a gardenia in her hair. She later named Lester Young "Prez" because she considered him the "president" of the tenor saxophone.

It was not until she started to sing with the bands of Benny Goodman and Artie Shaw in 1933 that she attracted national and worldwide attention. She also did a series of recording sessions with jazz pianist Teddy Wilson. On the recordings, Holiday was compared to her idol Bessie Smith and later to Ella Fitzgerald. As a member of the Artie Shaw orchestra, she became the first black female vocalist to sing and travel with an all-white band. Because of this, she suffered numberous embarrassments and abuses. Billie made over a hundred recordings and only a handful were blues. But her personal interpretation of each song gave it a natural blues flavor.

She made her film debut in *New Orleans*. Later the film division of Motown Entertainment Company produced a film of her life entitled *Lady Sings the Blues*, with Diana Ross in the title role.

One of the most degrading things a country can do to its artists is incarcerate them both mentally and physically. Because she had served time at a federal women's reformatory in Alderson, West Virginia, on a drug-related incident, Billie was refused a Cabaret card (a card all New York entertainers were required to have in order to work). Thus she was barred from working in New York clubs for twelve years. However, during this same period she was permitted to sing a welcome home concert at Carnegie Hall. After years of mental and physical abuse in a society that places commerical success over artistic integrity, Billie Holiday was admitted in a coma to Metropolitan Hospital in June of 1959 with a badly damaged liver. During this time she was still a heroin user and heavy drinker. The final humiliation was that as she lay dying in a hospital bed, she was arrested by federal marshals on a tip from a hospital nurse who claimed she found a bag of heroin in her handbag. But within hours "The Lady," Billie Holiday, was dead.

Dianne Reeves emerged as one of the most innovative and provocative of the new vocalists in jazz during the 1980s and 90s. Photo by Debra Feingold, courtesy of Blue Notes.

Suggested Readings and Listening

Books

Placksin, Sally. *American Women in Jazz.* (Wideview Books).
Billie Holiday Anthology: *Lady Sings the Blues* (Creative Concept Pub. Corp. 1976)

Records

Vaughan, Sarah *After Hours* (Columbia Special Products 66)
The Billie Holiday Story Vol. 1,2, 3 (Columbia)
The Best of Mary Lou Williams (Pablo (s) 2310756)
Brackeen, Joanne *Mythical Magic* (Pansa 7045)

CHAPTER 16

Jazz: A World Music

Jazz is now played by millions of people all over the world regardless of race, religion, or political belief. For years, governments have recognized the sociopolitical significance of jazz. In many instances the United States has used jazz musicians as unofficial diplomats to countries with whom our relationship has otherwise been cool. Generally speaking, jazz has been more readily accepted in foreign countries than in the United States. One reason is that in most foreign countries jazz did not suffer the stigma of having been born out of the injustices of slavery. To the foreigner, jazz was an art form representing a previously unknown culture. In the last twenty years, we in the United States have finally taken the first step toward recognizing African-American music, including jazz, as a definite art form. Music programs at major universities and colleges have hired professional jazz musicians to head programs in jazz. Although the colleges and universities with jazz programs are too numerous to mention, I am presently familiar with those at Indiana University (Bloomington)—David Baker; Oberlin College (Oberlin, Ohio)—Wendell Logan; Clark College (Vancouver, Wash.)—Lee Mack; University of Massachusetts—Max Roach and Archie Shepp; New York University (Stony Brook)—Warren Smith and Ken McIntyre;

The University of Pittsburgh Jazz Ensemble, Nathan Davis conductor, on tour in concert at a Jamaica Island school.

Rutgers University (New Brunswich, NJ); Southern University (Baton Rouge)—Alvin Batiste; Howard University (Washington, D.C)—Arthur Dawkins; Yale University (New Haven, CT)—Willie Ruff; North Texas State (Denton)—Neil Slater; University of Wisconsin—Bob Baca; Duquesne University—Mike Tamaro; University of Pittsburgh (Pennsylvania)—Nathan Davis; University of Michigan (Ann Arbor)—Louis Smith; and Berklee of Boston and the New England Conservatory. These are all still active.

Europe has made significant progress in forming a jazz community with enough political and economic muscle to support jazz. The European Jazz Federation which originated in Warsaw, Poland, with Chief Editor Jan Byrezek of *Jazz Forum* serving as a prime organizer, is an example of how to organize and promote jazz so it is not only profitable but educational. For the jazz fan interested in who's who in jazz in Europe and in the world, The European Jazz Federation's official magazine, *Jazz Forum*, was one of the major sources of information. The

Eric Gale, guitar; Rufus Reid, bass; Woody Shaw, trumpet; Nathan Davis, soprano saxophone; Johnny Griffin, tenor saxophone.

magazine was founded to inform jazz fans about jazz in eastern Europe. Later, its scope broadened to cover jazz in the world. *Down Beat* and *Jazz Times* magazines, in the United States, continued their fine tradition of reporting world jazz.

Jazz has come of age and is rapidly being accepted by more and more people throughout the world. It is second only to pop-rock (meaning the form of popular music that does not fall into the category of blues-rock) and to country and western music in the United States. The countries that actively support jazz include Austria, Argentina, Australia, Belgium, Brazil, Bulgaria, Cuba, Canada, Czechoslovakia, Denmark, France, Finland, Great Britain, West Germany, East Germany, Holland, Hungary, Italy, Japan, Norway, Poland, Romania, Spain, Sweden, Switzerland, the Soviet Union (on occasions the Soviets have supported extended tours of both European and American artists), West Indies (Trinidad, Martinique, Jamaica), and Yugoslavia.

It is impossible to name every musician in every country interested in playing jazz; however, I should mention those individuals who helped jazz develop in

Trumpeter Terry Clark, accompanied by pianist Mary Ann Morocco-Perry, bassist Paul Thompson, and drummer Michelle Hammond performing and lecturing to students at Falk Elementary School as part of the University of Pittsburgh's Annual Seminar in Jazz, 1994.

their own countries. A number of artists from both eastern and western Europe have international reputations as jazz personalities. In Belgium: Etienne Verscheuren (alto sax), Roger Vanhaverbeke (bass), Sadi (vibes), Bobby Jasper (sax), Nick Fissette (trumpet), Toots Thielemans (harmonica), Francy Boland (arranger), Freddy Sunder (guitar), Elias Gistelinck (composer); in Poland: Michael and Ursula Urbaniak (sax and vocal), Alan Boschinsky (trumpet); in West Germany: Albert Mangelsdorff (trombone), Michael Naura (piano), Klaus Doldinger (tenor sax), Peter Trunk (bass), Inga Brandenburg (vocal), Brian Auger (organ), Tubby Hayes (sax, vibes), John McLaughlin (guitar), Annie Ross (vocal); in Holland: Chris Hinze (flute), Rita Reyes (vocal); in Denmark: Bernt Jadig (sax), Kai Winding (trombone), Niels H.O. Pedersen (bass), Palle Mikkelborg (trumpet), Erik Moseholm, Svend Asmussen, and Alex Riel (percussion); in Czechoslovakis: Jan Hammer (piano), Miroslav Vitous (bass), Gustav Brom (The Gustav Brom Big Band); in France: Jean Luc Ponty (violin), Martial Solal (piano), Django Reinhardt (guitar), Stephane Grappelli (violin); in Yugoslavia: Dusko Goykovic (trumpet); in Austria: Friedrich Gulda (piano); in Sweden: Rolf Ericson

Grover Washington, Jr. with Nathan Davis at the University of Pittsburgh Annual Jazz Seminar.

(trumpet), Jan Johannson (piano), Moncia Zeterlin (vocal), Arne Domnerus (sax); in Norway: Jan Garbarek (sax), Karin Krog (vocal); in Canada: Oscar Peterson (piano), Don Thompson (bass/piano); and in Switzerland: Jurg Solothurnmann (sax).

In Asia, the most vibrant force for jazz is in Japan. During the late 1950s and early 1960s, Sleepy Matsumoto (sax), Isao Suzuki (bass), Jimmy Takeuchi (drums), and George Kawagauchi (drums) helped establish jazz in that country.

Saxophonist Jimmy "Lil Bird" Heath at the University of Pittsburgh Annual Jazz Seminar.

Jamaican jazz pianist Monty Alexander is one of the most exciting and explosive jazz pianists on the scene. Photo courtesy of James J.Kingsmann.

More recently, Terumasa Hino has emerged as a major voice on trumpet. These musicians, like their European counterparts, learned jazz by listening to American artists on records.

It was saxophonist/flutist Sadao Watanabe's articulate use of the then popular "bossa nova" beat that gained him an audience of young Japanese music lovers. Even the young Japanese who were not turned on to jazz were attracted to his music. This established him as one of the country's most popular jazz artists. Watanabe has hosted a fifteen-minute jazz program on the Nippon Radio Broadcasting Network.

One of the first American jazz musicians to spend a considerable amount of time living and working in Asia was pianist Teddy Weatherford. During the late 1930s, Weatherford took a band to Shanghai and remained there until his death in 1945. Clarinetist Tony Scott was also one of the first American musicians to travel and work throughout Asia. Scott, a self-styled ethnomusicologist, performed with shakuhachi player Yamamoto Hozan and koto player Shinichi Yuize (eventually recorded on Verve).

It was Watanabe who succeeded in establishing a jazz scene in Japan when he returned home from his studies at the famous Berklee College of Music in Boston and organized the first jazz workshop in Japan. It was through the workshop that many of today's Japanese musicians learned to play jazz. The school was sponsored by the Yamaha Instrument Company. Joining Watanabe were Masahiko Togashi (drums) and Masaaki Kikuchi (piano). During the late 1960s and early 1970s, Terumasa Hino (trumpet) and George Otsuka (drums) emerged as leaders of the Japanese jazz movement. Drummer Hideo Shiraki came to the United States during the 1960s to study with Max Roach.

Bassist Jacek Bednarek. Photo by Dionizy Piatkowski.

Saxophonist Sonny Stitt with student Akira Susuki at the University of Pittsburgh Annual Jazz Seminar.

Tenor saxophonist Dexter Gordon with trumpeter Woody Shaw and pianist Mike Longo at the University of Pittsburgh Annual Jazz Seminar.

British jazz vocalist Tina May is one of the most versatile of the new jazz singers of the 80s and 90s.

Afterward, he formed a group that included Terumasa Hino (trumpet) and Takeru Mumoka (tenor sax) to play the Berlin Jazz Festival (1965).

One of the first Japanese jazz musicians was pianist/composer Toshiko Akiyoshi. Akiyoshi first entered the American scene when she attended the Berklee College in 1956–57. Later she recorded with Herb Ellis (guitar), Ray Brown (bass), and J.C. Heard (drums). Akiyoshi later performed with former husband Charlie Mariano (alto sax). Presently, she and husband Lew Tabackin (sax) are co-leaders of one of the most exciting big bands in jazz.

Slide Hampton, one of the most important composers, arrangers, and orchestrators in jazz, founded the Jazz Masters, an all-star ensemble. Photo by Frank Micelotta, courtesy of Telarc.

Terumasa Hino is presently Japan's most exciting jazz artist. His high range, clear ideas, and stylish manner of dress have elevated him into a position similar to that of American trumpeter Miles Davis. Other musicians who have contributed to the development of jazz in Japan are Masaaki Kikuchi and Masahiko Sato (piano), Yasuo Arakawa (bass), Toshiyuki Miyama, and the New Herd Big Band. Recently, Japanese-American drummer Akira Tana, who was recommended to me by trombonist Slide Hampton, has become a favorite among U.S. jazz musicians.

In Africa, jazz seems to be less popular than other forms of Western music. Until a few years ago, American country and western music was one of the most popular forms of foreign music. Presently American "soul" music seems to have caught on and is considered a major form of music in most of Africa. Perhaps one of the reasons for the slow acceptance of jazz in Africa is that a country whose indigenous music is strong in character does not easily make way for the music of another culture.

In Ghana, E.T. Mensah (trumpet) is one of the country's most respected jazz artists. Mensah gained popularity when he joined Louis Armstrong in a trumpet duo of "Tiger Rag" during Armstrong's (1960) State Department tour of Africa. Most of his music during the 1950s before Armstrong's visit was patterned after European dance orchestras. This is understandable when one realized that most of the music industry in Africa is owned or controlled by the French or British. In 1960, my colleague Joe Harris and I had the opportunity to hear the Ghana Jazz Messengers in person at the Deutsche Industrie-Ausstellung in Berlin, West Germany. This group, led by saxophonist and percussionist George Lee, was patterned after Art Blakey's Jazz Messengers.

Percussionist Willie Amoaku from Ghana is one of the most dynamic percussionists to hit the scene since the days of Chano Pozo and Dizzy Gillespie.

Stan Plange (arranger/composer) is considered one of Africa's leading jazz arrangers. According to Dr. Willie Amoaku, his style resembles that of American composer/arranger Quincy Jones. South Africa is the only African country that has continually produced major jazz artists on a large scale. Some of the most popular artists are Miriam Makeba (vocal), Hugh Masakela (trumpet), Abdullah Ibrahim (formally Dollar Brand) (piano), and The Blue Notes. One reason for the emergence of so many excellent jazz artists from South Africa may be that the Kwela—a style of music similar to that of our earlier spasm bands—resembles our up-tempo jazz style. These bands, which began as street bands, were instrumental in introducing South African musicians to jazz.

Makaya Ntzhoko, the South African drummer featured on the LP *Live at the Domicile* with Benny Bailey (trumpet) and myself (sax), is a master in the use of polyrhythmic patterns. I am sure that had he been more extensively recorded by a major label, he would be one of the top drummers in jazz today.

To get a more comprehensive picture of jazz as a world music, I mailed out a number of questionnaires to various countries throughout the world. As with any such study, the return rate of the questionnaires was somewhere between two and five percent. But there were a number of surprises (which may, however, be attributed to local radio-TV programming, record availability, personal appearances by artists, local interest, etc.).

For instance, in Switzerland, Louis Armstrong, Duke Ellington, Charlie Parker, John Coltrane, and Miles Davis are the most popular artists. Drummer Pierre Favre was listed as the greatest innovator. It was not until the Cool Period that a non-American, German trumpetist Manfred Schoof, was mentioned as being a favorite. Other non-Americans named included Swiss drummer Daniel

Virtuoso bassist Santi Debriano has been one of the most active musicians on the New York jazz scene for the past several years. Photo by Baptiste Lingnel.

Humair (hard bop), French pianist Martial Solal, French organist Eddie Louis, Czech bassist Miroslav Vitous, Danish bassist Palle Danielson, the French vocal group the Double six de Paris, German trombonist Albert Mangelsdorf, violinist Jean Luc Ponty (France) and Poland's Michael Urbaniak and Zbigniew Seifert. The avant-garde, or free jazz, period showed an increase in the number of non-Americans listed in Switzerland: trumpeter Manfred Schoof (Germany), Tomasz Stanko (Poland), Kenny Wheeler (England), Maffy Falay (Turkey), saxophonist John Tchicai (Denmark), and Joe Harriott (Jamaica). Keyboardists included Missa Mengelberg. Percussion favorites were Han Bennink and Pierre Favre. The only vocalist mentioned was Ursula Dudziak (Poland). The bassist was David Holland (England). Trombonists included Albert Mangelsdorf (Germany) and Eje Thelin (Sweden).

In Switzerland, the serious study of jazz centers around the Konservatorium Basel, which has been operating since 1972. The Swiss Jazz School in Bern founded by Tony Hostettler and Heinz Bigler offers a number of courses in jazz ranging from improvisation to composition. Radio stations programming jazz include DRS, RST, and RSI—two three-hour programs weekly (two programs each). TV programming includes DRS, RSI, and RSR—two thirty-minute programs weekly (one program each).

From Lima, Peru, came the following information: the most popular jazz artists were Louis Armstrong (trumpet) and Django Reinhardt (guitar). The most popular local group was the Portena Jazz Band. As for radio programming, fifteen minutes a day is devoted to jazz, one to two hours to pop music, and three to four hours to European classical music. No universities were listed as having active jazz programs, but the Instituto Nacional de Cultura does have a program in African American music and supports a group in residence called Peru Negro.

In Holland the favorites were Louis Armstrong (trumpet), Lester Young (tenor sax), Charlie Parker (alto sax), and Duke Ellington (composer). Three artists not previously mentioned appeared—Perry Robinson (clarinet), Prince Lasha (clarinet), and trumpetist Lamar Wright. As for radio programming, six stations were reported devoting approximately ten hours a week to jazz programming. Financial support of ethnic music comes from small grants from both the national and local governments to support Dutch musicians who are devoted to playing their own music.

In France, the most popular musicians were Charlie Parker (alto sax), and Django Reinhardt (guitar). Saxophonist Michel Portal emerged as the favorite among native musicians. Recently, French pianist Michel Petrucciani has emerged as a promising new voice on the international scene. Trombonist Jimmy Harrison (formerly with Fletcher Henderson in the 1920s) and guitarist Floyd Smith (formerly with Andy Kirk in the 1930s) were mentioned. Flutist James Moody appeared to be the all-time favorite on flute. Aside from Django Reinhardt, the first non-Americans to emerge as favorites were Albert Mangelsdorf (Germany) and Argentine saxophonist Gato Barbieri.

The radio stations in France listed as having extensive jazz programming were France-Musique (MF) and France-Inter. The amount of time devoted to jazz programming was as follows: France Musique, 10 percent jazz, 80 percent European classical music, and 10 percent pop music. On France-Inter, 20 percent jazz, 30 percent European classical music, and 50 percent pop music. Europe #1, a commercial station, devoted no time to jazz, 10 percent to classical music and 90 percent to pop music.

For jazz education, the University of Paris—formerly the Sorbonne (Paris) Institute De Musicologie—offered courses in jazz history.

In Brazil, composer Duke Ellington and alto saxophonist Charlie Parker appear to be all-time favorites. Local favorites were percussionist Airto Moreiro and alto saxophonist Victor Assis Brasil. Veteran musician Jim Lannigan turned up as a surprise favorite in the bass-tuba category. Another surprise was vibraphonist Lem Winchester as a favorite (Winchester, a police officer, was one of the most promising vibraphonists during the 1950s, but killed himself playing Russian roulette). Other than Airto Moreiro (percussion), Czech bassist Miroslav Vitous and French violinist Jean Luc Ponty were the only non-Americans to be mentioned.

Brazil's Radio Elderade's program "Noite de Jazz" on Tuesday and Thursday from 11–12 P.M. appears to be the most active station programming jazz. Radio music programming is divided as follows: jazz—3–4 hours a week; classical music—50 hours a week; pop programming—120 hours per week on FM. Presently, Armando Aflalo has a series of programs entitled Jazz 60th Year for Radio Eldorado—Sao Paulo. The survey did not turn up any jazz programs at universities or colleges; but the State University at Bahia has taken the first steps toward establishing an exchange program in African music with the University of Pittsburgh.

One of the most interesting questionnaires I received was from the USSR. The favorite musician there appeared to be Charlie Parker (alto sax). The most popular native artists were alto saxophonist Georgy Giaranian (1959) and trumpeter Herman Lukyanov (1959). Two musicians not previously mentioned, David Baker (trombone) and Nathan Davis (tenor and soprano sax and flute) were other favorites. Other non-American favorites were Hungarian guitarist Attila Zollar, Danish bassist Niels H.O. Pedersen, German trombonist Albert Mangelsdorf, and Swedish pianist Jan Johansson. Another surprise was the name of the young trombonist Dave Bargeron. The only university or college offering courses in jazz was the Gnessins Music Institute, Moscow, which began in 1974.

The only Soviet radio station active in producing jazz was Tallinn Radio and Tallinn TV. Approximately 20 percent of the programming was devoted to jazz, 55 percent to pop music, and 25 percent to classical music. According to the survey, a minimal amount of time is devoted to the programming of folk-ethnic music. In addition to the Gnessins Institute in Moscow, the Academy of Sciences of the USSR has an institute for African Peoples with museums, exhibitions, and so on devoted to the study and preservation of African culture.

One of the later versions of the Paris Reunion Band at München's Allotria Club. Jimmy Woode, bass; Nat Adderly, trumpet; Woody Shaw, trumpet; Joe Henderson, tenor saxophone; Nathan Davis, tenor and soprano saxophone. Not pictured, Kirk Lightsey, piano.

In India, the most popular jazz artist is again Charlie Parker. The most innovative active artist appears to be Ms. Asha Puthi (vocalist). The name of Tommy Ladnier (trumpet) appeared for the first time. (Ladnier, who worked and recorded with musicians like Bessie Smith and Fletcher Henderson, was one of the most important trumpeters in the Louis Armstrong tradition.) Another surprise was the listing of Teddy Bunn, who was a guitarist in the New Orleans tradition. German trombonist Albert Mangelsdorf, guitarist Gabor Szabo (Hungary), and Jean Luc Ponty were among the non-Americans listed.

In Belgium, Louis Armstrong is considered the most important jazz artist. Tenor saxophonist Jach Sels (1920–50) was named the most innovative musician from Belgium. Surprisingly, Wayman Carver was named the most popular flutist (1920s) and Punch Miller (early 1900s) was mentioned. Non-Americans included Timmie Rosenkranz (Denmark), Bobby Jasper (Belgium), harmonica player Toots Thielemans, and vocalist Karin Krog (Norway). The names of Woody Shaw (trumpet), Philip Catherine (guitar), and Nathan Davis (tenor and soprano sax and flute) appeared as favorites among younger musicians.

As for jazz programming on radio and TV, composer/producer Elias Gistelinck (BRT) is responsible for one of the most active jazz radio programs in Europe. The BRT also underwrites several of Belgium's annual jazz festivals. Although there are no active jazz programs in Belgium universities, the BRT offers a number of historical jazz programs. The BRT (the Belgium Flemish radio group that broadcasts in the Dutch language) broadcasts some 25 hours of jazz weekly.

Jazz in Academia (The Teaching of Jazz)

The Monk Institute, with the assistance of major corporations and the support of the Clinton-Gore administration, provides young jazz artists with the opportunity to learn from the living jazz masters. The Institute has also established a working relationship with the U.S. State Department so that these young people can gain practical experience by touring and performing in various countries throughout the world. The Monk Institute selects the best young professional jazz musicians from around the world and provides them with an opportunity to work with current jazz masters in a classroom setting.

In Washington, D.C., the John F. Kennedy Center for the Performing Arts has established a program, founded by jazz vocalist Betty Carter, that uses the jazz masters concept to attract students from various countries. The program is under the direction of Dr. Billy Taylor, artistic director; Derek Gordon, education director; and Kevin Struthers, program manager. For approximately ten days young professionals from the U.S., western and eastern Europe, and Asia attend master classes consisting of performance practices, the history of jazz, business, etc. One of the unique things about this particular program is that each student is expected to bring a minimum of four original compositions that serve as the basis for the master classes. These original compositions are shared and performed by each of the 22 to 26 participants enrolled in the program. According to Dr. Taylor, this was Betty Carter's mandate—that the students be encouraged and mentored in developing their own original ideas, rather than jamming on songs they already know. As one who has worked with most of these programs, I have found this concept to be most rewarding.

The Thelonius Monk Institute is perhaps one of the most prestigious of the private programs teaching jazz, and its alumni are among jazz's elite.

Nathan Davis conducting students at the Thelonius Monk Institute summer program at Aspen. © 1998 by Steve Mundinger. All rights reserved.

The "Jazz AHead" program, established by vocalist Betty Carter at the John F. Kennedy Center for the Performing Arts, attracts some of the most talented young jazz musicians from around the world. Photo © Jeffrey Kliman

In Chicago, the Steans Institute at Ravinia (the summer home of the Chicago Symphony Orchestra) has developed a unique program under the direction of Penny Tyler, jazz coordinator; Jeffrey Sells, operations manager; and distinguished jazz educator and scholar David Baker, faculty chairman. Under David Baker's direction the program has attracted some of the premiere young professionals performing throughout the country. One of the impressive things about Ravinia is that classes are held in the campus-like atmosphere of the beautiful grounds of the Steans Institute in Highland Park, Illinois (a Chicago suburb). Featured are ongoing concerts and rehearsals by such artists as Chicago Symphony conductor Daniel Barenboim, cellist Yo Yo Ma, and violinist Itzak Perlman. Such an atmosphere gives the jazz students a chance to observe how professionals in other musical areas prepare their work. Participants are also expected to bring original material, which serves as the basis for the master classes

The Summer Jazz Program at Ravinia, the summer home of the prestigious Chicago Symphony Orchestra, is rapidly becoming one of the most important places for young musicians to study jazz. Photo by Cheri Eisenberg.

in analysis, rearranging, thematic construction, and melodic and harmonic revisions, taught by vising jazz masters.

One of the inspiring things about these three highly specialized programs is that they use the concept of the jazz masters as master teachers, and that each has a definite curriculum which is adhered to. Attempts to create similar programs have been made in Holland, France, Germany, Belgium, and England.

Of course one cannot forget the Berklee College of Music, founded in Boston, MA by Lee Berk and Robert Share. Of all the so-called private schools teaching jazz today, the Berklee College of Music has the longest and perhaps the most successful record. The school has produced more superstars in jazz than has any other similar institution or school.

One of the major problems in gaining support and funding for such programs is that jazz, in its purist form, is not considered a cultural preference in American society. The lack of exposure to jazz courses in our educational institutions is, in part, responsible for this lack of appreciation and understanding. Organizations such as the International Jazz Hall of Fame (Eddie Baker, founder and CEO), through its induction awards ceremony and proposed educational outreach programs; the American Jazz Museum in Kansas City (Rowena Stewart, executive director); along with the Smithsonian's various jazz programs are making great strides in eliminating this lack of appreciation.

Unfortunately, the majority of so-called jazz programs in both the U.S. and Europe fall into the trap of hiring a jazz musician simply because he or she is famous. This personality may have no idea of what it means to teach, yet he or she is thrown into a room with a group of young musicians and education is expected to happen. The sad result of such programs is that they too often end up as a lose-lose battle of the egos between the participants and the professionals. Little or no real learning takes place.

There is, of course, a valid school of thought that states the only way to learn to play jazz is by imitating or playing along with the masters. I personally developed my craft by playing night after night with Kenny Clarke, Donald Byrd, Eric Dolphy, Woody Shaw, and Sonny Stitt. But the fact is that in this twenty-first century, we have advanced to a higher level of education. There are numerous new textbooks, transcriptions and recordings. Why not take advantage of these by developing a constructive, well-thought-out curriculum that offers both oral and theoretical methods of learning?

The best way to achieve this is by making an honest attempt to hire professional jazz artists who are willing to take time out from their busy schedules and who want to devote the necessary time and preparation needed to work with students. As jazz education takes on new meaning in its quest for a rightful place in academia, we must never forget that the most important ingredient in jazz is originality. Instead of musicians accepting a gig to teach or giving a master class without focusing on this central concept, they should try to enhance the teaching of jazz by encouraging their students' originality. Why turn out a series of clones when we can take pride in helping to develop a new master?

In the United States, most major universities, colleges, and conservatories offer courses in jazz. The more serious of these programs are curriculum-oriented and have at least one or more active jazz musicians as teachers. By active jazz musicians, I am referring to musicians who have spent a good portion of their musical lives as jazz performers and who are committed to passing this knowledge on to their students. A major problem with many jazz programs is that they are taught by someone who has little or no experience as a professional jazz

Originally a tenor saxophonist, Billy Taylor developed into one of the most skilled and innovative pianists in jazz. He possesses one of the most fluid left hands of any pianist and has become one of the most distinguished diplomatic spokespersons for jazz through his work at NPR and the John F. Kennedy Center. Photo courtesy of Carol Pratt Photography.

musician. This may be attributed to the fact that many of the schools offering jazz courses are not willing to hire "specialists" who do not have a proper earned degree such as a Masters or Ph.D. Until the 1980s, it was almost impossible to find an active professional jazz musician who could or wanted to teach. If in fact they were willing, few if any had the necessary academic credentials to teach in the music department of an accredited institution. Ironically, some of the same institutions that would refuse to hire a Lionel Hampton or a Sonny Rollins to the faculty to teach jazz, would gladly hire a lesser-named classical performer to teach classical music courses. The core of the problem is the acceptability of jazz in relation to western European classical music.

On top of the problem of accreditation and degrees, there is also the issue of an institution's willingness to give the teacher-performer the freedom to continue some kind of performance schedule. Most jazz musicians are not willing to give up performing entirely to become a full-time teacher. Perhaps the most ridiculous argument put forward by some institutions is, "This is a research insitution and we are only interested in doing scholarly work—if you are only interested in performing, perhaps you should go to another institution, maybe a conservatory." The teaching of music should be the domain of those who can bring to it the experience of having produced music: either through performance, composition, or conducting as well as from having done research. The best teachers that I have had, classical or jazz, have been those who were able to personally demonstrate what they were trying to explain. This is especially true in Jazz. The old masters like Kenny Clarke and Johnny Griffin weren't entirely wrong when they advised me that "you can't really teach someone how to play jazz." They further explained that while it was possible to teach the theory of jazz, to teach someone how to swing was another story all together. That had to be learned from experience.

Yet another problem some jazz programs face is the assigning of classical musicians to teach jazz improvisation or jazz composition. Such an approach is just as bound to fail as would the assignment of an unqualified jazz musician to teach classical music. Many of the newer jazz programs would do well to take a look back in history. The Lenox School of Jazz in Massachusetts was one of the forerunners of today's jazz school. It was there that jazz masters such as Oscar Peterson, John Lewis, Ray Brown, George Russell, Gunther Schuller, and Max Roach served as master teachers for such young musicians as Ornette Coleman, Don Cherry, Joe Hunt, Larry Ridley, Chuck Isreals, David Baker, Nico Brunick, David Young, Al Kiger, and David Lahm. Another forerunner was the Advanced

School of Contemporary Music in Toronto, Canada, which was started in the early 1960s. Oscar Peterson, Ed Bickert, Ray Brown, Ed Thigpen, and Phil Nimnons were among the distinguished professional musicians who served as master teachers for advanced students such as Vince Genova (piano), Mike Taylor (bass), Vince Maggio (piano), Peter Appleyard (vibes), and Wray Downes (piano). A list of colleges, universities, and conservatories offering courses in jazz is available at the end of this book.

The Aesthetics of Jazz

Jazz as we know it today is an amalgamation of many styles. Blues is jazz and jazz is blues. Yet each style of jazz-blues represents an entirely different musical approach. The average jazz fan, especially if he or she is a "purist," tends to deny that blues is one of the main ingredients of jazz. Blues artists like John Lee Hooker, Sonny Boy Terry, and Brownie McGhee are often dismissed as ignorant or "low class" entertainers. Many jazz musicians have refused to perform with such blues artists because "It's below my dignity." Much of this anti-blues feeling among musicians vanished during the 1960s and 70s as a result of the economic success of young blues-rock groups and singers like the Beatles, the Rolling Stones, the Grateful Dead, and Jimi Hendrix. In some instances, the musicians accompanying these blues artists were too musically ill-equipped for these "over-hip" jazz purists. During the 1920s, Paul Whiteman and James Reese Europe turned to European art music rather than submit to the "crudities" of traditional blues.

Jazz musicians who played blues were often the victims of social and musical prejudice. They were not considered "true" musicians. That music is a cultural medium of inner expression is a widely-accepted fact. Jazz, however, has been accepted only recently. How can we distinguish between a type of music that serves as a vehicle for man's inner expressions and the type of music experienced by other members of a society?

In many instances, the type of music selected to represent the "cultural elite" of a particular society is that which best represents the society's financial and political accomplishments.

The word *aesthetics*, the philosophy of beauty, is used when scholars try to explain the art of music. The beauty of jazz music, as in all music, is in its overall rhythmical and tonal vibrations. The vibrations produced by the music create in the human mind and body a positive or negative response. Each one of us, whether we know it or not, responds to music. The old anecdote about the farmer who does not like music is far from true. Some of us do not respond to particular types of music such as jazz, European art music, folk music, and so on, but each of us does respond to some type of music.

Normally, when we refer to the aesthetics of a particular art form, we immediately associate the concept of beauty with that of pleasure. The philosophical concept of beauty in sound can be applied to such jazz innovators as Louis Armstrong, Bix Beiderbecke, Earl Hines, Lester Young, Charlie Parker, Miles Davis, Bill Evans, Stan Getz, John Coltrane, and Sarah Vaughan. The softness of the jazz sound produced by some of these artists and numerous others offered a new concept of beauty. The beauty of their tonal concept could not be found in any other type of music; it was a unique and original contribution to the world of sound.

The work of Lester Young (tenor sax) has never received the recognition given to other great artists in the field of music. Perhaps one reason is that those critics and writers who evaluated his work never fully comprehended what he was doing. And, in many instances, it was no doubt impossible to get close enough to him to discover his musical objectives. Without a doubt, Young influenced a whole generation of saxophonists, including Charlie Parker. His light, airy sound was like a soft, soothing breeze on a midsummer night. Yet at the same time, Young could preach the sermon of hurt—all with that same light, airy sound. This leads to the question whether the musical pictures evoked by the music are created solely by the musicians, by the listener, or both.

Those of us who have had the experience of being stimulated to the point of "no return" by such artists as Louis Armstrong, Lester Young, and Charlie Parker understand the ecstasy of listening to an exciting jazz artist. The marriage of trills and sub-toned musical sound can produce a feeling unlike any other. The fact that some people have never had such sensations can only be blamed on their lack of exposure to this particular art form rather than an inability to comprehend the music. If experiencing the total effects of a jazz performance depends on both the listener and the artist, what is the secret to uniting those two entities to ensure that one experiences the total musical offerings of a particular performance? The listener and performer are drawn together by the almost magical magnetism of rhythm and sounds from the overall musical presentation. The quality of sound, the manner or mode of presentation, and the physical and psychological makeup of both artist and listener determine the success or failure of a particular performance.

No two people respond in exactly the same way to a musical performance. We have all had different experiences that in part account for our psychological acceptance or rejection of a particular style of music.

One of the complaints of the "in" jazz musicians is that some of their more successful colleagues are in fact "classical." (Here the term "classical" refers to European art music in general and not just to European music of the latter part of the 18th century.) Some musicians who have turned to jazz without really understanding the true nature of the art form have acquired many "classical" techniques that permit them to present a flawless jazz performance. Some of these musicians honestly try to seek out the essence of the new style; yet others appear to snobbishly accept that they really are more brilliant than the less "capable" blues performer who does not possess the same amount of technique.

During my earlier years as an "expatriate" (1960s) living in Paris, I was amazed to find that most of the European jazz musicians were anxious to talk to me about the authenticity of jazz. They knew that jazz was a foreign art form in

The Berlin Jazz Festival salutes Kansas City Jazz. First row: Carmell Jones, trumpet; Queen Bey, vocalist; Jay McShaun, piano. Second row: Billy Mitchell, saxophone; Nathan Davis, saxophone. On the steps of Berlin's Gedächtniskirche, November, 1994.

which one needed years of cultivation before one could feel the true essence of the music. Merely playing the notes and clichés was only an imitation. Today, because of the many expatriates who lived with and embraced various segments of European culture, a number of young European musicians understand the art of true jazz.

It is interesting to compare the aesthetic value of the music created during the 1940s Bebop Period, the Cool Period of the 1950s, and the Avant-garde of the 1960s. The saxophone stylings of Charlie Parker, Lee Konitz, and Eric Dolphy represent a musical picture as diversified as that of the romantic and contemporary periods in music. Parker with his seemingly magical manipulation and Africanization of Western European melodic and harmonic techniques seems to dominate the other two saxophonists. Konitz, on the other hand, presents a picture of cool serenity and intellectualism. His almost flawless technical approach to sound and harmony gave him a unique position during the 1950s. Dolphy's approach to free style improvisation and his use of rhythmical-intervalic couplings placed him at the top of the list of avant-garde artists. Each of these artists (all of whom play the same instrument—the alto saxophone) offers something completely unique, yet each musician is playing jazz. Jazz has become many different things to many different people. Perhaps in the future, we will be forced to categorize jazz into even more distinct groupings or discontinue classifying the music according to periods.

One cannot rightfully speak of the aesthetics of jazz without referring to the music and personality of Duke Ellington. The very mention of his name evokes a memory of elegance and beauty in the field of music. If there ever was any doubt of the validity of true jazz, the dramatic sounds of Duke Ellington and his orchestra removed such doubt.

From a theoretical point of view, one could explain the Ellington sound by analyzing each note and chord and its proper role in the total composition. But this would be only a superficial explanation of his greatness. To understand the total substance of Ellington's music, we must be prepared to shed our pseudo-intellectualism and take a closer look at the philosophical nature of his work. The Ellington of the 1920s Harlem Renaissance period represented the attempt of black America to shed its punitive past in favor of a more lucrative Euro-American culture. The manner in which most of the jazz-dance orchestra of the 1920s dressed (most wore tuxedos, etc.) reflected their emulation of the European symphony orchestra. Ellington's group was no exception.

Perhaps Ellington's most outstanding musical contribution was his ability to effectively use tonal colors to teach a particular goal. Ellington did not merely assign harmonies to the various instrumental sections of his orchestra, but ingeniously mixed and blended together the various tonal colors of the orchestra much as Rembrandt or Picasso might have done with a painting.

Billie Holiday was more of a vocal stylist than she was a "singer," but her easy, laid-back style influenced generations of young vocalists and instrumentalists. The beauty of her untrained voice and her relaxed delivery produced a style that changed the entire concept of jazz singing.

Billie Holiday's relaxed style of performing has been the topic of numerous conversations among jazz musicians. The natural ability of a performer to relax and thoroughly concentrate on the music tends to make that performer a better performer. If this is the case, the success of a great performer depends on his or her ability to relax and at the same time present a stimulating performance.

Lester Young, the instrumentalist counterpart of vocalist Billie Holiday, possessed the ability to relax completely during a performance. Both of these remarkable artists could relax at will and called on this ability while performing.

Pianist Thelonious Monk is another musician who possessed this unique ability to relax completely during a performance. Although he may have appeared nervous to some, his ability to relax at the piano was more responsible for the germination of his musical ideas than his intellectual approach to improvisation. Someone once asked me why Monk didn't play more notes. Was it because he didn't have enough technique, or was it that he simply could not think that fast? I answered that the execution of a group of sixteenth notes didn't fit Monk's personality. Monk evidently didn't feel it was necessary to play in this manner, or else he would have done so. Musicians are like most of us in that they tend to master the necessary techniques required to reach a particular goal. Only the highly motivated or the extremely nervous go further.

The Art of Jazz Improvisation

The success of a jazz musician's performance depends on his ability to improvise freely within a given musical context. No amount of theoretical training will conpensate for a jazz musician's inability to express his or her inner feelings through improvisation. The beauty of Terry Pollard's piano and vibraphone solos and the miraculous footwork of an organ bass solo by Lou Bennett have one thing in common—spontaneity.

Artists such as Terry Pollard, Lou Bennett, organist Mike Carr, saxophonist Norman Williams, trumpeter Wynton Marsalis, his brother Branford Marsalis and the earlier Earl "Fatha" Hines, Art Tatum, and Teddy Wilson all understand the importance of spontaneity as opposed to learned repetition in jazz improvisation. Jazz musicians who play simply by repeating what they have heard are merely reproducing, not creating an original sound. Unfortunately, many cannot tell the difference.

If the average layperson has difficulty telling the difference between true jazz and a mere repetition, how can someone who has had no previous training in music tell the difference? The obvious answer is that to appreciate good jazz one does not have to be a trained musician. After all, our own inner feelings should be our main guide in accepting or rejecting a particular jazz artist. If we like the music, we should accept it on its own merit and not on the merit of general public acceptance. We should be aware that major record companies spend millions of dollars each year to influence our buying habits and our musical taste. Throughout the history of jazz, there have been artists who have not had any formal training. Many of these artists have been blessed with a relatively good ear. Some have even had perfect or absolute pitch (a form of tonal memory). Such artists can reproduce the exact pitch of anything they hear and thus can play anything they hear. Some musicians think that although perfect pitch is an admirable trait, relative pitch (the ability to hear pitches in relation to a fixed tonality) is more desirable. The ability to hear chord changes or harmonic progressions is important if one is to develop into a first-class improviser. Although a number of jazz artists with perfect pitch have been able to develop into top jazz performers without being able to read, two artists who excelled at performing by relying on "hearing the changes" were Chicago tenor saxophonist Nicky Hill and bassist Wilbur Ware. These two musicians had a phenomenal ability to hear harmonic progressions as fast as a trained musician could play them. Even before a jazz musician begins to improvise, he or she should be able to play a melody. During the early years of jazz, jazz musicians improvised from the melody without placing much emphasis on the harmonics associated with that melody. It was not until the 1930s and 1940s that harmonic improvisation overshadowed the technique of merely improvising from the melody. One of the shortcomings of improvising from the harmonic progression, omitting any reference to the melody, is that without referring to the melody, an improvisation on a given set of progressions in one song might sound exactly like any other improvisation. The melody is and should always be the major focus and primary reference.

Next, the jazz improviser must have command of the Jazz language. Music is a language, an international language. The jazz language consists of various phrases and musical motives utilizing scales, intervals, and arpeggios. Some players tend to use more scale type patterns. At one time in his career, John Coltrane concentrated more on scaler lines than broken chords or arpeggios. Some performers have a more intervalic approach. With whatever route an artist chooses to express himself or herself, the ultimate goal is to communicate. If he or she fails to communicate, everything else is lost. Dizzy Gillespie, Miles Davis, John Coltrane and Grover Washington, Jr. are all master communicators. To be able to communicate effectively with the audience and fellow musicians, improvisers should have thorough knowledge of their instruments. With this knowledge, they are then free to put technical considerations in the background and to concentrate solely on what they are going to say.

Without rhythm, music would cease to exist. A thorough and comprehensive knowledge of rhythms and the ability to execute them is essential to the jazz improviser. If the improviser possesses all of the other traits (harmonic awareness, melodic execution, concept, etc.) but cannot play in time or swing with the beat, he or she will find it next to impossible to perform with a jazz group. Rhythm, just like any other element or technique in jazz, can be learned. This is evident from the number of excellent young jazz drummers being produced all over the world.

Taste and concept are two of the most treasured attributes of any artist. Without taste and concept all of the previously mentioned techniques are meaningless. Good taste in jazz is an art acquired by listening carefully to those artists who possess good taste. Such artists as Louis Armstrong, Count Basie, Sarah Vaughan, The Modern Jazz Quartet, Miles Davis, Stan Getz, Oscar Peterson, Bill Evans, Monty Alexander, J.J. Johnson, and John Coltrane have all demonstrated impeccable taste in the past and should be role models for the young jazz improviser.

A New Breed in Jazz (1980s)

The 1980s gave birth to a new breed of jazz musician. Young and well-trained, this new group is best represented by New Orleans trumpeter Wynton Marsalis, son of jazz pianist and pioneer Ellis Marsalis. Together with his brother, saxo-

Wallace Roney, one of the most important and original young trumpeters to emerge in jazz during the 1980s and 1990s. Photo by Gary Guydosh.

phonist Branford, Wynton symbolized the determination of the younger jazz artists to benefit from the efforts of their forefathers. Trumpeter Terence Blanchard, alto saxophonist Donald Harrison, flutist Kent Jordan, and composer/pianist Geri Allen are among the new breed of outstanding young jazz soloists. Typically, these future masters of jazz are well-schooled in theory (in the case of the Marsalis brothers, both studied with their father, who is one of the finest jazz teachers this country has ever produced). In addition, many of these artists are equally proficient in European art music or classical music. This trend of jazz musicians being equally adept at performing classical music and jazz had begun on a large scale in Europe, in the 1960s, with artists like German pianist/composer Alexander Von Schlippenbach, and Danish bassist Niels Henning Orsted Pedersen. In the United States, clarinetist Benny Goodman was among the first jazz performers to commission and perform classical compositions. Throughout the history of jazz, there have been classical musicians who decided to change their emphasis in music from classical to jazz. However, this is somewhat different from the new breed of artist who is trained equally, from the beginning, in both areas.

The 1980s also produced another jazz phenomenon, the big band of Latin American bassist Jaco Pastorius. The band is one of the most innovative big bands to emerge since the Thad Jones/Mel Lewis big band of the 1960s.

The Critic and the Jazz Performer

One of the most important events in a jazz musician's career is his or her recorded and live performances. These performances represent the sum total of the artist's work. The critical review of these performances by both qualified and nonqualified jazz music critics has, in the past, greatly influenced the general public's acceptance or rejection of a particular artist. Until recently, we have not had a training ground for such critics. They were either hired by the journals or newspapers, or they volunteered to review certain jazz events because they loved the art form and wanted to see it flourish. Many of these "critics" had never heard jazz until they had reached maturity—and even then were exposed to the music only on a limited basis. Yet they were entrusted with informing the general public of the merits of a music many of them knew little or nothing about. Many of the newspapers and journals carrying reviews on jazz never even bothered to provide the new reviewers with such basic tools as a press card so that they could enjoy those special privileges normally accorded journalists.

Another problem is the critic whose specialty is European art music, but suddenly finds that he or she has been assigned to review a jazz event. Such reviewers can cause more damage than the untrained person simply because, by virtue of their knowledge of some music, they appear to be experts on jazz. Unfortunately, there are those who think that a critic trained in European art music is qualified enough to review a jazz event. That jazz was originally a non-European art form, with a history and technique of its own, is often overlooked.

There are also those "experts" who feel that because they were born in an environment where jazz existed they, and they alone, can serve as its spokesperson. This "over-hip" novice has done more to hinder the growth and acceptance of jazz by the general public than anyone. Such people tend to single out a particular style or type of jazz (free jazz, bebop, crossover, swing, dixieland, etc.) and denounce any other form of the music as false or not the "real thing." As a result of his or her philosophy of what is or is not jazz, many would-be jazz fans are turned off. These disappointed fans usually end up rejecting all forms of the music, reducing the number of people who would normally support jazz.

There is a style and type of jazz for almost everyone—especially if we remember that blues is jazz and jazz is blues and that the blues resulted from the African-American experience in North America. American pop-rock has its origins in the blues, just like bluegrass and other forms of American music.

In the past, the musician's reaction to the jazz critic has varied from pure apathy to outright violence. Several noted jazz artists have been known to physically reprimand critics who wrote unfavorable reviews of their performances. Still other musicians have publicly stated that an unfavorable review could not hurt their box office appeal, nor influence their musical direction.

During the 1960s, the so-called free jazz period, many young musicians found themselves the victims of unfair criticism by the general public, other jazz musicians, and the press. Like it or not, the critic's point of view affects thousands of people. Records are bought or sold on the strength of reviews. Many agents gauge the strength of their artists by the number of favorable reviews they receive. Fortunately, however, there are those musicians who are confident enough in their own musical judgment to decide for themselves what is and what is not good jazz. I have seen more undeserving artists become successful because of good reviews than good artists become successful in spite of bad reviews. Critics

Roots, a jazz group dedicated to the preservation and performance of the work of the great saxophonists in jazz, became one of the major voices of the 1990s. Photo by B. Seidel, courtesy of Mike Hennessey.

have a great responsibility and must do everything in their power to become familiar with the subject matter (painting, dance, music, sculpture, writing, etc.) so that they can make an honest and accurate appraisal of a performance.

One possible answer to the problem of inaccurate criticism in jazz is to establish courses in criticism at our colleges and universities. Such courses could fit within the academic framework of an already existing jazz program, or be offered as a special course of study in the music department, or in the school of continuing or adult education.

The Politics of Jazz

Politics in jazz?—why, that's impossible. After all, isn't jazz a "freedom" oriented music, completely separated from the everyday bickering of today's political activities? Quite the contrary. As a result of its worldwide popularity and the acceptance of its practitioners, jazz has become one of the most effective "tools" of our government in influencing our political relationship with other nations. The United States government has used, on several occasions, jazz music and musicians as "diplomats" when all other means have failed. Musicians like Duke Ellington, Benny Goodman, Woody Herman, Thad Jones, and Mel Lewis have done what trained diplomats have failed to do—enhance the image of the United States abroad. They did this by performing America's best export to date—jazz.

The idea of politics in jazz need not be a negative one. During the summer of 1977, I was fortunate enough to have been invited to play in Rossendal, Holland, with the Dutch pianist Jack Van Poll. This proved to be both an exciting and educational event. I learned from Van Poll that the young Dutch musicians had formed a group called BIM, which was composed primarily of improvising musicians. The purpose of the group was to ensure that its members were adequately paid for their musical performances. In response to their demand, the Dutch government agreed to match any sum of money paid each individual musician. Thus a BIM member is free to negotiate with a club owner or concert promoter for a reasonable amount of money and can expect the government to match that sum on completion of the job. In the United States, the National Endowment for the Arts has established traveling grants for young musicians who would like to travel and study with a professional musician of their choice. This is a step in the right direction, but is far from offering the continued financial stability of a program such as the one established between BIM and the Dutch government. In the 1980s, both the National Endowment for the Arts and a number of state Arts Councils made considerable progress in providing assistance to jazz artists. Many cities and counties throughout the United States now support jazz in area parks and recreational facilities.

According to Van Poll, BIM is not limited to musicians, but includes painters, sculptors, ballet companies, theater companies, and so on. Another interesting component of the program is that local BIM members are also free to negotiate with foreign promoters, with knowledge that the Dutch government will supply seed money (for general preparation for the job, rehearsals, travel, etc.) and match the host country's financial offer, up to a certain point. To qualify for membership in BIM, one need not be Dutch (American jazz musician Wilbur Little was a member). The main requirement for membership is that the artist must legally live and work in Holland. Future projects for the BIM include a sound, social security plan, a retirement plan, and sick benefits. Other countries like Sweden offer state financial concerts in public parks, and in museums and schools. Here are examples of politics working for the benefit of jazz musicians.

The European Jazz Federation, originally under the direction of *Jazz Forum* editor-in-chief Jan Byrczek, has done more than any other organization in Europe to pave the way for worldwide acceptance of European jazz musicians. In the United States, groups like the Collective Black Artist, the New York Jazz Composers Orchestra, and The Association for the Advancement of Creative Musicians in Chicago have exerted political pressure to obtain employment opportunities for young, American jazz artists. The National Endowment for the Arts has stimulated financial assistance for American musicians, but this is not enough. Young, American jazz artists must depend solely on commercial appeal if they intend to earn a living as jazz performers. What happens after the travel grant or the composer honorarium is gone? There are few club owners or promoters who will hire an artist who does not have commercial appeal. The answer to these and other similar problems is political. In the future, if we intend to ensure the continued success of America's number one cultural export—jazz—we must provide for its practitioners by voicing our opinion at the polls. In recent years, we have witnessed in the United States the resurgence of jazz social clubs similar to the Hot Clubs of the 1930s. This is a welcome trend since many of these organizations often co-sponsor concerts, festivals, and in some instances club dates.

The Business of Jazz

The Jazz Performer and the Record Industry

One of the most important vehicles for reaching an audience is the phonograph recording, CD, video, etc. If the musician is one of those artists fortunate enough to be able to communicate in the studio as well as in a live performance, he or she is a step ahead of the performer who cannot reach an audience through recorded examples. Without a current recording (one that is selling or being played at the moment), the jazz performer is not a valuable commodity and will find it difficult to get bookings. This was not always the case. During the early 1920s, club owners would display a sign stating that a "color band" was appearing. As a result, the club would be filled to capacity. It was not until after the success of such established artists as Paul Whiteman and Fletcher Henderson that jazz records began to sell in numbers large enough to attract the major labels. The Original Dixieland Jazz Band, an all-white group, was the first New Orleans jazz group to officially record a jazz record for a major company. The ODJB recorded "Dixie Jazz Band One Step" for Victor Records in 1917, and was in part responsible for the acceptance of jazz among whites in the United States.

Because of racial segregation in the United States during this period, record companies were forced to direct their marketing toward the more lucrative white audiences. With the success of Black Swan records, the first all-black-owned record company, black music, especially blues, had its first ethnic outlet.

Regardless of the intent of record companies, producers, and the jazz public, certain records have always appealed to particular social ethnic groups. Fortunately, many of our greatest jazz artists like Louis Armstrong, Duke Ellington, Count Basie, Sophie Tucker, and Belgium guitarist Django Reinhardt have always appealed to jazz fans regardless of color. In fact, traditional jazz purists have always, to a certain degree, been color-blind when it came to a good jazz music. All they wanted was the best, and if the particular artist happened to be black, they accepted the music on its own merit.

Today the jazz artist is still faced with the task of finding a suitable vehicle for reaching his or her audience. Because of the jazz artists' position, a position that finds them searching for a major label to help launch their product, they are often forced to compromise their ideas about their art and take the more commercial path often suggested by their producer or label. This has led many artists to establish their own independent labels and publishing companies. During the 1960s, especially with the development of free jazz, a number of independent labels emerged. One of the most successful of these independent labels was Bernard Stolman's ESP labels. Just as underground films began to win the public's approval, independently produced records began to appeal to a wider segment of the music audience. As a result, many jazz musicians, who had not previously had an opportunity to record, were now being recorded in large numbers in the same manner as artists like Miles Davis, John Coltrane, and Stan Getz. Many of the older, more established artists resented the easy access that the newer, unproven jazz artists such as Archie Shepp, Albert Ayler, and Guiseppi Logan, had to the highly-coveted territory of the established artists.

As a result of so many records, those of the established and major labels as well as those of the lesser known independents, there was an overflow of jazz records on the market. (During my many tours as a performing jazz musician, I have heard established jazz artists express their disapproval of the overabundance of jazz records on the market.) If the lesser known jazz artist was ridiculed for his or her, sometimes unorthodox, entrance into the jazz world, what effect did his entrance have on the record buying jazz public?

One good thing that emerged, from the introduction of so many lesser known, and in some instances unproven, jazz recording artists is that these artists broadened the concept of "modern jazz." They also proved that there was an audience, regardless of its size, for their music. In some instances, these independents kept the new music of that era alive.

In the 1970s, the larger, more established record companies began acquiring the smaller, independent companies. The president and chief executives of the smaller companies were often permitted to continue as chief executive officers of the new subsidiary, but the final decisions were not in the hands of the conglomerate or parent company. Thus, artistic considerations were often no longer the primary interest. On the positive side, the larger companies were in a better position to provide more exclusive and creative advertising and, above all, more capital for the actual recording session. It is well known that many jazz artists have longed to record with such luxuries as a full string section, similar to that of a typical chamber orchestra, or to have the luxury of overdubbing or re-recording previously unsatisfactory sections of a work. With the vast amount of capital available through the new conglomerates, this was now possible.

Numerous books and brochures have been written about how to "make it" in the record industry. Therefore, I will not attempt to single out any one book as the best. However, there are two books which I think get at the heart of the matter: *Music Business Handbooks and Career Guide* by David Baskerville, Ph.D. and *How to Make and Sell Your Own Record* by Diane S. Rapaport. These two books provide guidelines for the amateur as well as the professional in such areas as agents, distribution, publishing, royalties, demonstration records, bookings, and so forth.

"The New Traditionalists"

Jazz in the 1980s saw a trend toward traditionalism. Younger players like trumpeter Wynton Marsalis, tenor saxophonist Branford Marsalis, trumpeter Terence Blanchard, tenor saxophonist Courtney Pine, trumpeter Wallace Roney, alto sax-

Saxophonist Nathan Davis and wife Ursula join jazz legend Sonny Rollins backstage at Pittsburgh Hartwood Acres Summer Jazz Series.

ophonist Donald Harrison, tenor saxophonists Jean Tousaint, Joshua Redman and David Sanchez, trombonist Robin Eubanks, drummers Terri Lynn Carrington and Marvin "Smitty" Smith, and pianist Geri Allen set the tone for the new generation of the 80s. Their brash, new, bold, straight-ahead approach to improvised music was a welcome addition to the over-dramatized rock-oriented jazz of the 1970s. I do not wish to imply that all of the rock-oriented music of the 1970s was inferior, but the fact remains that many of the rock-oriented goups of this period have dropped out due to a lack of musical stability.

Established artists, like tenor saxophonist Sonny Rollins, drummer Art Blakey, alto saxophonist Phil Woods, and trumpeter Miles Davis, continued to create a musical climate that not only inspired the younger players, but they also tended to dictate the direction that the music should move in—especially Miles

Davis. With his strong dominant approach, Miles Davis legitimized the use of sound-altered electronic devices in music. Just as the musicians in the 1960s changed their negative outlook on Jazz Fusion (Jazz Rock), jazz musicians again followed Miles' lead into the adventurous area of midi-influenced (music—interface digital) jazz. It is also necessary to point out that in addition to Miles, keyboardist Joe Zawinul, tenor saxophonist Wayne Shorter, and keyboardists Chick Corea and Patrice Rushen were also in the avant-garde of the new midi revolution in jazz.

The fact is that the 1980s became a highly-diversified period in jazz history. It was possible to hear a variety of styles in jazz that draws from all corners of the globe. Perhaps it is an indication of our times that jazz, as well as other cultural offerings, are truly representative of a totally integrated global unity. Regardless of the various criticisms of the jazz fusion players, those artists who are well-trained in the foundations of music tend to survive the unpredictable changes that take place. One such musician, saxophonist Grover Washington Jr., was able to prove with the release of his straight-ahead LP "Then and Now" that he is one of the innovators of our time. His ability to penetrate the musical psyche of the jazz purist, as well as entertain the occasional jazz novice, shows a solid foundation that is capable of interpreting any style of music, whether it is classical, jazz, blues, ethnic-folk, or "middle of the road."

The timeless compositional style of Gil Evans is also an indication that good music is not limited to age. Evans' music is not only steeped in tradition, but it also embraces all that is good about the avant-garde.

CHAPTER 17

The 1980s and 1990s: New Directions in Jazz

The late Kenny Clarke, one of the most influential figures in the history of jazz, often used to say the more things change, the more they remain the same. This is evidently true when we take a look at the development of jazz during the eighties and nineties. The 1960s and 70s saw jazz develop along the lines of freedom in both expression and technique. Many of the jazz musicians during the 1960s, who played the music often referred to as avant-garde, were sincere in their efforts to further the concept of jazz, but lacked the necessary technique to develop those concepts. On the other hand, there existed certain musicians like Eric Dolphy, John Coltrane, Miles Davis and Cecil Taylor, who actually did possess the technique to express their ideas and concepts and to forge ahead in developing new areas and concepts in jazz. The 1980s and 1990s have seen what I call a complete turn-around or reversal toward the restatement of some of the earlier ideas developed by the jazz masters of the past. Without a doubt, the music of such young players as Wynton Marsalis, Joshua Redman, Terence Blanchard, Donald Harrison, and Benny Green has reached back into the past and borrowed from great masters such as Roy Eldridge, Louis Armstrong, Clark Terry, Coleman Hawkins, and Don Byas. This, then, tends to support Kenny's statement that the more things change, the more they remain the same.

The restatement of previously proven ideas in jazz should be viewed as a kind of assurance that the great music responsible for the stability and development of jazz will always be present. It is to the credit of these younger musicians that they have accepted the burden of carrying on the great work of the masters. Among these great masters, we also see the emergence of more women instrumentalists, which is a great sign. The fantastic work being done by pianist Geri Allen, the late Emily Remler on guitar, Germany's Barbara Dennerlein on organ, vocalist Cassandra Wilson as well as England's Tina May, is evidence that the jazz tradition is in good hands.

What is really important about the work of the younger musicians of the 80s and the 90s is its sincerity. I can remember speaking to a number of Europeans about the new crop of younger musicians emerging in the United States. Perhaps the most impressive, outside of Wynton Marsalis, were Terence Blanchard and his cohort with the Art Blakey band, Donald Harrison. The critics basically were impressed, not only with their ability to play and the freshness of their musical ideas, but were also openly impressed with their devotion to the past jazz masters. In many ways these two young musicians served as role models, along with the Marsalis brothers, Wynton and Branford, for the new generation. Not only did they play well, they were business oriented, dressed well, were

Wynton Marsalis has emerged as one of the most versatile voices in jazz.

Trumpeter Terence Blanchard and alto saxophonist Donald Harrison, both former members of Art Blakely's Jazz Messengers, represent the new breed of young jazz "lions" that emerged during the 1980s and 90s. Photo by Hans Neleman, courtesy of Sony Music.

very mannerable and respectful toward their peers, yet openly aggressive in their approach toward playing the music. Without a doubt, this open aggressiveness coupled with their show of respect and admiration for their peers is accredited to their association with the great master himself, Art Blakey. Blakey, aside from being one of the most important drummers in the history of jazz, was also one of the great teachers of our time. He demanded respect and total dedication to the cause of furthering jazz. He talked openly about this and insisted on it with his musicians. In 1982, Blanchard not only proved that he was capable of carrying on the long trumpet tradition associated with Art Blakey and the Jazz Messengers, but also gave the band a kind of new direction. After Blakey, Blanchard left with alto saxophone player Donald Harrison to form their own quintet, which also was responsible for recording a number of new albums. What was so highly unusual about Blanchard's entree onto the jazz scene, in the 1980s, was that he found himself in the awkward position of being compared to his fellow New Orleans cohort, trumpeter Wynton Marsalis. Much to his dismay, he found that there were those who basically compared his work to the same artists, Clifford

Brown and Miles Davis, as they did Wynton's. Some critics preferred Wynton; others preferred Terence. Without doubt, this must have been a very uncomfortable position for a young trumpeter. But much to his credit, Terence weathered the storm and began to forge ahead with his own identity. He has developed into quite a prolific composer having written film scores for Spike Lee's movies, such as the much heralded "Malcolm X," "Sugar Hill," and "Crooklyn," as well as serving as technical adviser on "Mo Better Blues."

Donald Harrison, together with Kenny Garrett, are probably two of the most influential alto players to come along since the 1960s. One of the most important influences in Harrison's life, as well as in the lives of Blanchard and the Marsalis brothers, is Ellis Marsalis. All four grew up in New Orleans and at one time or another studied under the direction of Ellis. Most of the younger musicians who come from New Orleans pay homage to veteran pianist Ellis Marsalis, father of Wynton, Branford, Delfeayo and Jason. Without doubt, Ellis has been an inspiration and a great teacher. This can be seen in the works of his young pupils who have begun to establish themselves in a formidable way in jazz. Donald also credits his period of study at Southern University, under the ample tutelage of clarinetist Alvin Batiste, as having a lot to do with his progress in music. He later attended Berklee School of Music, and subsequently Rutgers University. I first came in contact with both Blanchard and Harrison when they were with Art Blakey. One of the things that appeared evident about their way of playing was that they tended to be very aggressive and yet, at the same time, conservative. By conservative, I mean that they were able to venture out into new areas of music without sacrificing musicality. All too often we find that young artists who attempt to venture out into areas of new tonalities and rhythms, tend to forget the basis of music theory, especially those which deal with such areas as atonality, texture, phrasing, etc. This was not the case with Harrison or Blanchard. Donald's alto sound appears to be a combination of Lou Donaldson and Sonny Stitt rather than that of Charlie Parker. He has a tight piercing sound that tends to penetrate, as opposed to the softer more lush sound of Charlie Parker. He is quite impressive in the way he handles the high notes and is technically equipped to move around rather than using the high notes as a gimmick. Without doubt, he is one of the most important voices of the future. Kenny Garrett is another young alto saxophonist who has established himself as one of the more respected players during the eighties. Kenny's style is almost cliché-free. He possesses a penetrating sound and a formidable technique. I first became aware of Kenny's playing when he was a member of the group, Out of the Blue, which also featured another impressive, young trumpet player by the name of Mike Mossman. In that group, Kenny proved himself to be a strong soloist, but added to a tight anchoring, musical foundation that many young groups often lack. By this, I mean that he was able, when called upon, to produce some of the most lyrical solos that I ever heard, but at the same time was as comfortable playing a background role. This is something that is often lacking in many young players who feel that they must, at every chance, get out and prove how fast or how high they can play.

What is actually apparent, when looking at this most impressive group of young players, which also includes the talented Henry Butler, pianist, and the young piano player Marcus Roberts, is that they bring with them a new type of approach not often evident in the music of a lot of the other younger players. They bring a type of blues, New Orleans traditionalism with them. One could argue that there is no such thing as a New Orleans sound with these younger players. However, what is extremely evident is a kind of maturity that comes only from having had the combination of the traditional background, normally associated with players from an earlier generation, especially from the be-bop era with study of the technical aspects of jazz. True study of jazz can be seen in the music of many of the players who have emerged since the 1970s and 80s. There are a number of excellent schools around that have provided an opportunity for a number of these students to gain valuable experience. One of the advantages of having this particular type of academic background is that the students are able to get at immediately, through the art of transcription, the technical aspects of improvisation. By imitating certain soloists and analyzing their approach to improvisation, the young student is able to sound, at an earlier stage in his or her development, as close to the jazz master as possible. On many occasions, some of these students have been able to copy these masters so thoroughly that it has been virtually impossible to tell if the student is really thinking in that direction, or has actually memorized the solos of these artists. Here I am not, by any means, indicating that these younger players, and especially those from New Orleans, merely learn by copying the solos of the earlier jazz masters. What I am saying is that, without doubt, we can hear in their music that they have had this exposure.

Among some of the other younger players who have duly impressed the jazz world, during the 1980s and 90s, is the pianist, Benny Green. I first ran into Benny Green during the time when I taught on the faculty of Oberlin Conservatory, while he was appearing there as the accompanist for vocalist Betty Carter. Benny Green, together with Mulgrew Miller and Geri Allen, is perhaps one of the most mature sounding of the young pianists on the scene today. His style is reminiscent of many of the earlier players such as Wynton Kelly, Tommy Flanagan, etc., yet he maintains a kind of individual spirit that can only be associated with one as dedicated as Benny. In recent years, he has been working with the Ray Brown Trio and has also, on numerous occasions, appeared as soloist in and around New York City. I also had the opportunity of working opposite him in Spain and Pittsburgh, when he was a member of Art Blakey's Jazz Messengers. One of the things that is very evident about Benny is his musicality. His phrasing is unique in that he is able to follow through on his ideas and is able to blend together a type of sophisticated neo-be-bop style with a kind of progressive, post-sixties, free improvisation, often associated with Herbie Hancock.

Perhaps one of the most visible of the younger jazz musicians to emerge during the eighties is tenor saxophonist Joshua Redman. Redman, the son of another famous tenor saxophonist, Dewey Redman, and descendant of the famous Don Redman, who also was a saxophonist, has had one of the most spectacular careers in recent times. Without doubt, his affiliation with the much-heralded Thelonious Monk competitions, headed by one of the most spectacular and dynamic administrators that I've seen (Tom Carter, C.E.O. of the Monk Institute), has had a lot to do with Redman's success. His recent nomination as jazz musician of the year and album of the year award in *Downbeat's* fifty-ninth annual reader's poll, is evidence of his growing stature in the business. He has a fluid tone and excellent command of the high notes. Like many of the other young musicians I've mentioned before, Branford Marsalis,

Joshua Redman. ©*AFP/Corbis*

Kenny Garrett and Donald Harrison, he has chosen to return to the roots, often stating the well-documented musical ideas of such great artists as Illinois Jacquet, Coleman Hawkins, Ben Webster, etc. His affiliation with Warner Brothers, one of the giants in the business, has also played a very serious and intricate part in his quick rise to fame. Regardless of the stature of the musician, without the promotional mechanism in place an artist is often overlooked, and in some instances not even heard by the jazz public. If he continues along the same line, it is more than certain that Joshua Redman will be one of the major innovators of his time.

Another alto saxophonist worth mentioning is Bobby Watson. Although he is senior to many of the aforementioned newer players, the 1980s and 1990s have seen Bobby blossom into a serious and more widely-accepted artist. His work in and around New York has established him as one of the major alto saxophonists on the scene today. Not to take away from his early contributions as a member of the Jazz Messengers, however, during that particular period, many critics felt that he was actually searching for his own voice and had not yet arrived at the point where he could be considered one of the major players. As I mentioned before, the 80s and 90s have reintroduced Bobby as one of the more dynamic players of his generation. Antonio Hart is another example of a young alto saxophonist who has made quite a name for himself working with various groups, including the groups with his mentor and teacher, saxophonist Jimmy Heath.

Another alto saxophonist who has been able to break through and make a name for himself is Christopher Hollyday.

A young tenor saxophonist who is much heralded by fellow musicians in and around New York is David Sanchez, who has become well-known especially through his work with the units of veteran trombonist, Slide Hampton. Sanchez plays with a forceful, dynamic style often reminiscent of a combination of Coltrane and Dexter Gordon. No doubt his Latin background plays a role in his fiery approach to improvisation. Most of the veteran musicians and young musicians in and around New York consider young Sanchez to be among their favorites, if not their favorite, young tenor saxophonist. David Sanchez is probably a good example of the younger musicians who have come from Latin America to the U.S. and had quite an impact on the local scene. He has a very straight-ahead forward sound and in many ways is considered to be a leader among the newer breed of young, Hispanic musicians.

Santi Debriano, the young Panamanian bassist, is another musician who has made his mark on U.S. jazz. A very versatile bassist, he has recorded with a number of musicians throughout the United States and Europe. He appeared re-

Jazz saxophonist and clarinetist Eddie Daniels has a liquid, clear, full clarinet sound and has introduced a new generation of young jazz fans to the sound of the clarinet. Photo courtesy of GRP records.

cently on the first three albums by the group Roots and on my own CD, "I'm a Fool to Want You." He has blinding speed, possesses a full robust tone, and is equally comfortable playing free jazz, bebop, or swing.

Danilo Perez is another young, Hispanic jazz musician who has made quite an impression in the United States, primarily through his work with Dizzy Gillespie. He brings to jazz a formidable technique coupled with a thorough knowledge of Latin rhythms, as well as a soulful blues, funk style. In many ways, young Danilo represents the new breed of piano players who fuse together various styles without really sacrificing their musical integrity. Without a doubt, he is sure to develop into one of the most important pianists of our time. Also, among the young pianists, we must consider Cyrus Chestnut, who has begun to make quite a name for himself and is destined to become one of the major pianists of the 90s.

Eddie Daniels, although not considered one of the new breed of the 80s and 90s (he first established himself on the jazz scene during the early 1960s), the clarinetist/saxophonist is one of the freshest new voices to come on the scene, especially on clarinet. It can truthfully be said that he has reintroduced the clarinet to an entirely new generation. He plays with a fluid style, has an even tone throughout the instrument and is totally unique in his approach to the instrument. The clarinet requires difficult fingering and a clarinetist must negotiate through three different octaves, using different fingerings in each octave, making it a difficult instrument to play in comparison to the saxophone. (I was a clarinet major at the University of Kansas.) Another young clarinetist who has made a name for himself in a somewhat jazz-related area is Don Byron, who plays a number of various styles, but has been mostly associated with Klezmer music. As a member of the touring group Roots, I had a chance to work opposite him in Lubiana in 1994, and enjoyed his music immensely, especially his dark, warm sound.

Perhaps one of the most impressive of the young drummers is Lewis Nash. Nash is basically a horn-man's dream. He is able to keep steady time while at the same time playing complicated polyrhythms and swings beyond reason. Again, it was Dizzy Gillespie who launched Nash into the international spotlight. He is also an important voice in the continued subtle, but aggressive style of swing, coupled with grace and dignity, that was launched by the late Kenny Clarke.

Terri Lynn Carrington is one of the stars of the new breed of drummers working today, who first came to national attention through her work with Clark Terry, James Moody, and Wayne Shorter. Daughter of saxophonist Sonny Carrington, she was noticed on a national scale through her work as the drummer in the house band on the *Arsenio Hall Show*. She is also an exceptional teacher who does excellent clinics and workshops throughout the country; she swings as hard as any young drummer on the scene today.

Another trumpet player who has made quite a name for himself and has proven to be a leader on numerous occasions is young Roy Hargrove. Hargrove, who first hit the scene as a teenager, has taken the jazz world, especially Europe, by surprise. I can remember once playing the Stockholm Jazz Festival and seeing his name written boldly in capital letters as the headliner of the show, which included some very important jazz veterans. This kind of publicity often plays more of a negative role in an artist's career than is thought. Look back at the case of Julian "Cannonball" Adderley, when the critics and record industry billed him as a successor to Charlie Parker. Cannon felt that the publicity and the comparison tended to hurt his career rather than help it. This early promotion points the direction for the artists rather than allowing them to state the direction that they themselves would like to pursue. It also builds up a type of expectation, normally associated with the veteran artists, and deprives the younger artist of a

Belgian-born jazz guitarist and harmonica player Toots Thielemans is single-handedly responsible for establishing the harmonica as a legitimate jazz instrument. Photo courtesy of Abby Hoffer Enterprises.

chance to make his or her own statement, without expectations. In any case, there is bound to be some comparison, but the comparison is often unfair and brutal. Hargrove, however, seems to be untouched by such publicity and has forged ahead with a very aggressive and pure jazz style. In many instances his style seems to be more straight-ahead and is representative of the Clifford Brown-Blue Mitchell-Donald Byrd approach to the trumpet, which in my book, is pretty good company.

Perhaps one of the most dynamic young guitarists on the scene today is none other than Kevin Eubanks. Kevin has proven himself to be an exceptional musician who can adapt to any and all musical situations presented to him. His work as leader of the *Tonight Show Band* is evidence of his ability to adapt. I have personally worked with him, in a number of other situations, with Freddie Hubbard, Grover Washington Jr., Mulgrew Miller, etc. and I've heard him play some of the most dynamic and adventurous solos that I've ever heard played on the guitar.

Veteran artists, who have appeared on the scene during the 80s and 90s, have also had quite a lot to do with helping shape the music of the future. Some of these artists include, but are not limited to, such artists as Tito Puente, with his ever challenging and futuristic approach to Latin music; the re-emergence of Toots Thielemans on harmonica; and who can forget the re-introduction of veteran singer Tony Bennett. Perhaps due to the skillful management of his son he has become one of the most sought after jazz vocalists in history. Needless to say, his timeless style and impeccable tone allow him to skillfully manipulate the lyrics so that they not only convey the composer's intent, but also engage the listener. Tony is, without doubt, one of the most respected and highly praised jazz vocalists of the 90s.

Another younger vocalist who has made inroads is Kevin Mahogany from Kansas City. He, together with veteran singer Jimmy Scott, have been two of the most visible and dynamic male vocalists on the scene. Female vocalist Queen Bey who has been primarily billed as a blues singer, but is capable of singing any style, was also another welcome addition on the vocalist scene in the 90s. Dianne Reeves is perhaps one of the most important of the younger vocalists who have made a mark since the advent of such stellar vocalists as Sarah Vaughan, Carmen McRae, Nancy Wilson, etc. Reeves shows all the potential to be an equally important innovator as the aforementioned. Also Cassandra Wilson deserves credit for her adventurous style of improvisation. She is destined to become another of those important figures in the history of jazz. In England, vocalist Tina May is perhaps one of the freshest voices I've heard in quite some time. She possesses horn-like qualities, a pure sound, and is able to sing in any style from opera to blues. Tina, along with saxophonist Courtney Pine and pianist Julian Joseph, represent a new breed of British jazz musicians who have already begun to make their mark on world jazz, especially in Europe.

Although he is perhaps considered to be a veteran among trumpeters, Jon Faddis is one of the most impressive trumpeters to have emerged since Dizzy Gillespie. In spite of his ability to play almost any style and any range, he has not received the critical acclaim by the jazz press that has been given him by his fellow musicians. Perhaps the one word to describe him accurately would be genius. Wynton Marsalis with Terence Blanchard, Roy Hargrove, Mike Mossman, and most recently young Nicholas Payton from New Orleans, have forged together a kind of trumpet style that spans the entire history of the instrument. This style includes Buddy Bolden, Louis Armstrong through Roy Eldridge, Clark Terry, to Dizzy Gillespie, Miles Davis and Clifford Brown, and opens up a whole new concept of standards for young trumpet players. One of the most important things about the younger musicians is that they really do pay homage to their forefathers

Jon Faddis is one of the most impressive of the new breed of jazz giants to emerge during the 1980s and 90s. Photo by Teri Bloom.

and mothers. No one does that better than Wynton Marsalis. One of the most impressive things about Wynton, in recent years, is that he has returned to the music of his native New Orleans, and introduces it with a fresh, new spirit. It is one thing for the younger musicians to go back and reiterate the phrases of their idols during the be-bop era, the cool era, the hard bop era, etc., but more than anyone else, it was Wynton who started to focus attention on the music of earlier New Orleans—which, after all, is the music that gave birth to jazz.

Philip Catherine, the young Belgium guitarist, is quite an impressive soloist who carries on the long tradition established by another famous Belgium, Django Reinhardt. He is quite comfortable playing any style and has the technique and concepts necessary to execute his ideas.

Marvin "Smitty" Smith, the drummer, has done considerable work with Sonny Rollins. He has appeared at the University of Pittsburgh Jazz Seminar with a number of veteran artists, and has toured with his own group which included Kevin Eubanks. Rollins has, without a doubt, been a major influence on the scene. Marvin, according to Sonny Rollins, is one of his favorite drummers of the new breed. His work is not only exciting and vigorous, but shows that he is well grounded in the roots of the traditionalists, as well as more modern drummers who introduced the so-called floating time concept during the 1960s. They are not afraid to experiment and to seek an opportunity to introduce new ideas and concepts. Marvin "Smitty" Smith is one such musician.

Another musician who has just come into his own but has been around for quite some time is drummer T.S. Monk. Monk, the son of veteran jazz innovator Thelonious Monk, has assumed a leadership role in jazz, and has begun to establish himself as one of the most innovative drummers on the scene today. He has an association with the Monk Institute which, together with Tom Carter, has produced some of the most important musicians on the scene today, including Joshua Redman.

Bassist Christian McBride, according to most of the younger bass players, is perhaps one of the most important bassists to come along since Ron Carter and Buster Williams. His concept is well-developed and steeped in tradition. At the same time, he is an adventurer who often takes chances and wins. According to most of the critics who have heard him, his work is reminiscent of the Ray Brown school.

Veteran guitarist John Scofield and newcomers Russell Malone from Atlanta and Mark Whitfield are three of the most dynamic guitarists on the scene today.

I would be amiss if I didn't mention the new jazz saxophone repertoire orchestra, Roots, the brainchild of veteran producer Mike Hennessey. The group is booked and managed by Gaby Kleinschmidt, of GKP productions in Germany, and is a repertoire group primarily dedicated to preserving the music of the great saxophonists of the past—namely, such artists as Dexter Gordon, Sonny Rollins, Charlie Parker, Sonny Stitt, John Coltrane, Hank Mobley, etc. This group, although they primarily worked throughout Europe, is rapidly becoming a mainstay in the U.S. Members consist of Arthur Blythe (alto saxophone), Nathan Davis (tenor and soprano saxophones), Chico Freeman (tenor saxophone), and Sam Rivers (tenor saxophone). (Recently Sam Rivers left the group to pursue his own direction and was replaced by veteran tenor saxophonist Benny Golson, who is also serving as musical director.)

The Paris Reunion Band, also the brainchild of Mike Hennessey and put together by myself with Kenny Clarke's blessing, proved to be one of the most dynamic groups of the 1980s, having toured first in 1985. The original group consisted of Kenny Clarke on drums (however Kenny died before the first tour was to begin and he was replaced by Billy Brooks) Kenny Drew (piano), Jimmy

The original Paris Reunion Band consisting of former ex-patriot jazz musicians who had lived in Paris during the 1960s, on tour in England. According to many critics the band was one of the most exciting groups to emerge in the 1980s. From left to right: Ina Ditka—manager, Johnny Griffin—tenor saxophone, Kenny Drew—piano, Nathan Davis—tenor/soprano saxophone, Jimmy Woode—bass, Slide Hampton—trombone, Dizzy Reece—trumpet, Woody Shaw—trumpet, Mike Hennessey—producer. Not shown: drummer Billy Brooks.

Woode (bass), Johnny Griffin (tenor saxophone), Nathan Davis (tenor saxophone and musical director), Dizzy Reese (trumpet), Woody Shaw (trumpet), and Slide Hampton (trombone). The group received much acclaim for their numerous albums and their New York appearance at the Blue Note. Many critics called the Paris Reunion Band one of the most important groups on the scene during 1985.

Subsequently, the group toured Europe several times giving performances at major festivals, making CDs and videos. As with many groups with such enormous talent, the group began to disintegrate because of frequent personnel changes. Also, many of the artists felt that they would like to pursue their own direction with their own groups. However, during its five year period it proved to be one of the most dynamic forces in jazz.

The Future

What does the future hold for jazz? This is the question that has been asked by scholars, musicians, and jazz lovers, each time a new generation emerges. Perhaps the only answer to such a question is to look into the past for those artists who have established certain criteria that withstood the test of time.

One of the most inventive and underrated pianists on the scene today is veteran George Cables, who possesses all the qualities necessary to lead a new generation into the future. His ability to bring together various elements of blues, classics, stride and his flirtation with the avant-garde, makes him a formidable candidate for introducing new ideas capable of setting the pace of the new era in jazz. We could also speculate that a young artist such as Nicholas Payton may be the one that leads the way—or will it be Geri Allen, Wallace Roney or the Marsalis brothers, Branford and Wynton? One of the things that we can certainly say about the younger generation of musicians (80s and 90s) is that they are unafraid to assert themselves as carriers of the torch. In other words, this generation appears to possess a certain boldness and self-confidence that makes a statement of its own. As history recalls, the younger players of the 40s, and even the 30s, were often reluctant to assert themselves on the bandstand with the masters of that period. We are seeing a change of attitude today. Perhaps this is due to the number of opportunities given to them by record companies that are directly responsible for launching their careers. One of the tragedies of the jazz scene today is that many of the seasoned players who have proven themselves by having performed night after night, year after year, are often overlooked by the major record companies in search of the younger musicians through which they can recoup their initial investment. The seasoned players are often rejected by the record companies, simply because they are too old or because they ask for more money, and are, in effect, put on a shelf. Younger players emerge and are ready and willing to play if given the opportunity.

The standard set by today's young artists is higher than it has ever been. This is of course due to the numerous, excellent jazz programs existing around the country. Such schools as Indiana University in Bloomington with David Baker, North Texas State with Neal Slater in Denton Texas, the University of Pittsburgh, Rutgers with Ralph Bowen, Queens College with Jimmy Heath, University of Hartford with Jackie McLean, Oberlin College with Wendell Logan, James Williams at William Paterson College in New Jersey, Bunky Green at the University of North

Jazz trumpeter Wynton Marsalis and father pianist Ellis Marsalis. Photo by Ken Nahoum, courtesy of Sony Music.

Florida, Ted MacDaniel at Ohio State, Kenny Burrell at U.C.L.A., Mannes School of Music in New York City, Anthony Braxton at Wesleyan in Connecticut, Ernest Lampkins at Wiley College, Berklee, the New England Conservatory and as I have stated, surely the Thelonious Monk Institute, all have made a significant contribution toward the development and preservation of jazz.

The Thelonious Monk Institute is destined to become one of the premiere jazz schools in the world today. Under the able leadership of Tom Carter, together with T.S. Monk, son of Thelonious Monk, the Institute has already established itself as a force to be reckoned with in the area of jazz education and scholarship. Its annual contest is perhaps one of the most exciting and rigorous worldwide competitions in the area of jazz today.

Perhaps the one ingredient that students in many of these programs miss is the practical experience of performing live. By this, I mean that artists who de-

Terence Blanchard is one of the most promising of the young jazz artists of the decade.

velop solely in schools tend to sound, in some ways, superficial. In order to shed this superficiality, it is absolutely necessary for the young students to get much needed practical experience; just as the older bands during the 20s and 30s would travel throughout the country doing one-nighters. They needed to get the music to the point where they felt comfortable with it, before they would even think of going into the studio. The young artists of today must also get practical playing experience on the road, or in clubs or concerts, in order to become totally comfortable with the music—to give the same kind of performance as their elders.

One of the important things that has emerged recently in the area of jazz education has been the inclusion of practical courses in jazz programs that give students credit for actually going out on tour or playing in the local clubs. This idea of the student/mentor relationship is one that should be emulated throughout the country. Jimmy Heath has encouraged this kind of relationship with his

*Amina Figarova is one of the
new breed of international jazz
artists making an impact on
the scene today. Photo courtesy
of Amina Figarova.*

young alto saxophone student, Antonio Hart. At the University of Pittsburgh,
the University of Pittsburgh Jazz Ensemble, under my direction, arranges tours to
such areas as Jamaica, Trinidad and even Europe. There the ensemble is expected to perform nightly, in large and small ensembles, thus assuring that the artists
get the practical experience necessary to become seasoned and dynamic performers.

Can one actually teach improvisation, or teach someone to swing? This has
always been a question that has emerged whenever veteran artists get together.
Many artists feel that it is absolutely impossible to teach someone to play the
blues. This, of course, is not absolutely true. It is possible, without a doubt, to
teach theory and technique necessary to execute phrases, and harmonies, and
rhythms associated with blues. Once the student has learned these things, it is
then up to that student to put his or her personal feeling into the music. To deny
their personal feeling would negate the very purpose of jazz in the first place. So
it is definitely possible and necessary to teach jazz or blues, just as it is necessary

Joe Lovano, one of the most promising voices of the new millenium. Courtesy of Blue Note Records.

and valid to teach the theory of western European Classical music. But whether a student plays five licks from John Coltrane, and five from Charlie Parker, and five from Sonny Stitt, is irrelevant as far as creativity is concerned. What he or she can learn from these great masters is their theoretical approach. For the artist to assume that he or she is ready to perform and sign a record contract as a professional because he or she can play so many Sonny Stitt or John Coltrane or Sonny Rollins licks is absolutely absurd. Thus, we who are responsible for the training of these young artists must emphasize the concept of individual development. This, if done properly, will ensure that we see a bright and artistically rewarding future in jazz. The future, then, lies in the ability of our universities, conservatories, and colleges to attract seasoned veteran jazz performers, who also take the responsibility of becoming seasoned and dedicated scholars. They must be willing to make the commitment to living an almost unbelievable double life as a musician and as a scholar.

With such veteran musicians in place in our major universities, conservatories and colleges, jazz education and scholarship will then be ready to assume its rightful place alongside other universities, conservatories and colleges that have also hired veteran seasoned classical musicians as their faculty. Thus, the jazz student will be in a position of getting the best of both worlds, the academic and the practical sides of music. Once the university or academic institution has provided its students with the best possible faculty, it is then necessary for the institution to support that faculty member and his or her program by giving them the same support that they give to all other teachers of western European classical music or world music. One of the great disappointments in the area of jazz scholarship, at many of the universities and institutions throughout the United States, is that they have hired jazz faculty on a part-time basis and, in many instances, have assigned them lectureships rather than professorships. In many instances the jazz faculty member never reaches the point where he or she is awarded tenure. Happily, this is not the case at the University of Pittsburgh, where I am a full professor. At the University of Indiana at Bloomington, David Baker has been appointed, by the chancellor, a distinguished full professor of music. In some rare cases jazz musicians have also been awarded chair positions, as with Ellis Marsalis at the University of New Orleans. In order to ensure that jazz scholars and faculty will be able to carry out their mission of teaching and researching jazz in a proper manner, not only is it necessary for the institution to treat them equally, but it is also the responsibility of the jazz faculty and researcher to further his or her own education, and if possible, obtain the degrees that he or she is responsible for awarding to the students. This is only natural. It is important to realize that if we are to expect our students to achieve a certain level of proficiency and credibility, the faculty must also strive to achieve those goals. I'm sure that in the future we will see more masters degrees and Ph.D.s awarded to students who graduate from jazz studies programs in our major universities and colleges. These jazz students will not only be excellent performers, but will be excellent researchers, composers, producers, etc., just as in any other area of discipline. It is important for the jazz artist to set his or her own standard and to resist imitating classical music programs. There is enough energy, intelligence and will in the jazz community to establish criteria that will ensure the development and preservation of this wonderful music that we call jazz.

The Hidden Factor:
The Non-Artistic Factor

One of the most difficult things for a mature Jazz aficionado to accept is that a younger, more commercially-viable artist will soon replace his or her favorite artist as the 'new' star in Jazz. Whether or not this start is a "legitimate extension" of the more seasoned performer is, in most instances, irrelevant to the producers of the music. Cries of artistic injustice ring out: "Who is this trumpeter (saxophonist, etc.)—what qualifies him to fill the shoes of Charlie Parker or Miles Davis or Dizzy Gillespie?" If these voices of artistic protest are strong enough that they eventually translate into a drop in revenues, often the producers will respond by either changing their direction and focus or terminating the artist. What really matters is the viability of the artist to carry his/her financial weight. Thus, we find that the role of the producer of the music is a schizophrenic one at best. The producer, especially if he or she is an executive with a multi-national corporation, is limited as to what he/she can do in terms of producing a project based solely on artistic merit. If the new artist happens to be one who appeals to the projected market, then that is a welcome incentive. Such a scenario presents the producer with the option of stretching the creative boundaries of the artist.

The fact that Jazz is very important in the spiritual lives of most of us is relatively unimportant to many of the merchants who are responsible for the everyday availability of music to the prospective buyers. These are the kinds of factors that in a strange way affect the outcome of Jazz and eventually Jazz history. Another factor that influences the trends often found in the development of the careers of new as well as seasoned artists is the careful positioning of a certain artist in particular venues so that he or she receives the maximum exposure needed to succeed. Artists lucky enough to have a savvy producer-manager able to navigate this maze of promotional wizardry are probably destined for success. The fact that an artist may not have a capable producer-manager does not automatically insure failure. There is the most important fact of talent. Unfortunately, however, talent does not automatically guarantee success.

Perhaps one of the most important questions is who has the right to determine which artists are talented and which are not. History abounds with self-appointed artistic czars, pronouncing upon whether a given work is or is not good jazz, painting, literature, dance, cinema, etc. These so-called specialists are often placed in the position of determining the direction of the history of Jazz.

In the so-called war between business and the artist, in many cases the artist loses. He or she is labeled as being hard to work with and eventually is let go by the record company and replaced with another artist—who may not be as talented. Such an earth-shattering event can be fatal to the artist's career both creatively and financially. I have personally seen this happen to some of my close friends. Trumpeter Carmell Jones was, in the eyes of critics around the world, one of the best trumpet players in the post-Clifford Brown era. Carmell was, at the height of his career, placed in a position by his record company wherein he was denied the ability to record music of his own choosing, using musicians of his choice. Although this is a common occurrence with pop artists who are not considered major moneymaking "properties," it made little sense in Carmell's case since as a jazz artist he could never be expected to account for a huge volume of sales. (Jazz musicians are usually expected to sell only about ⅒ the percentage of a pop artist of similar stature.) Instead of permitting Carmell artistic freedom, the company informed him that they no longer needed his services. Then they proceeded to issue a new LP using his name but featuring previously-recorded material from several other artists on their roster. This was not only a breach of artistic and professional etiquette between the artist and his relationship with the only pipeline to his public—his label—but it was also a misrepresentation of the artist's current creative output. Although the material may have represented some of the company's best recorded efforts, it should not have been issued under Carmell's name.

Again the question arises, how does this affect the history of Jazz? The result is that we, the Jazz public, are now unwittingly presented with artistic work that is false. In many cases the compositions are not of the musician's choosing, and the supporting musicians are not those the artist would have used given the choice. Certain artists are known to perform better, or at least differently, when they play with certain other artists. Thus the overall concept of the recorded work may have been changed. This is major.

We, the Jazz public, have a right to ask ourselves whether we are hearing the real Carmell Jones or only a series of unrelated, pre-recorded works that "suggest" the work of the artist in question. The important lesson is that history, regardless of origins or intent, is often shaped by the business practices of the individuals and institutions closely associated with music performance and production. It is imperative to carefully examine the business practices that directly or indirectly affect the music, if we are to preserve and perpetuate the true history of this wonderful music we call Jazz.

The Future of Jazz in the New Millennium

One of the most important questions for Jazz enthusiasts around the world is, where is jazz going? What shape or form will it take? Will we be able to recognize it? Who will be the new stars? Will these new stars advance the cause of jazz or will they join the millions of quasi-jazz fans around the world who are satisfied merely to hear repetitions of previously improvised solos? This is just a sampling of the types of questions that surface whenever serious-minded jazz aficionados discuss the future of jazz.

Perhaps an answer to these complicated questions can be found in the number of young musicians participating in programs at our existing music institutions and the new independent programs which have developed in the past ten years. The fact that these new programs are recruiting young musicians from

The Carnegie Jazz Band—Jon Faddis, Music Director—is one of the most impressive big bands of the new millenium. © John Abbott. All rights reserved.

The Lincoln Center Jazz Orchestra, under the direction of trumpeter Wynton Marsalis (center), is one of the major big bands dedicated to the preservation of jazz classics. Photo by Anthony Barboza.

around the globe will undoubtedly change the future of jazz. This new breed of internationally-oriented jazz musicians will bring their own traditional ethnic roots to the new jazz.

Another source of new talent can be found in the recent contribution of the exciting jazz programs at Lincoln Center (under the able leadership of Wynton Marsalis, trumpeter and music director), Carnegie Hall (Jon Faddis, trumpeter and music director; George Wein, producer), the Smithsonian Jazz Orchestra (David Baker, musical director), the University of Pittsburgh Annual Seminar on Jazz (Nathan Davis, director), the Cleveland Jazz Orchestra, the Cincinnati Jazz Orchestra, the London Youth Jazz Orchestra, and the Rio Jazz Orchestra. In addition to presenting exciting concerts, these programs play an important role in educating the general public about the history of Jazz. Each of these programs is actively involved in preserving the music of past masters such as Duke Ellington,

Under the direction of jazz composer-scholar and cellist David Baker, the Smithsonian Jazz Orchestra is a major force in preserving the great music of the past and present

Count Basie, Dizzy Gillespie, and Thelonius Monk through creative programming of their works. Moreover, they are active in presenting clinics, lectures, workshops, and other educational offerings designed to promote and preserve jazz. The mere presence of such programs and their relationship to the immediate community as well as the country as a whole will play a major role in the direction jazz will take in the future.

Already, as a result of these types of programs, we have seen an upsurge of interest among young students (elementary and middle school) in Jazz—including such intricate styles as bebop and third stream. Probably one of the best examples of this effect can be seen in the number of young acoustic bass players at the middle and high school level, as well as the impressive number of exceptional young high school and college-age students who can accurately play and understand the music of the masters.

The New Generation

The number of younger players who have made a lasting impression on the jazz scene during the new millennium is impressive. Pianist Geri Allen is one of the new breed of jazz pianists who is able to combine a well-executed Western European technique with elements of traditional African-American blues, thus producing a kind of sophisticated melange of Jazz-World Music. I believe it is the future of jazz.

Further proof of this new direction can be seen in the piano stylings of Panamanian Denilo Perez and Cuban-born Gonzalo Rubalcaba. Both young pianists play with a fanfare and fire reminiscent of the finale of a modern-day opera. Three other pianists who represent a more traditional solid approach but also bridge the gap between the post 1960s wave and present are Mulgrew Miller, Cyrus Chestnut, and Alex Bugnon. Among the post-Freddie Hubbard/Woody Shaw trumpet era, Wallace Roney, Terence Blanchard, Roy Hardgrove and Nicholas Paynton have each made a significant contribution toward the future development of the trumpet in jazz. What is so impressive about this group of young trumpet players is their solid foundation in the jazz classics as well as a bold curiosity for exploring new territory.

The tenor saxophonists in this new group are a mixture of traditionalist and new wave. Joshua Redman and Branford Marsalis are among the most successful. Their brand of straight ahead, no nonsense improvisation is indicative of the younger players who feel an obligation to preserve the legacy of the masters like Coleman Hawkins and Don Byas. England's Mornington Lockett and Switzerland's Cyril Bugnon represent Europe's contribution to the new direction of jazz in the new millennium. David Sanchez and Ralph Moore are two of the more interesting young tenor players who not only maintain a connection to the masters but are daring and exploratory in their approach in improvisation. Two veteran saxophonists who have made their voices heard during the past decade are British alto saxophonist Peter King and American tenor saxophonist Joe Lovano. Alto saxophonists Kenny Garrett, Donald Harrison, and Antonio Hart are among the most impressive young artists on the scene today. Each possesses a distinct style and their playing displays a commitment to excellence.

In recent years the acoustic bass has suffered from the impact of rock more than any other instrument. Many upright acoustic players found themselves in the uncomfortable position of having to switch to the electric bass or not work at

Nathan Davis speaking at Honors Convocation Ceremony at the University of Pittsburgh.

all. Thus from the late 1970s until the mid 1980s revolution in jazz we find a void in the emergence of "real" bass players in jazz. However, due to the emphasis on acoustic music encouraged by the upsurge in jazz education programs, suddenly there has emerged a wealth of acoustic bass players. Four of the most successful young bassists on the scene today are Christian McBride, Bob Hurst, John Pattituci, and West African-born electric bassist Richard Bona. Bona, who hails from the Cameroonian village of Minta, is a fantastic technical whiz on the bass and is competent on several other instruments as well as vocals. This is typical of the new young breed of world jazz musicians—they play a number of instruments well.

Among the most promising young vocalists are Kevin Mahogany, Diana Krall, Belgium's David Linx, and England's Tina May. The direction of the guitar in jazz is solidly in the stewardship of Russell Malone, Kevin Eubanks, and England's Martin Taylor. Lewis Nash is one of the most sought-after drummers representing the new breed. He simply has it all. He swings with a passion, has the technique to play anything at any tempo, and above all has the taste and intelligence to complement any style or period in jazz. Winard Harper, Jeff Watts, and Terri Lynn Carrington are all exceptional drummers who are destined to make a major contribution to the new direction in jazz.

The new trombonists appear to come from the ranks of the already established professionals as well as a couple of newcomers. Among the most impressive are Delfayo Marsalis, younger brother of Wynton and Branford; Andre Hayward; Steve Davis; and Robin Eubanks. On the vibraphone, Stephon Harris is indeed impressive.

This partial list of young international jazz musicians, along with their many colleagues, represents the future of Jazz in the new millennium. Without doubt there will be new contributions from areas not represented on this list. These young men and women will, however, be among the forerunners of the musicians who will shape the course of the history of jazz to come.

Jazz Education Opportunities

Programs in the United States

Alabama:
Auburn University
University of Alabama
Wallace State College

Arizona:
Arizona State University
Mesa Community College
Northern Arizona University
University of Arizona

The following list was adapted form the "2000/2001 Jazz Education Guide," a special publication of *Jazz Times* magazine

California:
Cal Arts School of Music
Cal State Fullerton
Cal State Los Angeles
Cal Poly State University
Cal State Bakersfield
Cal State Northridge
Cuesta College
El Camino College
Fresno city College
Fullerton College
Harrison School of Music
Los Angeles Music Academy
Musicians Institute
San Bernadino Valley College
San Diego State University
San Francisco State University
San Jose State University
Thelonious Monk Institute of Jazz Performance (LA)
University of Redlands
University of Southern California

Colorado:
Naropa Institute
University of Colorado at Boulder
University of Denver
University of Northern Colorado

Connecticut:
Fairfield University
Hartford Conservatory
University of Hartford/Hartt School
Western Connecticut State University

District of Columbia:
Howard University

Florida:
Florida International University
Florida Southern College
Florida State University
Miami-Dade Community College
Seminole Community College
University of Miami
University of North Florida
University of South Florida

Georgia:
Clayton College and State University
Georgia State University
University of Georgia

Idaho:
University of Idaho

Illinois:
American Conservatory of Music
Augustana College
Benedictine University
Bloom School of Music
College of Lake County
Columbia College Chicago
DePaul University
Eastern Illinois University
Elmhurst College
Kennedy-King College
Milikin University
North Central College
Northern Illinois University
Northwestern University
Olive-Harvey College
Roosevelt University
Southern Illinois
University of Illinois at Chicago

Indiana:
Indiana University
Valpraiso University

Iowa:
Southwestern Community College
University of Iowa
University of Northern Iowa

Kansas:
Bethany College
Emporia State College
Hutchinson Community College
University of Kansas

Kentucky:
University of Louisville
University of Kentucky

Louisiana:
Grambling State University
Loyola University of New Orleans
McNesse State University
Southern University
University of New Orleans
University of Southwestern Louisiana

Maine:
University of Maine at Augusta

Maryland:
Catonsville Community College
Montgomery College
Towson University
University of Maryland

Massachusetts:
Berklee College of Music
New England Conservatory
University of Massachusetts at Amherst
University of Massachusetts at Lowell
Westfield State College

Michigan:
Central Michigan University
C.S. Mott Community College
Grand Rapids Community College
Interlochen Arts Academy
Michigan State University
Oakland University
University of Michigan
Wayne State University
Western Michigan University

Minnesota:
Musicians Technical Training Center
University of Minnesota at Duluth
University of Minnesota at Minneapolis

Mississippi:
Jackson State University
University of Southern Mississippi

Missouri:
Central Missouri State University
University of Missouri at Kansas City
Webster University

Montana:
University of Montana

Nebraska:
Northeast Community College
University of Nebraska at Kearny

Nevada:
Community College of Southern Nevada
University of Nevada

New Hampshire:
University of New Hampshire

New Jersey:
New Jersey City University
Princeton University
Rowan University
Rutgers, the State University
William Patterson University

New York:
Aaron Copland School of Music/Queens College
Audrey Cohen School
Brooklyn Conservatory
Brooklyn-Queens Conservatory
City College of New York
College of Saint Rose
C.W. Post of Long Island
Eastman School of Music
Five Towns College
Hunter College
Ithaca College
Lehman College Long Island University
Manhattan School of Music
The New School
New York University
Purchase College
SUNY Fredonia
Syracuse University

North Carolina:
Brevard College
East Carolina University
Elon College
North Carolina Central University
UNC at Asheville
UNC at Chapel Hill
UNC at Greensboro

Ohio:
Bowling Green State University
Capitol University
Oberlin Conservatory of Music
Ohio State University
University of Akron
University of Cincinnati
Youngstown State University

Oregon:
Clackamas Community College

Pennsylvania:
California University of PA
Duquesne University
East Stroudsburg University
Indiana University of PA
Millersville University
Moravian College
Temple University
University of the Arts
University of Pittsburgh
West Chester University

Rhode Island:
University of Rhode Island

South Carolina:
University of South Carolina
Winthrop University

Tennessee:
Middle Tennessee State University
University of Memphis
University of Tennessee

Texas:
Bee County College of Music
Coastal Bend College
Collin County Community College
Houston Community College
Lamar University
Southwest Texas State University
Stephen F. Austin University
Texas Christian University
University of Texas Arlington
University of Texas Austin
Weatherford Community College

Utah:
University of Utah

Virginia:
Hampton University
James Madison University
Virginia Commonwealth University
Virginia Tech University
Virginia Union University
Shenandoah University

Washington:
Cornish College of the Arts
Whitworth College

West Virginia:
Shepard College
West Virginia University

Wisconsin:
Lawrence University
University of Wisconsin at Eau Claire
University of Wisconsin at Madison
University of Wisconsin at Stevens Point

Wyoming:
Casper College
Northwest College

International Programs

Australia:
West Australian Conservatorium of Music
Elder Conservatorium
Sydney Conservatorium

Austria:
Aim-Hohner Musikschule
Brukner Konservatorium
Musikhochschule Graz

Belgium:
Conservatoire De Liege
Conservatoire de Bruxelles
Jazz Studio Tritonus
Koninklijk Vlaams Muzic Conservatorium

Canada:
Banff Center for the Arts

Denmark:
Det Alternative Rytmiske
Nordjysk Musk-Konservatorium

Finland
Helsinki Pop/Jazz Conservatory
Sibelius Academy

France:
AIMRA
American School of Modern Music
CIAM
CNSMDP- Conservatoire de paris
EDIM
IACP
International Music School

Germany:
Folkwang Hochschule essen
Hochschule der Kunste Berlin
Hochschule fur Musiki-Hanover
Hochschule fur Musik Dresden
Hochschule fur Musik Frankfort
Hochschule fur Musik Koln
Hochschule fur Musik Hanns Eisler
Jazz & rock Schule Freiberg
Neue Jazzschule Munchen
Staatliche Hochschule fur Musik Stuttgart

Greece:
Philippos Nakas conservatory

Hungary:
Ferenc Liszt Academy

Ireland:
Newpart Music Center

Italy:
Associazione Musicale Dizzy Gillespie
Associazione Siena Jazz
Centro Jazz Torino
Civici Corsi di Jazz di Milano
Suono Improvisio

Netherlands:
Brabants Concervatorium
Hogeschool Voor de Kunsten Groningen
Hogeschool Voor de Kunsten Arnhem
Royal Conservatory

Norway:
Music Conservatory of Trondheim

Portugal:
Associacao Filarmonica De Faro
Centro de Ensino Musica de Braga

Spain:
Escuela de Musica Creativa
Escuela de Musica Virtelia
Estudio Escola de Musica
Taller de Musicos

Sweden:
Royal University of College of Music
Skurups Folkhogskola
University of Goteberg

Switzerland:
Conservatoire de Montreaux
Conservatoire Populaire de Musique de Geneve
Ecole de Jazz et de Musique Actuelle
Jazzschule Basel
Jazzschule Luzern

United Kingdom:
Leeds College of Music

Endnotes

Chapter 1
What Is Jazz?

1. Eileen Southern, *The Music of Black Americans: A History*, (New York: W.W. Norton, 1971), p. 18.
2. John Storm Roberts, *Black Music of Two Worlds*, (New York: Praeger, 1972), p. 147.
3. Paul O. Tanner, David W. Megill, Maurice Gerow, *Jazz* (McGraw-Hill, 9th edition), p. 88.

Chapter 2
New Orleans

1. Marshall Stearns, *The Story of Jazz*, (New York: Oxford Univ. Press, 1956), p. 53.
2. Southern, p. 7.
3. Southern, p. 9.
4. Sidney Fox, *The Origins of and Development of Jazz*, (Chicago: Follett Educational Corp.), p. 13.
5. Stearns, p. 53.
6. John Chilton, *Who's Who of Jazz: Storyville to Swing Street*, (London: Bloomsburg Book Shop, 1972), p. 35.
7. Chilton, p. 211.
8. Frank Driggs and Harris Lewine, *Black Beauty, White Heat*, (New York: W. Morrow, 1982), p. 52.
9. Driggs and Lewine, p. 55.
10. Stearns, p. 47.

11. Jack V. Buerkle and Danny Barker, *Bourbon Street Black*, (London: Oxford Univ. Press, 1973), p. 18.

Chapter 3
Ragtime
1. Stearns, p. 105.
2. David R. Baskerville, "Jazz Influence on Art Music to Mid-Century" (dissertation, Ann Arbor: University Microfilms, 1972), p. 29.
3. Driggs and Lewine, p. 62.
4. William J. Schaefer et al. *The Art of Ragtime*, (Baton Rouge, La.: Louisiana State Univ. Press, 1973), p. vi.
5. Baskerville, p. 99.
6. Terry Waldo, *This Is Ragtime*, (New York: Hawthorn Books, 1976), p. 86.

Chapter 4
Religion and Jazz
1. James H. Cone, *The Spirituals and the Blues: An Interpretation* (New York: Seabury Press, 1972), p. 32.
2. Stearns, p. 66.

Chapter 5
Minstrelsy and Its Effect on Jazz
1. Stearns, p. 87.
2. Stearns, p. 90.
3. Stearns, p. 83.

Chapter 6
The Blues
1. Stearns, p. 76.

Chapter 7
Chicago and New York During the 1920s
1. John Chilton, *Who's Who of Jazz: Storyville to Swing Street*, (London: Bloomsburg Book Shop, 1972), p. 162.
2. Gene Fernett, *Swing Out, Great Negro Dance Bands* (Midland, Mich: Pendell Publishing Co., 1970, p. 31.

3. Chilton, p. 116.

Chapter 8
Kansas City: The Focal Point of Jazz During the Late 1920s

1. Nathan Davis, "Charlie Parker's Kansas City Environment and its Effect on His Later Life" (Ph.D. dissertation, Wesleyan University).

Chapter 9
Swing

1. Leonard Feather, *Encyclopedia of Jazz*, (New York: Horizon Press, 1966), p. 229.
2. Gene Fernett, *Thousand Golden Horns*, (Midland, Mich.: Pendell Publishing Co., 1966), p. 34.
3. John Chilton, *Who's Who in Jazz*, (Philadelphia: Chilton, 1972).
4. Barry, Ulanov, *History of Jazz*, (New York: Viking Press, 1952).

Chapter 10
Bebop

1. Howard H. Kendler, *Basic Psychology*, (Mends Park, Calif.: W.A. Benjamin, 1974), p. 631.
2. Nathan Davis, "Charlie Parker's Kansas City Environment and Its Effect on His Later Life" (unpublished dissertation, Wesleyan University).
3. Davis.
4. Stearns, p. 155.
5. Leonard Feather, *The Encyclopedia of Jazz*, (New York: Horizon Press, 1960).
6. Ortiz M. Walton, *Music: Black, White and Blue*, (New York: William Morrow, 1972), p. 99.

Chapter 11
Cool and Third Stream

1. Leonard Feather. *The Encyclopedia of Jazz in the Sixties*, (New York: Horizon Press, 1966).
2. Bill Cole, *Miles Davis*, (New York: William Morrow, 1974), p. 195.
3. Feather, *The Encyclopedia of Jazz*, p. 445.

Technical Studies

Agnostini, Dante. *Solfege Rythmique*. Paris: K. Clarke & D. Agnostini, 1972.

Baker, David. *Techniques of Improvisation*. Chicago: Maher Publication, 1971.

Baker, David. *Arranging and Composing for the Small Ensemble*. Chicago: Maher Publications, 1970.

Colo, William Shadrack. *Miles Davis: A Beginning Study*. Unpublished manuscript.

Delamont, Gordon. *Modern Harmonic Technique*. New York: Kendor Music, 1965.

Delamont, Gordon. *Modern Arranging Technique*. Delevan, New York: Kendor Music, 1965.

Harris, Eddie. *Intervalistic Concept*.

Mancini, Henry. *Sounds and Scores*. Northridge Music, 1967.

Sebesky, Don. *The Contemporary Arranger*. New York: Alfred Publishing Co., 1975.

Yusef Lateef's Method on How to Improvise Soul Music. Teaneck, NJ: Alnur Music, 1970.

Discography of Jazz Recordings

I. African—West African Ancestry

Anthology of Music of Black Africa. Everest, SDBR 3254/3, 1969 *Music of West Africa.* Roulette, SR-9003.

II. West Indian Influence

Black Music of South America. Nonesuch, H72036. *West Indian Spirituals and Folk Songs.* Musical Heritage Society, M.H.S. 15/5.

III. Religious Influence

Reverend Gary Davis, 1935–1949. Yazoo L-1023.
Voodoo Trance Music—Ritual Drums of Haiti. Lyrichord, LLST 7279 *Anthology of Black Gospel Music.* Legacy, Leg. 114.

IV. Secular Songs (Work Songs, Game Songs, etc.)

Afro-American Spirituals, Work Songs, and Ballads. Library of Congress, Music Division, Recording Laboratory (1956), AAFS L3.
Negro Work Songs and Calls. Library of Congress, Music Division, Recording Laboratory (1959), AAFS L8.
Negro Blues and Hollers. Library of Congress, Music Division. Recording Laboratory (1962), AFS L59.

V. Ragtime

Addenda (Folkways Jazz Anthology, vol. II). Folkways, FJ2811.
Ragtime, James P. Johnson. Biograph, BLP 1009Q.
Blues and Rags, Eubie Blake. Biograph BLP 1011Q-1012Q.
Jelly Roll Morton Plays Jelly Roll. Olympic, 7131.

VI. Dixieland

King Oliver in New York. Victor, LPV-529.
New Orleans (Folkways Jazz Anthology, vol. 3). Folkways, Fl2803.
Sound of New Orleans (Jazz Odyssey, vol. 1). Columbia, C3L30.
The Blues Heritage (Oliver, Armstrong, Smith). Olympic, 7104.
Smithsonian Collection of Classic Jazz. W.W. Norton Co., P6 11891. (11892-11897).
Mardi Gras Time, Dukes of Dixieland, Audio Fidelity, AFSD 5862.
Jazz Funeral at New Orleans, George Lewis. Olympic, OL7117.
Louis Armstrong: An Early Portrait. Milestone, MLP 2010.
King Oliver Creole Jazz Band. Olympic, OL7133.

VII. Chicago—1920s

Chicago No. 1 (Folkways Jazz Anthology, vol. 5). Folkways, FJ 2805.
Chicago No. 2 (Folkways Jazz Anthology, vol. 6. Folkways, FJ 2806.
The Sound of Chicago. 192-40 (Jazz Odyssey, vol. 2). Columbia, C3L32.

Boogie-Woogie Piano Players
Blue Note's Three Decades of Jazz, 1939–49, vol. 1. Blue Note, BST 89902.
Boogie-Woogie (Folkways Jazz Anthology, vol. 10). Folkways, FJ 2810.
Jazz Piano Anthology. Columbia, KG 32355 (C32356-32357).

VIII. The Blues—1920s

Country
The Blues Box. Verve Folkways, FTS-3011-3.
Country Blues Classics, vol. 1. Blues Classics, BC5-6.
Country Blues Classics, vol. 2. Blues Classics, BC5-6.

Guitar Wizards, 1926–1935. Yazoo, L-1016.

The Young Big Bill Broonzy, 1928–1936. Yazoo, L-1011.

The South (Folkways Jazz Anthology, vol. 1). Folkways, FJ 2801.

Negro Blues and Hollers. Library of Congress, Music Division, Recording Laboratory, AFS L59.

The Real Blues, John Lee Hooker. Everest, 1089.

Leadbelly. Everest, FS 202.

Josh White. Everest, FS 209.

The Legendary Leadbelly. Olympic, 7103.

Negro Prison Songs. Everest, TLP 1020.

The Blues Tradition. Milestone, MLP 2016.

Folk

American Negro Slave Songs. Tradition. 2108.

Mississippi Blues. United, US-7786.

Early Blues. Blind Lemon Jefferson. Olympic, 7134.

Urban (Rhythm and Blues)

The Blues Box. Verve Folkways, FTS-3011-3.

Hoodoo Man Blues. Junior Well's Chicago Band. Delmark, DS-9612.

Dinah Washington Sings the Best in Blues. Mercury, MC 20247.

Memphis Slim. Everest, FS 215.

LA. Midnight. B.B. King. ABC, ABCX 743.

Blues Bash. Big Joe Williams. Olympic, 7115.

Classic

Any Woman's Blues. Bessie Smith. Columbia, G. 30126.

The Blues (Folkways Jazz Anthology, vol. 2). Folkways, FJ 2802.

Jazz Singers (Folkways Jazz Anthology, vol. 4). Folkways, FJ 2804.

The Bessie Smith Story. Columbia, CL 855-858.

IX. New York—1920s (Harlem Renaissance)

Big Bands

The Ellington Era. Vols. 1 & 2. Columbia, C3L27 (C12046-CL2048).

Big Bands (Folkways Jazz Anthology, vol. 8). Folkways, FJ 2808.

The Sound of Harlem (Jazz Odyssey, vol. 3. Columbia, C3L33 (C12160-2162).

Duke Ellington, vol. 2: The Early Years. Everest FS-249.
Fletcher Henderson, vol. 2. RCA Victor, 741.071.
Luis Russell. Columbia, PG 32338.
Harlem in the Thirties. Fletcher Henderson. Olympic, 7118.
Bix Beiderbecke—1928. Olympic, 7130.

Harlem Piano School
Ain't Misbehavin', Fats Waller. RCA Victor, LPM 1246.
Piano (Folkways Jazz Anthology, vol. 9). Folkways, FJ 2809.
Boogie-woogie (Folkways Jazz Anthology, vol. 10). Folkways, FJ 2810.
Piano Starts Here, Art Tatum. Columbia, CS9655.
Jazz Piano Anthology. Columbia, KC 32355 (C32356-32357).
James P. Johnson—1921-1926. Olympic, OL 7132(E).

Society Dance Bands
Paul Whiteman, vol. 1. RCA Victor, LPV-555.
Greatest Bands in All the Land, vol. 3. Bygone, BB SWT 1503.

X. Kansas City (Territory Bands) Late 1920s
Count Basie in Kansas City. RCA Victor, LPV-514.
Kansas City Suite. Count Basie (music of Benny Carter). Phonodisc Forum SF 9032.
Boogie-Woogie (Folkways Jazz Anthology, vol. 10). Folkways, FJ 2810.

XI. Swing Era (1930s)
Benny Rides Again, Benny Goodman. Chess, LP 1440.
Blue Note's Three Decades of Jazz, 1939–49, vol. 1. Blue Note, BSST 89902.
Just You, Just Me, Lester Young. Parker, PLP-409.
The Essential Coleman Hawkins. Verve, V6-8658.
Duke Ellington. BYC 529081.
Billie Holiday. Everest, FS 265.
Artie Shaw. Everest, FS 263.
Teddy Wilson. Everest, FS 263.
Big Bands Uptown (Redman, Hopkins, Carter, Millinder). Decca, DL 79242.
The Core of Jazz, Johnny Hodges. MGM, SE 47237.
South Side Swing, Earl Hines. Decca, DL 79221.

Jimmie Lunceford. Decca, DL 79237.
Charlie Christian. Everest, FS 219.
Collector's History of Classic Jazz. Murray Hill, 927942.
Anthropology, Don Byas. Black Lion, BL-160.
Django Reinhardt, vol. 3. Everest, FS-255.
The World's Greatest Jazz Band. Everest, FS-314.

Cassettes
Things Ain't What They Used to Be, Johnny Hodges and Rex Stewart.
Body & Soul, Coleman Hawkins.
Stuff Smith.

XII. Dixieland (New Orleans) Revival (Late 1930s–Early 1940s)

Records
Spreadin' Joy: The Music of Sidney Bechet. Classic Jazz, 5.
Sidney Bechet, vol. 1–2. Blue Note, 81201–81202.
New Orleans Legends. BYG, 529.062.
New Orleans, Kid Ory and Jimmy Noone. Olympic, 7109.
Al Hirt at the Mardi Gras. RCA, LSP-2497.
Maxine Sullivan and Jack Teagarden. FS 307.

XIII. Bebop (1940s)

Harlem Jazz Scene 1941. Esoteric Records, ES-548.
The Essential Charlie Parker. Verve Jazz Essentials, V-8409.
Dizzy Gillespie. RCA Victor, LPV-530.
Bird and Diz. Verve, V6-8006.
Underground, Thelonious Monk. Columbia, CS 9632.
Max. Argo, LP 623.
Portrait of Carmen, Carmen McRae. Atlantic, SD 8165.
Gene Ammons/Boss Tenor. Prestige, 7534.
The Greatest of Dizzy Gillespie. RCA Victor, LPM 2398.
King Pleasure. Everest, FS 262.
Sarah Vaughan. Everest FS 250.
Blue Note Gems of Jazz (Tadd Dameron, J.J. Johnson, James Moody, Fats

Navarro, Bud Powell). Blue Note, BST 82001.
Boppin' a Riff, Fats Navarro. BYG, 529.102.
Smithsonian Collection of Classic Jazz. W.W. Norton & Co. P. 6 11891 (P11892-118970.)
Famous Solos, Buddy DeFranco. 1974.
Anthropology, Don Byas. Black Lion, BL-160.
Invisible Cage, Bud Powell. Black Lion, BL-153.
Woody Herman. Everest, FS281.

XIV. Progressive—1945–50

Artistry in Rhythm, Stan Kenton. Capitol, T167.

XV. Cool—1950s (West Coast)

Cool Samba. Battle, BS 96123.
Dave Brubeck's Greatest Hits. Columbia, C1 2484.
Birth of the Cool, Miles Davis. Capitol, T762.
Jazz at Oberlin. Fantasy, 3-11.
Andre Previn: The Early Years. Everest, FS-247.

XVI. Hard Bop (Late 1950s) (East Coast)

Livin' it up, Jimmy Smith. Verve, V6-8750.
Mercy, mercy, mercy, Cannonball Adderley. Capitol, ST 2663.
Respect, Jimmy Smith. Verve, V6-8705.
Alfie, Sonny Rollins. Impulse, A-9111.
Night Train, Oscar Peterson. Verve, V8538 (D).
Genius and Soul = Jazz. Ray Charles. Impulse, A-Z.
Mingus, mingus, mingus. Impulse, A-54.
'Round About Midnight, Miles Davis. Columbia, CS 8649.
The Jazz Messengers. Phillips, B07175L.
Royal Flush, Donald Byrd. Blue Note, St-8410i.
Fearless Frank Foster. Prestige, 7461.
Soul Brothers, Milt Jackson and Ray Charles. Atlantic, 1279.
Genius of Lee Morgan. Tradition, 2079.
Big Soul, Johnny Griffin. Milestone, M-47014.

Montmartre Collection, vol. 1, Dexter Gordon. Black Lion, BL-108.

XVII. Third Stream (Late 1950s—Early 1960s)

Third Stream Music. Atlantic, 1345.

XVIII. 1960s Avant-Garde, New Thing, or Free Jazz

OM, John Coltrane. Impulse, A-9140.
E.S.P., Miles Davis. Columbia, CL 2350.
Out to Lunch, Eric Dolphy. Blue Note, 84-63.
Groove Street, Larry Young. Prestige, 7237.
Fire Music, Archie Shepp. Impulse, A-86.
First Recordings, Albert Ayler. GNP-9022.

Blues Revival

Touch of the Blues, Bobby Bland. Duke, CLP 88.
Big Joe Williams. Everest, FS 218.
Sonny Terry. Everest, FS 206.
Concert at Newport, John Lee Hooker. Vee Jay, VJS 1078.
Super Black Blues, vol. 2, Curtis Hones. Goody, GY 10.007.

Big Band Revival

Woody Herman's *Big New Herd at the Monterey Jazz Festival*. Atlantic, 1328.
Happenings, Hank Jones and Oliver Nelson. Impulse, A-9132.

OTHERS—Records

Happy Girl, Nathan Davis. SABA, SB 15025.ST.
The Hip Walk, Nathan Davis. SABA, SB 15063 ST.
Happiness, The Russian Jazz Quartet. Impulse, A-80.
Jazz Samba, Stan Getz and Charlie Byrd. Verve, V6-8432.
Bitches Brew, Miles Davis. Columbia, GP 26.
My Favorite Things, John Coltrane. Atlantic, 1361.
Natural Black Inventions: Root Strata, Rahsaan Roland Kirk. Atlantic, SE 1578.
Impromptu: Billy Taylor. Mercury, MG 20722.
Makatuka, Nathan Davis. Seque, LPS 1000.
Moses Alive, Mose Allison. Atlantic, SD 1450.

Moody & the Brass Figures, James Moody. Milestone, MSP 9005.
I Remember Django, Stephane Grapelly. Black Lion, BL-105.
Live in Tokyo, Albert Mangelsdorf. Enja, 2006.

XIX. Jazz—Jazz Rock

Blood, Sweat and Tears. Columbia, CS 9720.
Bitches Brew, Miles Davis. Columbia, GP26.
Watermelon Mon, Mongo Santamaria. Milestone, M-47012.
Big Fun, Miles Davis. Columbia, PG 32866.
Body Heat, Quincy Jones. A & M, SP3617.
High Energy, Freddie Hubbard. Columbia, KC 33048.
Spectrum, Billy Cobham. Atlantic, SD 7268.
Open Our Eyes, Earth, Wind & Fire. Columbia, KC 32712.
Thrust, Herbie Hancock. Columbia, PC 32965.
Between Northingness and Eternity. Mahavishnu Orchestra. Columbia, KC 32766.
XX. 1970s
Fusion Atmaj, Michael Urbaniak. Columbia, KC 33184.
Mysterious Traveler, Weather Report. Columbia, KC 32494.
Giant Box, Don Sebesky. CTI, CTX 6031-6032.
Butterfly Dreams, Flora Purim. Milestone, M-9052.
Don't Mess with Mr. T., Stanley Turrentine. CTI, 6030.
Sahara, McCoy Tyner. Milestone, MSP 9039.
One, Bob James. CTI, 6043.
High Energy, Freddie Hubbard. Columbia, KC 33048.
Black and Blues, Bobbie Humphrey. Blue Note, BN-LA 142-C.
Spanish Steps, Hampton Hawes. Black Lion, BL-122.
Bad Benson, George Benson. CTI, 6045.
Upon This Rock. Joe Farrell. CTI, CTI6042.

Big Band
Different Drummer, Buddy Rich. RCA Victor, LSP 4593.

Free, Semi-Free (Avant-Garde)
Science Fiction, Ornette Coleman. Columbia, KC 31061.
Joe Henderson in Japan. Milestone, 9047.

New Music
Treasure Island. Keith Jarrett.

Others
The Raven Speaks, Woody Herman. Fantasy, 9416.
Soul Zodiac, Cannonball Adderley. Capitol, SVBB-11025.

Soul
Fulfillingness First Finale, Stevie Wonder. Tamia T6-33251.

Record Collections

Collector's History of Classic Jazz. Murray Hill #927942.
The Smithsonian Collection of Classic Jazz. Smithsonian Institution,
    Washington, DC #P6 11891.
History of Classic Jazz. Riverside #SDP 11.

Bibliography

Armstrong, Louis. *Louis Armstrong—A Self-Portrait*. New York: Eakins Press, 1971.

Baskerville, David Ross. "Jazz Influence on Art Music to Mid-Century." Dissertation, Ann Arbor, University of Microfilms, 1972.

Bechet, Sidney. *Treat It Gentle*. New York: Da Capo Press, 1975.

Berendt, Joachim. *The Jazz Book*. NY: L. Hill, 1975.

Blesh, Rudi. *Shining Trumpets*. New York: Da Capo Press, 1975.

Blesh, Rudi and Harriet Janis. *They All Played Ragtime*. New York: Grove Press, 1959.

Buerkle, Jack V., and Danny Barker. *Bourbon Street Black*. New York: Oxford University Press, 1973.

Carl Gregor, Duke of Mecklenburg. *International Jazz Bibliography*. Strasbourg, France: P.H. Heitz, 1969.

——. *Die Theories des Blues—im Modernen Jazz*. Baden-Baden: Koerner, 1971.

Carr, Ian. *Music Outside*. London: Latimer New Dimensions, 1973.

Charters, Samuel Barclay. *The Bluesmen*. New York: Oak Publications, 1967.

——. *Jazz: New Orleans, 1885-1963*. New York: Oak Publications, 1963.

Chilton, John. *Who's Who of Jazz: Storyville to Swing Street*. London: Bloomsbury Book Shop, 1970.

Cohn, Mik. *Rook (From the Beginning)*. New York: Stein and Day, 1969

Cole, Bill. *Miles Davis*. New York, William Morrow, 1974.

Cone, James H. *The Spirituals and the Blues: An Interpretation*. New York: Seabury Press, 1972.

Connor, D. Russell and Warren W. Hicks. *BC on the Record*. New Rochelle, NY: Arlington House, 1969.

Davidson, Basil. *The African Slave Trade*. Boston, MA: Little, Brown, 1980.

Davis, Nathan. *Charlie Parker's Kansas City Environment and Its Effect on His Later Life*. Ph.D. Dissertation, Wesleyan University.

Davis, Ursula Broschke. *Paris Without Regret*. Iowa City: University of Iowa Press

Davis, Nathan. *African American Music (A Philosophical Look At)*.

Davis, Ursula Broschke. Cinema: The Hidden Persuader. New York: Simon and Schuster.

DeLerma, Dominique-Rene. *Black Music in Our Culture*. Kent, Ohio: Kent State University Press, 1970.

de Toledano, Ralph. *Frontiers of Jazz*. 2d ed. New York: Frederick Ungar.

Dexter, Dave. *The Jazz Story: From the '90s to the '60s*. Englewood Cliffs, NJ: Prentice-Hall, 1964.

Down Beat Magazine. Chicago: Maher Publications.

Feather, Leonard. *Encyclopedia of Jazz in the Sixties*. New York: Horizon Press, 1966.

——. *The Encyclopedia of Jazz*. New York: Horizon Press, 1955.

Fernett, Gene. *Swing Out: Great Negro Dance Bands*. Midland, Mich.: Fendell Publishing Co., 1970.

——. *Thousand Golden Horns*. Midland, Mich.: Fendell Publishing Co., 1970.

Fisher, Miles Mark. *Negro Slave Songs in the United States*. New York: Russell & Russell, 1968.

Francis, Andre. *Jazz*. Translated and revised by Martin Williams. New York: Grove Press, 1960.

Franklin, John Hope. *From Slavery to Freedom*. New York: Knopf, 1974.

Frazier, E. Franklin. *Black Bourgeoisie*. New York: Free Press, 1965.

Garland, Phyl. *The Sound of Soul*. Chicago: H. Regnery Co., 1969.

Gitler, Ira. *Jazz Masters of the Forties*. New York: Macmillan Co., 1966.

Grossman, Stefan. *Delta Blues Guitar*. New York: Oak Publications, 1969.

Hadlock, Richard. *Jazz Masters of the Twenties*. New York: Macmillan Co., 1965.

Harris, Marvin. *Culture, Man, and Nature*. New York: Thomas Y. Crowell, 1971.

Harrison, Max. *Charlie Parker*. New York: A.S. Barnes & Co., 1960.

Harvard Dictionary of Music. Cambridge, Mass.: Belknap Press of Harvard University Press, 1969.

Heilbut, Tony. *The Gospel Sound*. New York: Simon and Schuster, 1971.

Hentoff, Nat and Nat Shapiro. *Hear Me Talking to Ya*. New York: Rinehart, 1955.

Herskovits, M.J. *The Myth of the Negro Past.* Boston: Beacon Press, 1958.

Hodeir, Andre. *Jazz: Its Evolution and Essence.* New York: Grove Press, 1956.

——. *The Worlds of Jazz.* New York: Grove Press, 1972.

Jackson, George Pullen. *White and Negro Spirituals.* New York: J.J. Augustin, 1943.

Jazz Forum (the magazine of the European Jazz Federation). Vols. 2, 11, 16, 24, 28, 30, 75.

Johnson & Johnson. *Black World.*—Special Issue. November 1973.

Jones, LeRoi. *Black Music.* New York: William Morrow and Co., 1967.

——. *Blues People.* New York: William Morrow and Co., 1963.

Kaufmann, Mrs. Helen. *From Jehovah to Jazz.* New York: Dodd, Mead & Company, 1937.

Keil, Charles. *Urban Blues.* Chicago: University of Chicago Press, 1966.

Kendler, Howard H. *Basic Psychology.* Menlo Park, CA: W.A. Benjamin, 1974.

Kennington, Donald. *The Literature of Jazz.* London: Library Association, 1970.

Kmen, Henry A. *Music in New Orleans.* Baton Rouge: Louisians State University Press, 1966.

Kofsky, Frank. *Black Nationalism and the Revolution in Music.* New York: Pathfinder Press, 1970.

Leonard, Neil. *Jazz and the White Americans.* Chicago: University of Chicago Press, 1962.

McAllester, David Park. *Readings in Ethnomusicology.* 1949. Reprint. New York: Johnson Reprint Corp., 1971.

McCarthy, Albert J. *The Dance Band Era.* Philadelphia: Chilton Book Co., 1971.

Machlis, Joseph. *The Enjoyment of Music.* 4th ed. New York: W.W. Norton, 1977.

Merriam, Alan P. *A Bibliography of Jazz.* 1954. Reprint. New York: Da Capo, 1970.

Mingus, Charles, ed., by King Nel. *Beneath the Underdog.* New York: Alfred A. Knopf, 1971.

Nathan, Hans. *Dan Emmett and the Rise of Early Negro Minstrelsy.* Cambridge, Mass.: Belknap Press of Harvard University Press, 1961.

Nettl, Bruno. *Folk and Traditional Music of Western Continents.* Englewood Cliffs, NJ: Prentice-Hall, 1965.

Nketia, J.H. Kwabena. *African Music—in Ghana.* Evanston, Ill.: Northwestern University Press, 1963.

Oliver, Paul. *Savannah Syncopators.* New York: Stein & Day, 1970.

Oliver, Paul. *The Story of the Blues.* Philadelphia: Chilton Book Co., 1969.

Ostransky, Leroy. *The Anatomy of Jazz.* Seattle: University of Washington Press, 1966.

Panassie, Hugues. *Dictionnarie du Jazz.* Paris: A. Michel, 1971.

Paskman, Dailey. *Gentlemen Be Seated.* New York: Doubleday, Doran, 1928.

Reisner, Robert C. *Bird: The Legend of Charlie Parker.* New York: Citadel Press, 1962.

Roberts, John Storm. *Black Music of Two Worlds.* New York: Praeger, 1972.

Rublowsky, John. *Black Music in America.* New York: Basic Books, 1971.

Russell, Ross. *Bird Lives: The High Times and Hard Life of Charlie (Yardbird) Parker. New York: Charter Books, 1973.*

——. *Jazz Style in Kansas City and the Southwest.* Berkeley: University of California Press, 1971.

Russell, Tony. *Black, White, and Blue.* New York: Stein and Day, 1970.

Schafer, William J., et al. *The Art of Ragtime.* Baton Rouge, La.: Louisiana University Press, 1973.

Schuller, Gunther. *Early Jazz: Its Roots and Musical Development.* London: Oxford University Press, 1968.

Shemel, Sidney. *This Business of Music.* New York: Billboard Publications, 1971.

Simon, George Thomas. *Simon Says.* New Rochelle, NY: Arlington House, 1971.

Simpkins, Cuthbert O. *Coltrane.* New York: Herndon House, 1975.

Southern, Eileen. *The Music of Black Americans: A History.* New York: W.W. Norton, 1971.

Spellman, A.B. *Four Lives in the Bebop Business.* London: Macgibbon & Kee, 1967.

Standifer, James A. *Source Book of African and Afro-American Materials for Music Educators.* Washington: Contemporary Music Project, 1972.

Stewart-Baxter, Derrick. *Ma Rainey and the Classic Blues Singers.* New York: Stein & Day, 1970.

Stewart, Rex William. *Jazz Masters of the Thirties.* New York: Macmillan Co., 1972.

Stearns, Marshall. *The Story of Jazz.* New York: Oxford University Press, 1956.

Tanner, Paul, and Maurice Gerow. *A Study of Jazz.* 5th ed. Dubuque, IA: Wm. C. Brown Co., 1984.

Ulanov, Barry. *A History of Jazz in America.* New York: Viking Press, 1952.

Waldo, Terry. *This Is Ragtime.* New York: Hawthorn Books, 1976.

Walton, Oritz M. *Music: Black, White and Blue.* New York: William Morrow, 1972.

Williams, Martin, ed. *Jazz Panorama.* London: The Jazz Book Club by arrangement with the Crowell-Collier Press, 1965.

Work, John W. *American Negro Songs.* New York: Howell, Soskin & Co., 1940.

Index

Title	Artist	Jazz Essential Collection
1. Struttin' with BBQ	Louis Armstrong	Vol. 2
2. Dipper Mouth Blues	King Oliver	Vol. 1
3. Froggie Moore	King Oliver	Vol. 1
4. Black Bottom Stomp	Jelly Roll Morton	Vol. 1
5. King Porter	Jelly Roll Morton	Vol. 1
6. Sugar Foot Stomp	Fletcher Henderson	Vol. 1
7. Concerto for Cootie	Duke Ellington	Vol. 1
8. Tiger Rag	Art Tatum	Vol. 2
9. Singing the Blues	Bix Beiderbecke	Vol. 2
10. One o'Clock Jump	Count Basie	Vol. 3
11. King Porter Stomp	Benny Goodman	Vol. 2
12. Easy Living	Billie Holiday	Vol. 4
13. Body and Soul	Coleman Hawkins	Vol. 3
14. Slippin' and Slidin'	Sidney Bechet	Vol. 1
15. Lester Leaps In	Lester Young	Vol. 3
16. It Don't Mean a Thing	Django Reinhardt	Vol. 4